T0304946

Love from Venice

Love from Venice

A Golden Summer on the Grand Canal

GILL JOHNSON

HODDER &
STOUGHTON

First published in Great Britain in 2024 by Hodder & Stoughton Limited
An Hachette UK company

3

Copyright © Gill Johnson and Isalem Limited 2024

The right of Gill Johnson to be identified as the Author of the Work has been
asserted by her in accordance with the Copyright, Designs and Patents Act 1988.

All rights reserved. No part of this publication may be reproduced,
stored in a retrieval system, or transmitted, in any form or by any means
without the prior written permission of the publisher, nor be otherwise
circulated in any form of binding or cover other than that in which it
is published and without a similar condition being imposed on
the subsequent purchaser.

A CIP catalogue record for this title is available from the British Library

Hardback ISBN 9781399721653
Trade Paperback ISBN 9781399721660
ebook ISBN 9781399721677

Drawings © Isabella Ross 2024

Typeset in Celeste by Palimpsest Book Production Limited, Falkirk, Stirlingshire

Printed and bound in Great Britain by Clays Ltd, Elcograf S.p.A.

Hodder & Stoughton policy is to use papers that are natural,
renewable and recyclable products and made from wood grown in sustainable
forests. The logging and manufacturing processes are expected to conform
to the environmental regulations of the country of origin.

Hodder & Stoughton Limited
Carmelite House
50 Victoria Embankment
London EC4Y 0DZ

www.hodder.co.uk

To my brother Hugh Johnson

CONTENTS

AUTHOR'S NOTE

AS I REFLECT on my life at the grand old age of ninety-one, surrounded by my children and grandchildren, my mind wanders back to the summer of 1957. As a twenty-five-year-old woman, I looked after two young boys in Venice whose family embraced me and introduced me to a glittering and exotic world, the vivid memories of which have filled my heart and mind ever since. It was not just a golden summer, but a life-changing rite of passage.

The inspiration and genesis of this memoir dates from the discovery of a 'lost' file of letters that I wrote from Venice to my fiancé David Ross in 1957. The more I think about it, the stranger and more precarious the survival of these fifteen or so dispatches becomes. David rarely kept letters. Perhaps he thought that my scribbles conjured something of that halcyon age of Venice suspended between the last days of the European Grand Tour and the arrival of mass tourism. Having withstood the vicissitudes of David's life in Paris and later London, the letters were packed away and forgotten about, until I rummaged through his papers in 2015. Visions and memories of 1957 flared up, igniting a richly digressive series of reminiscences. What David intended by saving the letters remains a mystery;

he died in 2009. I hope *Love from Venice* helps fulfil whatever private, unspoken purpose he had in mind.

The very generous way in which I was welcomed in and became part of the Brandolini d'Adda family was a gesture of trust that I would never want to dishonour. I hope *Love from Venice* goes some way to record and repay the great warmth and affection that the family showed me throughout my stay.

Whimsically, I dated some letters, but left others blank. For those dateless, I have deduced their day by comparing the events described in the letters with the entries in my diary of 1957. I give the date in square brackets.

PROLOGUE

'*ECCO IL MOTOSCAFO*,' said the Conte, as we arrived at Mestre and got out of the Cadillac.

Chafing restlessly at its mooring, the spotless white launch trimmed in blue awaited us by a quayside. The captain, barely a boy, held out an arm and gestured for me to come forward. Looking down, I paused to measure the gulf and, with what felt like great daring, made the leap from shore to ship. Ruy and Leonello scrambled aboard with Daisy the corgi. Fräulein Rasch, the German nurse, held Nuno's hand and half hoisted, half dragged the three-year-old on to the heaving vessel. The Conte embarked with practised ease, as if stepping on to weighing scales, then turned to help the Contessa, heavily pregnant, wearing dark glasses and a broad-brimmed hat. I gazed towards the horizon. In the distance, Venice shimmered, looking like a pile of precariously stacked architecture floating above the water.

We took our places on soft-cushioned armchairs. With her elegant lines, the *motoscafo* stood out from the other lagoon traffic.

'*Attenzione prego!* Hold on, please,' said the captain, as he fired the powerful engines.

With a growl, we surged towards Venice across the couple of miles of shallow water that separate her from the mainland, a strait that had not only protected her physically from invasion but had also kept her at one remove from the shifting kaleidoscope of northern Italian politics, internecine warfare and territorial quarrels that characterised so much European history.

Throwing up a plume of sun-sparkled water, we passed the white passenger ship that plied to and from Athens, and wove between barges laden with coal, lumber and fruit. Venice in those days was the third-largest port in Italy.

Arriving at the mouth of the Grand Canal, the captain throttled back. Gurgling and spluttering, the *motoscafo* began its stately passage down Il Canalazzo, nodded to and bowed to by passing gondolas. Viewed from a *motoscafo* glissading along the water, the Grand Canal seemed more compact, smaller, foreshortened and more intimate than it appears in photographs, which tend to give it unwarranted breadth, scale and panorama. The palazzi floated past in a cavalcade of architectural styles – Byzantine, neo-Byzantine, Gothic, Renaissance, baroque and neo-classical. The Venetian palette was glowing with warm, muted colours and tones – pale rose and umber, blanched and bleached by centuries of sun.

Once I'd overcome my initial excitement at being in Venice, I was able to observe the palazzi more closely. Although colourful and glorious, La Serenissima bore signs of distress and decay. Broken windows, mouldering balconies and rat-gnawed masonry spoke of neglect and impoverishment. Some dilapidated palazzi looked as if they wouldn't be able to hold out for much longer; others exuded an impeccably romantic air of aristocratic desertion and melancholy.

I had little idea where or how the ride aboard the *motoscafo* would resolve itself. In the preceding weeks, reality had outrageously and flamboyantly outrun my expectations. I was a twenty-five-year-old woman from London come to Venice following a series of blind coincidences, why-not impulses, half-thought-out motivations and a brainstorm of rose-tinted thinking all set off by a romantic possible wild-goose chase, all to look after the eldest two boys of one of the pre-eminent families in Europe, never mind Italy, never mind Venice. I was finding it hard to tell fantasy from reality, fairytale from fact. I kept thinking I'd made it all up and that my imagination had taken a strange turn, but then I remembered that my mind is not so creative. Having been to Venice once before, I knew that she would only compound this bafflement.

I glanced at the Conte, who had pulled his straw hat low over his head and appeared to be trying to sleep. I turned to Ruy and Leonello. They sat in identical poses, their chins resting on the cross of their forearms, which reposed on the gunwale of the *motoscafo*, as they stared at the passing palazzi.

'A Venetian palazzo is only ever a few years of neglect away from becoming a safety hazard,' said the Conte, from under his straw hat. He pushed it back, sat up and looked straight ahead, his profile backdropped by a miscellany of marble columns, lacy latticework, mosaics, arches and various items of laundry hanging out to dry on balconies, 'but it usually passes through a phase of domestic utility first.'

'It is so lovely to return to Venice,' I said. 'The atmosphere, the light and the colour are so very different from Paris, which seemed so, well, depressing.'

The Conte gave this statement some thought. 'Really, it is such a pity,' he said.

After a lull, which I'd hoped the Conte would fill but didn't, I asked, '*What* is a pity?'

'The Parisians appear to have made a habit of being invaded by unwelcome foreigners and are suffering the consequences – not something we Venetians would tolerate. People come here for love, not destruction. The distress you see here,' he gestured, with an epic sweep of his arm, at a crumbling façade with bed linen hanging off it, 'has nothing to do with war damage. It is a combination of poverty and other priorities. The old money is still here,' he gave a fatalistic shrug, 'but in places it is wearing thin.'

'Was Venice affected by the war?'

'Hardly.' The Conte shook his head. 'All sides agreed to leave her alone. I think many of the generals had spent, or were hoping to spend, their honeymoons here. This is the magical city of romance, the place where people learn, or remind themselves, how to have civilised fun. You have been to Venice before, yes?'

'Three years ago. Mainly to see paintings.'

'Ah, so you know it a little.'

'I sort of understand Venice.'

'Ha!' The Conte turned away with a smile and a dismissive gesture. 'Impertinence! *Impossibile capire Venezia!* It is impossible to understand Venice. The best one can hope for is a vague knowledge of *how parts of it work or don't work*, but that's not the same.'

There was another lull as the *motoscafo* nosed its way through traffic. The Conte continued: 'Even for someone like myself, whose family . . .' he shook his head almost with disbelief '. . . goes back generations, Venice seems almost incredible. Look at these magical palazzi, with their enticing façades that welcome you in, and compare them with the cold, dark, castellated paranoia that is so much of European architecture of the time. If you take her high point, let's say some time between the Fourth Crusade's sacking of Constantinople in 1204 and Vasco da Gama's discovery of the sea route to India in 1498, you have to consider that Venice's long glide has been a very drawn-out affair, one false sunset after another.'

'So why do people grumble and say, "Venice isn't what it was"?'

'Show-offs! What do these people want? A time machine? Tell me somewhere that *is* what it was. They presume to know what Venice was. But all one knows about Venice's past is the sum of what Venetians pretend to know or want you to know.'

I took in the rich and ancient anthology of architectural styles that floated past. 'I suppose Venice has done a pretty good job of keeping faith with what she once was, whatever that was,' I said dreamily.

'No one does degradation better than the Venetians,' said the Conte. 'Venice's so-called decline has been so drawn out that you wonder if it really is a decline or something else, like something miraculous. Venice hovers in the alchemy between science, art and magic. It seems a miracle that she has survived so long, no?'

I nodded. The Conte continued, 'She could have fallen to the King of Italy, the Lombards, the Saracens, the Dalmatian pirates, or the Magyars. Or she could have been taken over by the Ottoman Empire, like Constantinople was. Or she could have been levelled by Napoleon or flattened in the two world wars. Or she could have burnt down or simply been wiped out by plague. Or she could have sunk. Or she could simply have died of neglect. Go out into the lagoon and you will find islands that once hosted great cities and towns. All gone. Ruined, with grass growing. But Venice continues, as she always does. And just when you think she is finally about to sink into the lagoon, something comes along to save her. Who knows what it will be next?'

'Instead of worrying about Venice's decline, one should celebrate the fact that she still exists,' I ventured, adding momentum to the flywheel of the Conte's conversation.

'Exactly. Venice has resisted the carnage of time without having to become boring and modern. The early Venetians built her from nothing and in the most unlikely of places, seventy tiny islands in a lagoon, chosen deliberately because they were out of the way. Yet for centuries this city was the centre of the world. Unlike the Parisians, we're happy that our best years are behind us. We see brilliant prosperity in decay. Who can resist nostalgia, art and romance? They are so much more alluring than growth and efficiency.'

I wondered how the Conte had learnt to speak such fluent and idiomatic English, and with such a good accent. I didn't feel it my place to ask.

We passed beneath the Rialto Bridge, which spans the Grand Canal at its narrowest. After a few more metres, the longest straight of the Canal would stretch out before us. I had forgotten how lovely Venice is.

Heads turned. While the English avoid staring, Venetians embrace it, but less demonstratively than other Italians and certainly less than the French. However, even the most unwavering Englishman could scarcely have failed to look twice at the gleaming *motoscafo* and the impressive figure of the Conte who, not unconscious of his appearance, received the glances of passers-by without reluctance, and occasionally responded with a nod or a faint gesture as if he were cupping butterflies.

We continued for the full extent of the long straight, until we reached the sharpish left-hander preceding the Accademia Bridge. As we neared Palazzo Mocenigo, where Byron wrote *Don Juan*, the captain eased off.

'*Ecco* . . . Palazzo Brandolini,' said the Conte. We drifted at a thirty-degree angle towards a 'Golden Age' Gothic pile almost opposite Mocenigo. Unlike most of the other palazzi, this one looked freshly minted.

As the captain manoeuvred the *motoscafo* towards the landing stage, I peered up at the façade. All four storeys looked like a cliff of carved marble. The *portiere* opened the water gate, and bowed. He offered me an arm as I stepped ashore. The boys jumped, Ruy taking Daisy by her lead. Fräulein Rasch followed, muttering, '*Danke*,' as she stepped ashore with Nuno, and scuttled off into the bowels of the palazzo. The Conte made an impeccable disembarkation and helped the Contessa out.

I mounted shallow steps to a black and white marble floor that lay before me, at the end of which, and to one side, stood the *portiere*'s lodge. To the rear of the palazzo, a colonnade gave on to a formal walled garden with parterre, boxwood traceries, roses, oleanders and herringbone paving. In mid-garden a marble wellhead was fretted with ironwork.

The Conte gestured: 'Please. This way.' A red-carpeted staircase rose regally to the floor above, up which Ruy and Leonello had already clambered. But the stairs were not the object of the Conte's open-handed gesture. Adjacent to the staircase stood a gilt and padded red-velvet sedan chair with golden curlicues, large enough to seat four.

'Please. Take a seat,' said the Conte.

I wondered why he wanted me to sit down – I hardly needed a rest. But I did as I was told. The Conte and Contessa sat next to me. Then the Conte pressed a button. An electric motor whirred into life. The sedan chair wobbled upwards towards a hole in the ceiling and into the heart of the palazzo. After much wobbling and whirring, it came to a stop.

Surely, I thought, there is another way into the palazzo besides this peculiar contraption. Why is this being laid on for me? A sense of impostership X-rayed through me.

The sedan chair now still and silent, the Conte and Contessa waited as monumental doors opened before us. I beheld . . . well, I was unsure what I beheld. I had never seen anything quite like the perspectives that opened up before me, never seen so much marble on such a scale, or so many romantic baroque curlicues, or so much spun glass, scrollwork, arabesques and ornate twiddles, or so many painted ceilings hung with Murano chandeliers forested with candles, or so many massive mirrors gorgeously framed in gold, which duplicated and multiplied the scene. On the walls and ceilings, nymphs, sirens, satyrs, bathing naiads and the indispensable naughty *putti*, some of them life-size and most of them garlanded and vined, gambolled and frolicked in a fantasy classical landscape. I felt almost ant-like in the vast interior.

As I moved about, gilded and tapestried halls and salons opened up to me, peopled with marble busts and set with thrones and vaguely episcopal chairs. The windows were swagged in a palette shot with discords of orange-vermilion, cyclamen pink, sage green and mauve. I could hardly see for looking. Sprays of fresh flowers, jasmine, honeysuckle, roses and lilies scented the air and sparked further riots of colour. I wasn't sophisticated enough not to be awed. This was no-expense-spared good-as-you-can-get make-believe and magic. Even were I sophisticated enough, I should still have been awed.

'I must rest,' said the Contessa, as she walked slowly towards a large doorway. 'I see you later. *Ciao.*'

I turned to the Conte. He was watching me trying to take it all in. 'It's not much of a palazzo really,' he said, 'but it's home. Fifteenth-century Gothic, restored two years ago for my niece's wedding. The *piano nobile* is traditionally where Venetians entertain. The scale, proportions, furniture, artworks, décor . . . mainly for show. If you were Venetian and owned a palazzo, money was assumed. Taste mattered more. Dynasties wither away, money ebbs and flows, but you hope your eye endures.'

We walked down a corridor of polished antique wood to a comparatively cosy dining room: a beautiful space lined with green velvet overlooking the garden. Perfume from the flowers outside drifted in through the open window. In mid-room, a circular table was laid for two.

Domenico the butler and his assistant Angelo appeared as silently as a prayer, wearing white gloves. They served prosciutto with melon, then green gnocchi with tomato sauce, followed by small steaks, artichoke hearts and fresh garden peas – home cooking for much of northern Italy, although without the white gloves.

Five years' working at the National Gallery had taught me that when treading on uncertain ground in matters of art, the best protection against seeming an ignorant fool was to maintain a sprung silence. However, I was too guileless to conceal my interest in one particular detail. My eyes kept darting towards a frescoed frieze around the upper part of the room.

'Palma Vecchio,' said the Conte, hardly pausing to look up.

'Music to my eyes,' I said.

I felt a low-level jolt of excitement at the thought of eating in a private dining room that Palma Vecchio had stood in and decorated. In the National Gallery, this fresco would have been considered sacrosanct, a landmark in the Italian High Renaissance; here, it was part of the décor. I had no one to share my excitement with, except the Conte, but he seemed blasé about dining before a masterpiece. I thought, Where else in the world is like this?

'Heavily influenced by Giovanni Bellini,' continued the Conte, tearing into a piece of bread.

'Giovanni Bellini is one of my favourites.' I tried to sound convincing. The irony was that I genuinely did admire Giovanni Bellini, most famous of the Bellini clan, the others being Jacopo and Gentile. 'You feel that Bellini, or whoever painted as Giovanni Bellini, had a wonderful eye.'

'Indeed. Not only was he Palma Vecchio's master but Titian's too. Where would Venetian art be without the Bellini family? Now tell me, how is London?'

'She's recovering from the war, and has one or two scars,

but otherwise she is on the mend. Lovely city but a bit dreary. I'm glad to have the chance to travel.'

'Do you like opera?'

'Up to a point,' I lied. 'I prefer music for relaxing to, rather than to get worked up about. I'm more interested in choral music. I sing in a choir. I like baroque.'

The Conte stopped eating and looked at me with an expression of genuine curiosity. 'What do you like about baroque?'

'It's the sort of music you don't have to listen to in order to enjoy,' I said. 'Just hearing it is enough. It allows you to get on with other things.' I must have come across as quite the Philistine.

'In Venice we had Vivaldi who wrote some of the most famous concerti ever – although the *Four Seasons* is an unusual piece for a Venetian composer, all about shepherds, meadows and birds. Before Vivaldi we had Monteverdi, the maestro at San Marco, and before him Giovanni Gabrieli. Venice is the birthplace and cradle of the baroque that is so important for the development of Western music. And there is nothing more baroque than opera – all art forms working in unison and always taking the pretty route.'

There was a pause. 'What is the opera like in Venice?' I asked.

'Drama, ritual, love, romance, tragedy, comedy, gossip, lust, power, vengeance, magic, mystery . . . and then the curtain goes up. Everyone plays their part.'

'I suppose that sums up Venice, doesn't it?' I said. 'It is hard to know where the art ends and real life begins.'

'Define "real".'

Domenico and Angelo entered as soundlessly as before. Angelo cleared while Domenico hovered.

I tried to simulate an air of nonchalance at the sheer magnificence of my surroundings as if they were nothing less than that to which I was accustomed. It wasn't easy. On my previous visit to Venice, I had stayed in a cheap *pensione* in a squalid *calletta* between San Marco and the Rialto. I looked up to the palazzi along the Grand Canal as temples of mystery and imagination, as in a scene by Canaletto. I could barely believe that here I was inside one such temple, and that I had become part of such a scene.

CHAPTER ONE

'Who Are These Italians?'

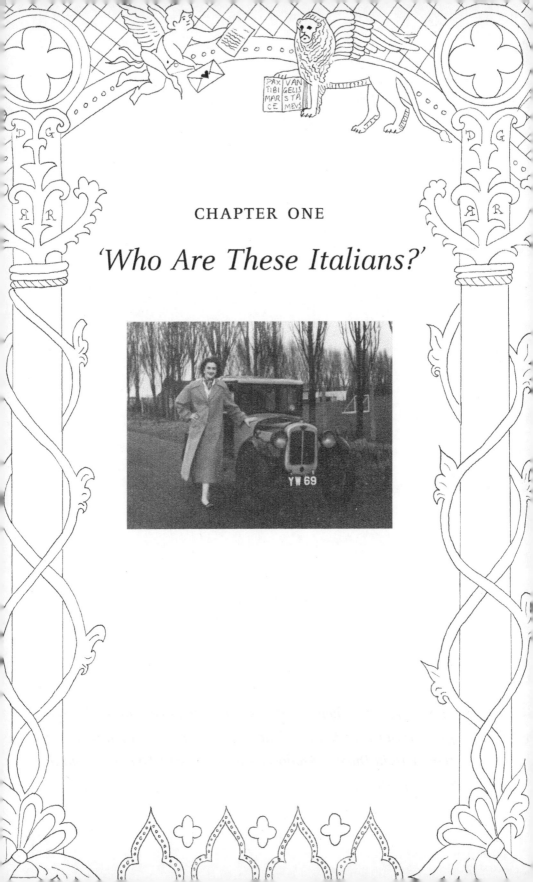

Previous page: *When David Ross, my then boyfriend, left London for Paris in March 1957, I had to sell my 'pet' 1929 Austin 7, seen here in Duke's Meadows, Chiswick, west London. I had no one to push it.*

HOVERING BETWEEN YOUNG adulthood and whatever came next, I had been working at the National Gallery in London, helping run the Publications Department, whose main business was shifting postcards, posters and calendars. Occasionally I assisted Sir Philip Hendy, the distinguished director of the Gallery.

'The Gallery sprinkles its fairy dust,' said Sir Philip, on one of our tours of inspection. 'A job here is a form of ennoblement.'

'Hmm.' I nodded pensively. Despite being promoted to assistant manager of Publications, I wasn't seeking art-world 'ennoblement' or even a career in the art world.

While at the Gallery, I interviewed candidates for a position as my assistant. I lit upon the friendliest-looking, nicely dressed, attractive in her own way. Her name was Jean Eaton.

'I should warn you, sweetie,' she confided, 'I don't have a degree in fine art. In fact, I have no formal qualifications at all.'

'Neither do I,' I whispered. 'Neither does anyone here, not even the director. The more "educated" or "qualified" you are, the less adapted you are to real life.'

Slightly naughty, somewhat irreverent and often insightful, Jean was soon promoted from 'colleague and friend' to 'colleague and confidante'. We shared a tiny office overlooking a dark courtyard. Through tears and giggles, we compared love lives. She was the sister I felt I had never had.

A year later, I was a bridesmaid at her wedding. Were anyone to search for the bottom rung of the property ladder in west

London in the mid-1950s, I should know exactly where to find it: a certain basement flat near Gloucester Road Underground station, which Jean shared with her husband as well as the District Line that ran beneath. Later, Jean announced she was leaving the Gallery. A twinge of loss and the thought that she was inching ahead in the egg-and-spoon race of life spurred me to get on too.

In the summer of 1956, Jean invited me to a ball at Londonderry House in Mayfair. I dug deep into the dressing-up box. My bridesmaid's dress needed only slight adjustment.

As my eyes travelled around the marble statues, full-length portraits, and Louis Something furniture of Londonderry House, Jean surveyed the room and said, 'Your dress looks a lot better than some of these gruesome outfits, sweetie.' She grabbed champagne. 'Come and meet a friend.' Deftly elbowing her way through the silk-swathed throng, she led me to a tall, dark, broad-shouldered man in full Highland regalia.

'Sweetie, this is David Ross. David, meet Gill Johnson.'

I had to remember to breathe. It wasn't the ill-fitting dress. We danced. David was good on his feet. I managed to establish that he was an architect, living in London with his mother. We agreed to keep in touch.

Over coffee the following morning, Jean filled me in. 'David? Only child. His childhood and upbringing were utterly miserable. His Siberian mother had a breakdown . . . His father, half Russian half Scottish, was a military attaché and probable spy who died of cancer or drink or both years ago . . . David is a superb dancer: flawless technique, I'm told, whatever that means. Good linguist . . . French girl in the background . . . But, sweetie, he's probably not your thing . . . Russian-Scottish?

Vodka and whisky don't mix. Still, one never forgets a man in a kilt . . .'

The wedding ring gleamed on Jean's finger. She was already sliding comfortably into domestic orthodoxy: curls cut short, roll-neck jumper, dark green skirt with unassertive check, stockings, low-heeled court shoes, no make-up or jewellery.

The first time David took me out was in August 1956. Nikolai Bulganin (Premier of the Soviet Union) and Nikita Khrushchev (First Secretary of the Communist Party of the Soviet Union) were invited to Covent Garden. David seemed more interested in the ballet than in me. 'Uplifting,' he said, over a glass of wine in the interval. After dinner in a very of-the-moment restaurant in Chelsea, we had our first kiss.

'I wonder how he got hold of tickets to Bulge and Krush,' said Jean, the following day. 'David has no money.'

David and I began to 'go out', with the emphasis on 'out'. In those days, relationships developed slowly, subject to parental oversight and scrutiny. Here was a problem.

I lived with my parents, sister Pauline and younger brothers Brian and Hugh in Morpeth Mansions, an 1880s red-brick mansion block in Victoria. Before the war, Winston Churchill had lived a few doors away in a flat that Frances Stevenson, Lloyd George's mistress, had previously occupied. My bedroom, a rear-facing former maid's quarters off the kitchen, was strewn with well-thumbed first editions of Georgette Heyer novels. Heyer portrayed self-determined women set in an age when women were possessed and controlled. For some, her novels were romances. For me, they were so much more: a source of comfort, guidance and inspiration, dust-jacketed with beautiful Regency heroines in corsets and dramatic poses.

Heyer's characters and Artur Barbosa's illustrations captured the life I craved. Still, my room felt like a dungeon.

With Nanny – Florence Bird, but known as 'Nanny' – we were seven. Brian and Hugh were at Cambridge; Pauline led a Flying Dutchman's existence as an air hostess. This left me at home to bear the filial burden. Although London was hardly poor, Londoners *felt* impoverished. Post-war rationing extended to 1954. Shelves were bare. Buddleia flourished in the blitzed gaps of peeling terraces. Everyone was waiting for things to improve. In my parents' Victorian parlour, the grave *tick . . . tock* of the grandfather clock seemed to emphasise and elongate the wait.

Whenever I came home, I would face a barrage of questions from my mother about why certain chores, cooking, cleaning and ironing, hadn't been done, chores that, since Nanny was no longer up to them, I was expected to carry out despite my full-time job. As my mother was a stranger in her own kitchen, I did the cooking.

My mother was half German, half English. The German half came from her father, Theodore Bruno Kittel, a German steel magnate turned banker from Leipzig. Having married Lydia Slater (my grandmother-to-be) from Worcester, Theodore moved to London, worked in the City, and owned factories in Sheffield. Despite taking British citizenship in 1898, he was jailed during the Great War and interned on the Isle of Man for 'unpatriotic behaviour' after he was spotted reading a German newspaper on the Underground. Someone had it in for him; I heard he could be quite arrogant.

When not in bed, my mother drifted about like a mournful mannequin. My siblings and I joked that the only useful thing she ever did was produce *us*. Her mood swings were best avoided. Speaking in German, her mother tongue, she would, wittingly or not – it was hard to tell – say cruelly unkind things, especially to Nanny, whose shock-absorbent qualities were beginning to degrade. A relict from grander days, Nanny was among the most important figures in our lives, but her waning influence brought us face to face with my mother's strangely undeveloped, un-diagnosed personality.

My mother's repertoire of hysterics, tantrums, flouncings off, 'grand moments', *de haut en bas* put-downs, slammed doors (her speciality) and her death stare, which haunted its victims as terrifyingly as certain renditions of Lady Macbeth's mono-logue, 'Come, you Spirits that tend on mortal thoughts . . .', began to tell on my father. I never dared ask if their marriage was a mistake. He might have answered, 'Yes.'

Maybe I was the one in denial. I dreaded aggravating the tension in case it forced my father to take sides. And were he to take my side, I was frightened that my mother should thereby be driven to finding new ways and more occult methods of being beastly to my father.

After a particularly difficult Sunday lunch, when my mother flew into a rage over the correct way to carve a chicken, my father confided to me, 'If I'm honest, Gilly, I don't think I could bear to live at home without you.'

From then on, I began to hate the reasons I loved my father. He was one of ten children from a landed family near Darlington in County Durham. Scholarly, loving and long-suffering, he trained as a barrister, then chaired an association of insurance companies. When he refused a knighthood, my brothers and I joked that he did so to prevent our mother becoming 'Lady

Johnson'; she was unbearable enough as she was. On his Irish side, my father claimed descent from the Marquess of Waterford.

With complete clarity, I knew I could no longer endure playing Cinderella. Without the shred of independence that my job gave me, my life might have become one of unmitigated misery. However, while the Gallery was a possible ticket into the art world, ennobled or not, it wasn't a guaranteed one-way journey, not for a young woman. A wrong word, an ill-judged first impression or a simple misunderstanding could damn me. The Gallery threatened its own form of institutional concubinage and, ultimately, chatteldom. I didn't want to risk ending up a spinster wearing out my days like one of those sad women with their lunchboxes who sit in the galleries pretending to be security guards. Not that I had unusual hopes. All I wanted was to leave home, marry and have children. But neither of my parents, for different reasons, wanted this. My mother depended on me; my father needed me as an emotional shield against my mother.

'This David person . . . no one we know seems to have heard of him,' crushed my mother over tea one weekend. Her grandiosity, hitherto subcutaneous, was becoming more apparent in middle age, as character defects often do. 'What kind of a name is "Mr David Ross"?'

David's Russian extraction was bad enough. My parents' main objections were his dim prospects and lack of money, tantamount to a 'fault' that a title might recompense were David to have one, which he didn't.

'I intend to marry for love and to live happily.'

There was a rattle of Crown Derby at the mention of marriage.

'David is just a penniless architect,' persisted my father. 'You can do better.' My father never discussed money, as if the Irishman in him didn't notice and the Englishman didn't care. He made an exception for David.

'He's my kind of penniless architect,' I said. 'He's perfectly turned out, and he went to Marlborough and Cambridge. What more do you want?'

I hardly cared what my mother thought. I did, however, worry about my father's harsher censure. With his cold-blooded attitude, he hoped that, if I *must* marry, I'd make a brilliant money marriage to someone with boundless promise and ambition, a future Cabinet minister, a law lord, a senior diplomat or a prominent editor. But I instinctively knew that such people would never bring happiness. It seemed my parents were more interested in being proved right than in knowing about David's finer qualities. So I concealed him. Hence the emphasis on going *out*.

Ironically, David's family was far more distinguished than mine. His grandfather, Sir Archibald, mechanised the Russian and British fleets. His great-uncle, Sir Denison Ross, a Middle Eastern scholar and friend of Kemal Atatürk, was the first director of, and professor of Persian at, the School of Oriental Studies, later the School of Oriental and African Studies (SOAS). It was typical of David not to mention this. He was oblivious to my parents' disapproval. Had he known, he might have put them right. But he kept quiet.

Our romance developed at cafés, theatres, concerts and cinemas. Music and art bound us. I told David how at school I had been spotted by Dr Reginald Jacques, then musical director of the Bach Choir. 'Dr Jacques would take me to dine at the Athenaeum,' I said. 'He told me that he had once conducted

Brahms's *A German Requiem*, in which a member of the choir had herself been conducted by Brahms.'

At my suggestion David joined the Bach Choir. We even discussed ecclesiastical architecture or, rather, David talked about ecclesiastical architecture; I tried to look as if I might be listening. It was a lovely way to begin a relationship. I imagine some people fall in love and marry straight away, only to find terminal incompatibilities.

David's mother Tania struck me as fabulously exotic when I met her over dinner at her flat on Gloucester Walk in Notting Hill. Born in Siberia, tossed by the Russian Revolution, forcibly uprooted to Vladivostok, then fortuitously plucked to Newcastle-upon-Tyne, she was further pummelled by the convulsions that led to the Second World War. When the war ended, she hoped for blue skies and normality, but her husband, Brigadier Ross, fell ill with throat cancer and died in 1948, leaving a slender provision. Father and son hardly knew each other. By the time I met David, his and his mother's lives had been a succession of grievous losses and miseries. In his case, his loneliness was compounded by his not getting on with his mother. David found her irritating and embarrassing. In temperament, they were miles apart: she was loud and emotional; he was quiet and brooding. Like his late father, he was a linguist; she, on the other hand, never mastered English. David minded about his mother, but didn't love her.

We got about in my 1929 Austin 7 – my 'pet'. David didn't seem to notice the bald tyres, the rusty bodywork, the loose wooden floorboards, the windows that didn't close and the door locks that didn't lock.

As with some pets, mine needed walking; David didn't seem

to mind that either. After grinding to a halt one evening outside the Ritz, he hefted me half a mile along Piccadilly to a garage off Belgrave Square. Breaking down was part of the fun; motoring was a middle-class mating ritual. David must have pushed me further than I ever drove him. This, I felt, was a good test and indicator, so to speak. I began to see him as a catalyst in a plan that was germinating in my mind to flee home.

Just when I fancied I'd stepped into a Botticelli-esque interlude of grace, beauty and romance, a thunderclap shook me one day in December 1956. Over lunch, David announced that he'd entered, and won, an architectural competition. He'd been offered a job in Paris. He'd leave in four months.

Well . . . I . . .

Someone had taken a meat cleaver to my Botticelli fairy-tale and replaced it with a Hieronymus Bosch nightmare. I went crashing round to Jean's flat.

'Samaritans hang up on you, sweetie?' she asked, when I stormed in. 'Your face is a picture – painted by Edvard Munch. How are you feeling?'

An ironing board stood in the sitting room. A BBC voice read news on the wireless. The aroma of a stew filled the flat.

'Disappointed? Deflated? Devastated?' I said, throwing myself on to the sofa. 'It definitely begins with a capital D.'

'Let's begin with Drink, shall we, sweetie?' Aproned, Jean turned down – but not off – the wireless, and fetched glasses of whisky.

'David never mentioned anything about an architectural competition,' I said, concluding my summary of his bombshell. 'It's quite in his character not to talk about his job, but *this*? I feel he's being secretive.'

'Think through the rage, sweetie,' said Jean, returning from the kitchen with the bottle.

'Worse, he hasn't invited me to join him in Paris,' I cried.

'I expect he wanted to spare your emotions,' soothed Jean. 'The gentleman in him didn't want to upset you. The courtier in him didn't want to risk looking a fool.' She hung up a shirt on the mantelpiece. 'Anyway, how could he ask you to Paris? *You're not married.*' The gleaming ring on Jean's finger seemed to laugh at me. I could have sworn I saw a matching glint in her eyes.

'How are you supposed to get married without having the chance to know who, or what, you're marrying?'

'You can't,' she called, over the clatter of pots and pans in the kitchen. 'It's like pinning the tail on the donkey.'

'There I was, dreaming of what to wear at our wedding. I even caught myself wondering what colour eyes our children would have. And to think he was quietly engineering an exit.'

'His job here does sound rather . . . linear?' Jean reappeared wearing oven gloves.

'Have I simply strung together a few dreams with wishful thinking?' I took another draught of whisky.

'Perhaps you have allowed yourself the luxury of getting lost in rose-tinted mist,' said Jean. 'Perhaps he doesn't trust – or doesn't dare to trust – his happiness. Perhaps he feels happier when slightly unhappy, if that makes sense.'

'Oh, God, he's not a manic depressive, is he?'

'No. Just Russian,' said Jean, plumping and arranging cushions. 'Perhaps you could find it in yourself to be delighted on David's behalf.' She sat down on a chair, picked up her glass 'After all, "delighted" begins with D.'

Jean wasn't being as helpful, supportive and empathetic as I'd hoped. She no longer *needed* me. I heard voices, each in a different key of disappointment, ringing in my head, among them Jean's earlier caution: *French girl in the background . . .*

'I'm worried he's spiralling out into a different orbit,' I said. 'If he goes to Paris and consummates this French thing, he might never come back, and I'll lose him for ever.'

Jean gave me a level look.

Finally I blurted out, 'I'm thinking of leaving the National Gallery, moving on, doing something else.'

'Aren't you throwing in the towel a little early, sweetie? You're only twenty-five.' Grabbing the bottle, she splashed more whisky into my glass. I raised my hand, too late.

'*Twenty-four!*' I said. 'I suppose I *have* been feeling pleased with myself lately, having been promoted and all that. But I don't want to be left stupid and festering in London, waiting like a sad Labrador. And I could do with seeing less of my parents.'

'So what are you going to do, sweetie?'

'I don't know.'

'Maybe it's time for a holiday,' said Sally-Anne, my hairdresser, when I went for an appointment at Peter Jones on Sloane Square. 'I mean, if *he*'s going away, you might as well too.'

'Quite! I need to dig out my passport.'

'You need less certainty in your life,' said Sally-Anne.

I looked at her in the mirror of her hair station.

'Make sure you don't go to Paris, that's all,' she went on.

'No?'

'He mustn't think you're chasing him. Go anywhere but Paris.'

Sally-Anne always referred to David as 'he'. Presumably her head was already stuffed with the names of the boyfriends, husbands, sons and lovers of other clients.

'And what about my job?' I already knew what I thought about my job, but I wondered what the canon of hairdresser's wisdom had to say on the matter.

'What about your job?'

'Common sense would say that the job comes before the wild-goose chase.'

'Common sense will only get you so far,' said Sally-Anne, through several hair clips clenched between her teeth. 'You need to give up your job, take a running jump off a cliff, and hope that you grow wings on the way down.'

I forced a weak smile. I had definitely reached a 'moment' in my life. I was standing, if not on a cliff, then certainly on a cusp. There was no place for doubt or hesitation. I had to act. Flicking through a magazine while sitting under a hair-dryer, I spotted a small advertisement for Universal Aunts. Their motto caught my eye: 'Anything for Anyone at Any Time'. I tore it out and squirrelled it into my handbag.

As soon as the Christmas holidays were over, I gave in my resignation: five months' notice. I would leave the Gallery at the end of May. With flaming bridges behind me, I would set off into the future. Naive? Everyone of my background was, in those days.

My mother took my resignation with a pained look. My father weighed in: 'You can't leave the Gallery. You need a job, security and a position.'

'I have other priorities,' I said. 'I have held down a decent job. I know I can do it. I've earned the right to do what I want.'

'But why throw it away? You've been promoted. Things are about to get interesting.'

'I'm throwing nothing away. This job was never meant to be a vocation. I love the National Gallery, but I refuse to grow old there, and I certainly don't want to plot and connive my way up to the top. It is time to move on!'

'And do what?'

I could tolerate a little light questioning, but this was an inquisition too far. 'Follow the yellow brick road!'

I saw in my father's eyes a look of terrified loneliness. He could see I meant it. I could almost hear him thinking that his loving daughter was intending to leave home, and that no one would replace that love. It meant abandoning my father to a cold and lonely fight with my mother.

'How do you know where it leads?' asked my father, quietly.

'I'll tell you in twenty years.'

Meanwhile, strategic thinking was called for. To provoke a reaction in David, I pretended to audition suitors. I adroitly rotated boyfriends, or friends who happened to be boys. From my diary, I cannot remember who 'John', 'Stuart' and 'Jack' were, never mind their real names. In February, I managed to get one up on David by going on a skiing trip to Switzerland.

While on the slopes, to my pleasant shock, a telegram arrived on 14 February: 'Romeo to Juliet'. I easily deduced that it was from David. Even as I write this sixty-six years later, I can still feel the emotions that overcame me. It was so unlike David.

Returning to London, I found that my Austin 7 had become a maternity ward. A cat had climbed in through the uncloseable windows, and littered in the footwell. Happy that a pet had nested in my 'pet', I left the clowder alone. A few days later, it vanished. This felt like another spur.

My other-boyfriend feint worked. From mid-February to David's departure in March, my diary was awhirl with theatre visits, dinners, film expeditions and concerts, all with David, and anything to keep away from home. I said goodbye to him in a tearful farewell at Victoria Station as he boarded the boat train to Paris.

I wanted to travel too, but in a way that aligned with my parents' sensitivities. Had I told them I was about to go abroad on my own, they would have clamoured, *A young girl travelling abroad alone? Unthinkable!* They would have howled even louder if I'd said I was travelling to see David. Whatever I did, they would have objected. I needed to find the least objectionable excuse. From my handbag, I pulled out the advertisement for Universal Aunts.

'I want an adventure,' I announced to the middle-aged woman seated in the sparse office of Universal Aunts in Belgravia, hung with framed testimonials, where I'd dropped in one day in early May. 'Somewhere abroad,' I persisted. 'Anywhere but Paris.'

The woman put down her sandwich, picked up a paper napkin, and dabbed her Cupid's bow lips.

'We are not travel agents, you know.' She held out a mottled hand. 'Gertrude Maclean.'

'Gill Johnson.'

Miss Maclean's resigned what-might-have-been air reminded me of a forlorn nun who had taught me piano and French in a convent in the Borders of Scotland where I was evacuated during the war.

'I quite understand,' I said, maintaining an upright posture. 'It's just that I saw your advertisement at the hairdresser's, and thought I'd come by in my lunch-break.'

'You have a job?'

'At the National Gallery.'

'Your position?' said Miss Maclean, picking up a pen.

'I'm assistant to the head of Publications but . . .' I paused.

Miss Maclean looked up.

'. . . I have handed in my notice.'

Miss Maclean whipped off her glasses. 'Miss Johnson, I am knee-deep in handwritten letters accompanied by stamped, addressed envelopes to the back of beyond from girls who'd kill to work at the National Gallery. You are staring at the catch-net of the unenfranchised, the dispossessed and the unloved. Why do you think you're different?'

'I don't. I just feel in need of excitement, a bit of fun.'

'*Fun*.' Miss Maclean spat out the word as if it were an inedibly tough part of her sandwich. 'Most of the women we meet are trying to get *into* a job, not out of one.' She stared at me, purse-lipped. 'So. Tell me about yourself.'

'I've just turned twenty-five. I'm single, educated – up to a point. I don't have many qualifications but I know how to tie shoelaces. I live in London with my parents – it's all right, there haven't been any homicides. At least not yet. I feel just like I'm . . .'

'Persephone dragged into the cold netherworld of the dead.'

'That's it!'

'I hear that a lot,' said Miss Maclean. '"Anywhere but Paris". What's wrong with Paris?' She leant forward slightly, then added, '*What* is in Paris?'

'. . .'

She leant further forward, and said, '*He*'s in Paris, isn't he.' It wasn't a question.

I had no idea that I gave so much away.

'Y-yes.'

'Nothing wrong with a *cri de coeur*,' said Miss Maclean, sitting back in triumph. 'Hear them all the time. How long will *he* be in Paris?'

'He says a year.'

Miss Maclean's blue-grey eyes turned cold, so I pre-empted the next question: 'You need to know if I'm reliable.'

'Are you?'

'Ask Sir Philip Hendy, the director of the National Gallery.'

'If you get along so well with Sir Philip, why did you hand in your notice? I have better things to do than to help you play games with your sweetheart. Missing out on the marital merry-go-round is the least of the problems that I have to deal with.'

'I don't want five years at the National Gallery to become fifty.'

'Why should they? You could work anywhere. The art world would be at your feet. Think of the glamour.'

'I don't need glamour,' I said. 'I'm happy with happiness. But I refuse to wait at home while he's pursuing his Parisian pipe-dreams.'

'So, you're ready to toss your cards into the air and see where they land.'

'I'm hoping you might make such a move unnecessary,' I said. 'Or at least give me an idea of what cards I hold and where they *might* land.'

'And if *he* snaps his fingers . . .?'

'Am I on the next train to Paris?' I shook my head. 'No. Absolutely not.'

Miss Maclean brightened. 'Good,' she said. 'We try to avoid impulsive behaviour. Now, I don't suppose you hold a driving licence.'

'I do.'

'What languages, other than the Queen's English?'

'German and French.'

'Italian?'

'With a bit of pantomime, I can get by.'

Miss Maclean put on her glasses, picked up an envelope and held it lightly in her fingertips. She placed it on the desk between us. I saw that the return address, although upside-down to me, consisted of three words on two lines, and was embossed in red.

'Have you ever been in charge of children?' asked Miss Maclean.

'I have two younger brothers. I like children. I used to be one myself.'

'Grown-ups? Have you been in charge of adults?'

'At the Gallery, I work in a team. We're very—'

'I mean *staff*.'

'Ah! When I stayed at my Aunt Ida's dairy farm, I gave the farmhands their orders in German. My grandfather came from Leipzig.'

Miss Maclean paused and looked at me objectively. 'As it happens,' she said, 'a letter arrived this morning offering a rather unusual position to a young woman with languages who can drive and look after young children. The job description does not seem onerous. However, the position demands an unusually high calibre of candidate. I've considered a number of girls. I wonder if it might appeal to you.'

'I'd be completely fine with that,' I said. 'Why not?'

I was still unable to make out the small, upside-down legend of the return address. I felt like a cheating schoolgirl trying to peek at a classmate's test paper. 'Is this job in Europe?' I asked.

'Yes.'

'I'm interested.'

Miss Maclean nodded slowly.

'The return address,' I said, looking at the envelope. 'Are three words enough?'

'Plenty,' said Miss Maclean, 'No street address necessary – none possible, in fact.' She picked up the envelope, and withdrew the letter. 'The family name is Brandolini d'Adda.' She flourished the document. 'This letter is from Conte Brandolini d'Adda. The Contessa wants someone to look after their boys aged nine and seven for the summer. I understand she is expecting another child.'

'What is the address?'

'Palazzo Brandolini, Venice.'

The following day, blossom confetti'd brilliantly in the spring sunshine as I arrived at Pelham Place, an elegant Georgian terrace.

'Good afternoon,' I said. 'Is this the house of Oliver Messel? My name is Gill Johnson.'

'Ah, yes,' said the handsome butler, a young man of Scandinavian physiognomy wearing a striped butcher's apron. 'Do come in.'

We climbed stairs. The drawing room ran the entire length of the house.

'Do take a seat,' said the butler. 'Mr Messel will be with you shortly. Tea?'

'Thank you.'

Miss Maclean had forwarded me to Oliver Messel who was acting as referee for the Venice position. I had little idea who Mr Messel was other than an interior designer.

Number 17 Pelham Place was two houses joined laterally. I'd never felt such an exhilarating sense of light and space, and yet there was nowhere to sit. The space was filled with . . . Well, what? It was a sensational Aladdin's Cave of fantastic *brocante*: flowery china, bunches of roses, a papier-mâché bust wearing a wig, and a pair of gilt, marble-topped tables. On the floor lay a heavy-looking roll of canvas, a pile of dishcloths and several sheets of gold paper. Hanging on the walls were two mirrors encrusted with a gold floral motif, and festooned with engraved or embossed invitations. To either side of one mirror hung grotesque theatrical masks, hatted, plumed, sequined and swathed in silk. In mid-room, Regency armchairs filled with papers addressed a dark-green silken couch.

I noticed some sketches lying on a sofa: they looked like a

playful fantasy of what a grand interior might look like. I was standing in the crèche and nursery of an artist's inspirations and creations.

A boyish-looking Latin-dark man appeared as if from nowhere.

'Oliver Messel. How do you do?' He smiled warmly. 'Thank you for coming. Please,' he said, scooping a pile of books and papers from a sofa.

Trim, dapper in white shirt with sleeves rolled up, alert, lively, Messel had the air of a sprite: dark, intelligent gaze, eyebrows plucked into miniature proscenium arches and a high forehead. 'Have you come far?' he asked.

'I live in Westminster,' I said. 'It was such a lovely afternoon that I walked.'

'London is so gorgeous at this time of year, isn't it? Now, a dear friend in Venice is looking for someone to take care of two children for the summer. Your name has been sifted.' Messel grinned. 'That's right, isn't it? Hah! As you can probably tell, I've not done this sort of thing before. Normally I'm the one being interviewed. Anyway, her name is Contessa Cristiana Brandolini d'Adda.'

'That name means nothing to me, I'm afraid,' I said. 'Miss Maclean mentioned something about a well-known family in Venice.'

'Cristiana is an Agnelli,' Messel said. He paused and put on an expression of sudden seriousness. 'I expect you've heard of her brother Gianni Agnelli?'

I had to reach deep into my knowledge of Italian. 'Lambs?' I said.

'Ah, *parla italiano*!' Messel relaxed, leant back and smiled.

'The Agnelli own Fiat in Turin. You know those little Cinquecento cars?'

'Ah, yes.'

'Gianni runs the shop. Cristiana is married to Brando Brandolini d'Adda, lovely man. He's a conte of some sort. His family go back centuries. I've done a few bits and pieces for them. I've no idea what exactly the job entails, but they've asked me to help. I understand the boys had an English governess.'

'If these boys are Italian, why did they have an English governess?'

'Ah, that's because English is the common language of the jet set,' said Messel.'

'I've heard of the jet set, but know nothing about them, except that people talked about them breathlessly.'

'They're the rich, glamorous, international, wafer-thin upper crust of European and American society that travels around the world in jet aeroplanes. Whether they're Greek, French, Italian, German, South American, Swedish, Danish or Russian, they need English if they are to be taken seriously. The important thing is that the jet set looks to the English not only for their language but also for their manners, style and [cough] taste in interior decoration.' Messel couldn't resist a smile. 'They all secretly want to be English gentlemen and gentlewomen. Some of the more intelligent ones even manage to fathom the English class system, and the really clever ones, like Brando and Cristiana, even understand the English sense of humour. Cristiana and Brando are what you might call critical nodes.' Messel winked and grinned. 'Now, I understand you love art.'

'Yes.'

'So, if I said, "Bellini"?'

'The painter or the Venetian cocktail, and if the painter, which of the three Bellini?'

Messel smiled. 'Do you know anyone in Venice?'

'Only dead ones, like Titian and Veronese.'

'Yes, it's always handy to have a bit of background knowledge.'

Interview over, we descended to the hall. While Messel dug about for his card, I peered at a pile of parcels by the front door: 'Ernest E Lupowitz III, Sutton Place, New York', 'Mme de Boisseau, Avenue Montaigne, Paris', 'Alfred Pleydl, Beverly Hills' and 'Royal Opera House, Covent Garden'.

Feeling a tingle of excitement and liberation, I deferred my journey home, and walked to Gloucester Road to meet Jean. Could Mr Messel produce me like one of his creations, wrap me up and affix a label for dispatch to Venice? This adventure, if it came off, could be breathtaking and life-changing. I wanted it more than ever.

'I know Italians are brought up to believe in miracles but isn't this asking a lot of God?' said Jean, chopping carrots. 'What do you know about childcare or teaching English?'

'I'm not even asking for a minor miracle. I could look after children and teach English in my sleep.'

'I expect,' said Jean, 'Mr Messel will be feeling relieved. He was probably dreading having to interview a queue of dull women who can only pretend to speak Italian and haven't a clue which country Venice is in. Still,' she put down the chopping knife and bit the end off a carrot, 'I can't see how this job is an improvement on the National Gallery.'

'Is chopping carrots and ironing an improvement?'

'Well . . .'

'Exactly. Who cares about an "improvement" when there is a far greater good at stake?'

Walking home from Gloucester Road, I had two and a half miles in which to wonder if David really was a 'greater good' or if I was imagining it.

Back home, I found my mother at her dressing-table awaft with Chanel No 5 mixed with the aroma of gardenia bath oils.

'*Venice?*' she cried, at her triple mirror, when I told her about the job. 'I thought you didn't want to be an au pair, and, if you do, why not be an au pair to your own family?'

'Let's not go into that.' I flung her a nonchalant look. 'I just walked into the offices of Universal Aunts.'

I felt that my mother's interest was piqued by Venice. My parents loved Venice. They'd honeymooned there. Perhaps their marriage was credited to Venice. Would something similar happen to me?

All of a sudden, my parents' lives were thrown into confusion. It was one thing for me to hand in my notice, quite another to leave home. That the convergence of these two eventualities seemed to coincide with the arrival of David was multiply alarming, especially to my father, whom I suspected of jealousy. However, he knew, and I knew that he knew, that he wouldn't want to alienate his favourite daughter for ever.

'And who will help at home?' asked my mother.

At that moment, Nanny stumbled in, bearing the look of a threadbare cushion. I half convinced myself that Nanny could take over my role within the household. Despite her loss of resilience, I was casting her as an unlikely peacekeeper between my parents. Wasn't that half the point of staff – to hold families together while keeping them apart?

The mood changed significantly when the telephone rang on its wobbly side table. My mother went to pick it up. I could make out the booming voice of Aunt Ida, who would occasionally ring for a 'quiet' chat. My mother held the receiver a few inches from her ear.

'. . . and Gill has been interviewed for a job in Venice,' she said to Aunt Ida, 'working for an Italian family.'

My mother mentioned the news of my possible job in Venice simply as something that might interest Aunt Ida. She slightly looked up to her elder sister, her only sane sibling and one to whom she had been indebted since Aunt Ida had looked after us during the war.

'An Italian family?' cried Aunt Ida. 'Who are these [crescendoing boom] *ITALIANS*?' My mother opened the angle of the receiver.

I visualised Aunt Ida as if she were standing before me. Indomitable, enthusiastic, generous, intelligent, faintly patronising and often mistaken for a hybrid of Lady Bracknell and one of Bertie Wooster's aunts, she was a tough-love fairy godmother. During part of the war, I lived with her at Bryckden Place, her Victorian pile on thirty acres of east Sussex. I was the dream niece, who bore neither blot nor stain, over whom she could wield influence absolved of direct responsibility.

The legend of her chaining herself to the railings outside Buckingham Palace in 1914 in support of the suffragettes indicated a daring and liberating spirit. Professionally, she was a phenomenon. While her whisky distiller husband golfed, she rolled up her sleeves. She invented milking machines that enabled her to juggle her dairy herd while leading a comfortable and civilised life. With her unshakeable belief in progress, and the essential goodness of new things, Aunt Ida was a step up from many other aunts. While my mother came across as spoilt, Aunt Ida conveyed a sense of grandeur tempered by humour. She and my mother were a study in opposites: Aunt Ida's lightning to my mother's thunder.

Neither of my parents had bothered to ask, 'Who are these Italians?' I could tell they thought I wouldn't get the job. Aunt Ida, however, had no such qualms.

'The family name is Brandolini d'Adda,' said my mother to Aunt Ida.

'That name rings a cracked bell,' said Aunt Ida. 'What is the job?'

'She hasn't yet been offered one.'

'Never mind that,' said Aunt Ida, brusquely. 'What's the job description?'

'Sort of au pair to the children, teaching them English, and generally looking after them.' My mother glanced at me for approval. I nodded.

'I see,' said Aunt Ida. 'We need to make it abundantly clear that Gill goes into battle at the very top. She's officer class.'

'Gill simply had an interview today,' said my mother, trying to dampen Aunt Ida's spirit, 'with a man called Oliver Messel, who I underst—'

'*Oh. I. Know. Oliver.* His parents are neighbours. Oliver knows Anthony. They met in Hollywood. Oliver designs film sets or something. Let's see . . . Hollywood is eight hours behind.

Anthony will be having his elevenses. I'll call him. Leave this with me. Tell Gill to pack.'

The idea of my cousin Anthony Dawson, the Hollywood villain and arch baddy, having elevenses seemed laughable, but I let it go. Aunt Ida was willing to make intercontinental calls on my behalf, while it wouldn't have occurred to my mother even to get out of bed. More importantly, Aunt Ida's leap into unprompted action was the first credible endorsement of my proposed adventure. I wasn't simply daydreaming in an unemancipated age: I was making sensible decisions.

Powerful machinery began to turn. A universal aunt in a real sense, Aunt Ida was an effective operator. Her voice and manner could assume a chilling authority. I wondered if she really *did* know Oliver Messel.

When the telephone rang the following morning, I smothered it.

'Is Miss Johnson there?' said the voice. I recognised Miss Maclean.

'Speaking,' I said.

'Gertrude Maclean. Universal Aunts.'

'Ah, yes, lovely to hear from you.'

'I'm delighted to say that the job in Venice is yours should you choose to accept it. The term of the contract will run from the fifth of June. You will be paid the sum of . . .'

I had already glazed over and floated off, chloroformed by euphoria and the sound of the Hallelujah Chorus ringing in my head. Did Miss Maclean say eighty lire a month or eight hundred or eight thousand or . . .? It didn't matter. What was a life worth? Money didn't figure, never did, never will.

'. . . First-class rail tickets will be sent by post. While the start date is fixed, your tickets allow you to travel whenever you wish. They, er, include a stopover in Paris. Enjoy your time as a Universal Aunt, Miss Johnson.'

My mother took the news with a plumping of pillows. My father managed to seem pleased, especially when I mentioned 'return ticket', and proceeded to give a fine dissection of Venetian diet, morals and lavatories. Meanwhile a letter arrived from David. He referred to 'a complete black depression'. Work had dried up. He was out of a job. His boss had told him, 'You can leave this evening.'

'It's ridiculous,' he wrote. 'I worked myself out of a job!'

Things weren't going as well as David had hoped. He was regarded as cheap expendable labour 'at the other end of a pencil'. Perversely, I gleaned a sprig of comfort from this news. On the other hand, I was about to 'toss my cards into the air and see where they land' and 'step off a cliff and hope to grow wings'. What grounds did I have for thinking I'd fare any better? I rang David. Unprompted, he suggested we meet in Paris.

I set my departure: 31 May. David said he would meet me at the Gare du Nord. For the next three weeks, I became a blur of activity. One important task was to sell my Austin 7. Its value depended on how much petrol was in the tank. One unfortunate prospect had his trousers ripped off by the gear mechanism, which had become exposed. I managed to offload the car to Dickie Du Cann QC, for fifteen pounds.

'Venice and Britain are quite similar,' said Sir Philip Hendy, at my leaving party. 'Maritime, mercantile, tolerant, not particularly religious, and coming to terms with post-imperial decline.' He was in art-expert mode.

'Fascinating,' I prompted.

'Like Britain,' he continued, 'the Venetians skilfully defended themselves from larger interests by divide-and-rule, or divide-and-avoid-being-invaded. No would-be assailant was lucky enough, brave enough nor clever enough. The old power structures and families of Venice therefore persisted. And when you add in the great art of Venice,' he said, rounding off, 'I'm sure, Gill, you will feel quite at home.'

CHAPTER TWO

'I Never Thought
I'd Leave Paris in Tears'

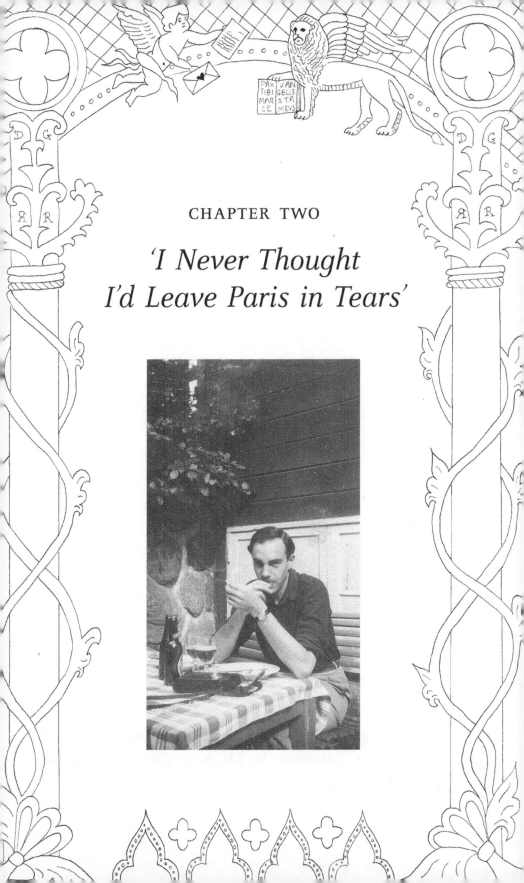

Previous page: *A rare photograph of David seen here in Paris in early 1957. Throughout his life, he preferred being behind, not in front of, the lens.*

MY FATHER SAID he'd drive me the short distance to Victoria Station, to see me off on the Golden Arrow. My mother, meanwhile, preferred to stay in bed.

'Does she think of anyone besides herself?' I asked my father, as I stood on the pavement outside Morpeth Mansions watching him heave my trunk containing my entire wardrobe, several Georgette Heyer romances, a guide to Venice and, on Aunt Ida's instruction, as many packets of cigarettes as I could fit in ('Hard currency!' she said). When thinking about my mother, I would rarely stop at 'fair'. I would overshoot, ignore warning signs and go past red. It was time to move on.

'Now, now, darling. Your mother is . . . your mother,' said my father, closing the boot of his green-grey Jowett Javelin, while clouds gathered overhead. 'At least from now on you won't have to worry about her,' he said pointedly, as he fired the engine, looking grimly ahead. From this, I read, 'From now on, I will have to battle my wife alone.'

Unless travelling abroad, my mother preferred to stay in rather than go out. When I was younger, on Christmas Eve, my father would take me to the service of Nine Lessons and Carols at King's College, Cambridge, where he had been a scholar. What felt like the greatest Christmas treat was greeted by my mother with an adjustment of bedclothes.

At Victoria, my trunk was sealed, tagged and dispatched, not to be seen again until Venice. I kissed my father goodbye, and was crying by the time I stepped aboard. As the train scraped out of the station, I leant from the window and waved to the blurred figure receding on the platform. I'm sure my father cried too.

I'd been feeling guilty at leaving home. Uncritical, enchanted, perhaps wrong-headed, I loved my father partly because my mother was so beastly to him. Until now, I had stayed strong in my refusal to sacrifice my own happiness on the altar of my father's asymmetrical love for my mother, but now the reality of leaving my job and my home and saying goodbye struck me forcefully and emotionally. As tears flowed, I wondered, Would it be worth it? Would David be worth it? Did David even love me?

The first-class carriage of the Golden Arrow seemed a wheeled palace, padded and mirrored in vaguely Edwardian luxe, with exotic inlays and decorated marquetry. I peered around, hoping to see countesses, exiled monarchs, crowned and coroneted heads or even an abdicated king or two, or just someone who might change my life. All I saw were a few armchaired businessmen, one or two couples, and a steward who had developed a knack of removing the crown tops off tonic-water bottles by levering them against a flourish in the ornate décor.

As the train picked up speed, so did my imagination. Sadness gave way to a razor-edge sensation of mild adrenaline, escapism, expectation and anonymity. As we rattled through Kent, the sun broke through and I began to feel less accountable to my previous self, as if I had shed something and finally cut loose. Hope sparkled before me.

Gazing out of the window, I thought of my grandmother,

Lydia Slater, whose family had owned shoe factories in Worcester and were well-heeled in every sense. She must have had ambitions beyond the usual four walls of the family house, and probably experienced similar thoughts and emotions to mine. After school in the Cotswolds, she was 'finished' in Paris, then went on to study music in Leipzig. By the time she met my grandfather, Theodore Kittel, on a train in Saxony, she was an accomplished woman.

Alighting at Dover, I embarked on a ferry to Calais, where I boarded the Flèche d'Or to Paris. As the train rolled across the Picardie countryside, it passed the same land on which my father had fought in the Great War. Shot at Ypres ('Like being hit with a sledgehammer'), he said that trampling over dead comrades in the trenches was far worse. Against the odds, he made it home in one piece, with a lodged bullet to spare.

'Does the train pass through Ypres?' I asked the ticket inspector.

'*Non, Mademoiselle.* Ypres is in Belgium. We pass thirty kilometres to the west.'

'I'm so glad,' I said. 'Thank you.'

As the train approached Paris, the wheels hammered away on the joints of the track. To my fevered mind, they sounded as if they were calling: 'He won't be there! He won't be there! He won't be there!' I hadn't seen David for ten weeks. Would I recognise him? Would he recognise me? If I tried to conjure him in my mind's eye, the image soon faded into vague and dislocated impressions.

The Flèche d'Or hit its target bang on time. Politely rebuffing several blue-overalled porters on the platform, I walked slowly amid the din of passengers and whistles towards the barrier.

I spotted David. He was the only person not looking up or wandering about. Unlike my father, he was not a blur. He was leaning against a pillar writing on a newspaper. As I walked forward, he continued writing, oblivious to my approach. I realised that he wasn't writing: he was sketching the roof of the Gare du Nord on a copy of *Le Figaro*. He looked up. Our eyes met. After a momentary pause, his face lit up. This was the moment I'd hoped for.

I was shocked by what greeted me through the windows of the taxi. Dreary, dirty, sullen and in places very run-down, Paris was like a dystopian nightmare. Elegant eighteenth-century façades and grand boulevards were riddled with bullet holes and the wounds of bitter conflict. Every few yards, a bunch of dead or dying flowers, or a small plaque, commemorated a victim of the war. This was not the Paris of Toulouse-Lautrec and Seurat; it was the Paris the Nazis had left behind.

'I thought Paris in the spring was meant to be beautiful,' I said. 'There is hardly any greenery. The only flowers are *in memoriam*.'

'Parisians are not allowed window boxes,' David explained. 'After the Revolution, boxes were banned because people stored stones and ammunition in them.'

David was full of snippets like that. He was the gentlest of men, but when waging wars of wits and battles of general knowledge, he was always well-armed.

A few rusty green buses lurched about the boulevards alongside the occasional black Renault and Deux Chevaux, all of which had to avoid the many handcarts and bicycles that filled the streets. The real 'colour' of Paris lay in the rising perfumes and aromas. The city was high with the powerful stench of drains, intermingled with the smoke from a million Gauloises, a few whiffs of scent, the wafts of delicious cooking and the fresh 'green' bouquet of fruit-and-vegetable stalls.

'Parts of Paris are excellent,' said David. 'I'm still trying to work out which ones.'

He lived in the Hôtel Danube, directly opposite L'Université on rue Jacob in the *6ème arrondissement*, the intimate old Paris across the Seine from the Louvre, a tight mesh of narrow streets and high-roofed buildings on the Left Bank.

The proprietor, a pale, defeated-looking man seated at Reception, gave me a glare of fastidious suspicion bordering on hostility.

'Why did he look at me like that?' I whispered to David, as we made our way to his room.

'According to French law, were you to give birth while resident here, we would have the right to live here and raise a family. If you'd been pregnant, they would have turned us away.'

I wondered if that was the *real* reason.

David's room was on the first floor. Containing most of his possessions, it was quite stark. Begrimed cream walls framed a threadbare brown carpet. Daylight washed in from two windows overlooking rue Jacob. After sunset, a pitiless yellowish glow seeped from a raw bulb wired to the ceiling. The room was furnished, if that's the right word, with a bed, two chairs, a small writing table, a sink and an early model of a bidet: tin, with wooden legs. To fill it, you held it under a running tap. If you wanted a bath, you had to give a day's notice so that a fire could be lit beneath a boiler.

Under its carapace of chipped and peeling paint, of stained

and curling wallpaper, and the occasional growth of mushrooms, the hotel had undeniable character and oozed period charm.

In the 1920s and 1930s, with a café on every corner and the Boulevard St-Germain cutting across it, the *6ème arrondissement* was the intellectual core of the city, crucible of the avant-garde, crèche of the quasi-avant-garde, hotbed of the rebel avant-garde, seat of the cubists, fountainhead of futurists and so on. Welcome to the brains of Paris.

David seemed *au fait* with all the cross-currents of intellectual life. At the Hôtel de l'Abbaye, where breathing was like chewing a Gauloise, we would sit at a table while he, to borrow a Russian expression, 'skimmed stars from the firmament', pointing out famous, notorious and challenging minds that were uprooting and bouleversing European art and thinking.

'As far as I can see, there's nothing famous, notorious or challenging about their dress sense or appearance,' I said. 'They all look rather grubby and badly dressed to me, or is that just the clouds of cigarette smoke? At least in England they keep the lunatics in asylums.'

'What you are witnessing in this part of Paris,' said David, gesturing vaguely in the direction of an interestingly fragile, intense and almost flower-like man, who might have been Jean Cocteau, 'is simply a rather more public form of artistic self-preservation than you might find in England. I'm trying to think of the English equivalent that might mean something to you . . . If you were, let's say, John Constable who can't sell his greatest masterpiece . . .' Constable's *The Hay Wain* failed to find a buyer when first shown at the Royal Academy in 1821, but when I was working at the National Gallery it was the best-selling postcard '. . . or a J. M. W. Turner who struggles to sell anything at all, then it is perhaps not surprising that you might want to try something new, something different, something radical, anything in fact to help you try to stay sane.'

After the war, the area became gentrified and was – *is* – considered desirable. Rue Jacob was lined with bookshops, dress shops, art galleries and emporia dedicated to *objets d'art* and antiques. If not the most glamorous or salubrious street, it had earned itself a place in the history of respectively the arts and, curiously, that of the United States. At number 56, Benjamin Franklin, John Adams and two representatives of George III signed the Treaty of Paris in 1783 bringing to an end the American Revolution. James Whistler, the late nineteenth-century American painter, rented rooms in rue Jacob. At number 20, Whistler's compatriot Natalie Clifford Barney, the playwright, poet and novelist, kept a salon for more than sixty years. At number 14, an impoverished Richard Wagner lived for five months trying to complete *The Flying Dutchman.* Nearby, the novelist Nancy Mitford rented a flat on rue Monsieur. Rue Jacob was well placed if you wanted to drink in the historic, artistic and cosmopolitan atmosphere of old Paris.

I found the Parisians, however, unfriendly to a degree that mocked the *entente cordiale.* The men were brusque; the women turned their backs on me. Going shopping felt more like going into battle. Every inch of ground had to be fought for. I soon disliked the Parisians as much as they me.

'Was *this* what we fought the war for?' I asked David after a particularly bruising encounter in the local *boulangerie.*

I got scant sympathy. David had a deep, soulful love of France, her history, countryside, food, wine, people, literature, language and even Paris. He felt perfectly at home. Having spent part of his childhood in Tours, he was fluent to a degree that rendered him almost suspect in the eyes of many Englishmen, including my father, and yet David managed to pre-empt any actual suspicions by the complete absence of supercilious ostentation in his accent, enunciation and articulation of French. Speaking French, he *became* French. It helped that he looked slightly exotic, certainly not Anglo-Saxon. At times, however, even he found that Paris fell short. None of his friends were French, at least none of his male friends.

'Come on, cheer up,' he would say unconvincingly. 'Having had their city occupied by the Germans, it is perhaps understandable that, with their innate sense of superiority, Parisians should want to reassert themselves.'

'Innate sense of superiority?'

'It's the Parisian way of coping with the fact that so many people dislike them. Their "superiority" allows them not to notice their compatriots' loathing.'

'So people dislike them even more,' I said.

'And so they become more "superior".'

'And so on, until . . .'

David puffed out his cheeks, exhaled and shrugged, just as a Frenchman would. The only French thing to which David took exception was the politics. 'Which Republic are we on?' he said. 'Third or Fourth? I forget. Whatever it is, the system doesn't work. *Comme toujours!*' (The Fourth Republic fell a year later, triggered by the Algerian crisis.)

In letters that he had written to me soon after arriving in Paris, David had described his frugal existence earning '350 francs an hour, no more than a tip'. (Following the war, the French franc was devalued several times. In 1957, 350 francs was the equivalent to half-a-crown or 12.5p). After the early disaster of losing his job, he'd survived on random meals from friends. However, he had later got a new job at 400 francs an hour, which at least allowed him to breathe and eat. His office was 'much nearer to my hotel and the atmosphere is much more sympathetic,' he wrote. 'There are three women, each one is nice-looking, and probably married. Women in an office always make the atmosphere a bit warmer, even if they may be as plain as frying pans.' I recognised that his love of France was only half the reason why David tolerated the hardships of Paris. The other half was that, like me, he needed to flee home, and his femme fatale mother.

Speaking of frying pans, David had neither kitchen nor access to one. Was this, I wondered, a reaction to his inability to cook? That would have been entirely justifiable. The real shock of Paris was the food. Not only plentiful, it was also exceptionally good. The French have never understood breakfast as the English do, but lunch and dinner were perennial pleasures of artichokes, pâté, fish, *fruits de mer* and great steaks served *saignant*. At Le Petit Saint-Benoît, Le Comptoir des Saints-Pères, Café de Flore, Les Deux Magots and Le Procope, where Victor Hugo, Balzac and Napoleon had taken coffee and brioches, David's napkins were kept in pigeonholes, his wine stored in racks. The ingredients were no better than in London, but Parisian chefs knew what to do with them.

'Part of it is that the French place great faith in the routine of ordinary life,' said David one day over lunch at Le Petit Saint-Benoît, a favourite *boîte*. He nodded to the woman at the till, counting out the day's takings. 'Someone polishing the Holy Grail could not look more devout.'

In David's modest library, pride of place went to his 1939 copy of the *Michelin Guide to France*. It spoke to three of his passions: eating, travelling and books. 'A very useful volume,' he said, over lunch one day at a restaurant attached to an oyster-importing firm at Les Halles, then Paris's chief food market, where we sat surrounded by barrels of every strain of bivalve. 'And not necessarily in the ways you might think,' he added, while wielding pliers, claw-crackers, gouges and forceps as he tucked into *fruits de mer*, an iced platter of crustacea and shellfish. 'Just before the Second World War,' he said, splitting the claw of a crab, 'the British secret service were looking for ways to eavesdrop on the Nazis. One intelligence officer, Olwen Brogan, reckoned that if they occupied Paris, the senior Nazis would likely gravitate to the best restaurants. So she consulted the 1939 *Michelin Guide*, identified the relevant establishments, and fitted them with bugs. She reckoned right, I'm told.'

'I didn't know the Nazis went into battle with copies of the *Michelin Guide*,' I said.

David swirled a glass of Muscadet into a pale green maelstrom. As he bowed his head over the glass as if in prayer, a look of exalted concentration came over him. Eventually he resurfaced, and, eyes closed, intoned, 'Ah, this is the bit where you see God.'

'Oh, for goodness' sake.'

Walking in the Bois de Boulogne, while we were contemplating a summer holiday aboard David's Vespa, he stopped, removed his signet ring, and gave it to me.

'I can't afford an engagement ring,' he said, 'but this belonged to my father.'

This was the moment I'd been longing for. It felt like an

anticlimax. I suppose I'd hoped for a tiny casket containing something set in velvet. David had decided I was going to be an important person in his life, maybe important enough to marry, but he had no money and therefore couldn't afford a ring. There was nothing else he could do but give me his signet ring. Still, I detected a note of reluctance. Besides, the ring was too big.

'You look after it for me,' I said, handing the ring back. 'Canals and jewellery don't go together, especially if the jewellery doesn't fit.'

Later, I rang the Brandolini d'Adda to confirm my arrival time in Venice. When I replaced the receiver, I noticed David rummaging about among the papers on his writing table. Producing a card, he scribbled on it, folded it, placed it in an envelope and sealed it.

'Perhaps this will do as a substitute until the real thing arrives,' he said giving me the envelope.

My few days with David in Paris represented my first 'big deal' romantic experience, when humdrum matters like the time of day, the time of night, the world outside, and whether you are asleep or awake all seemed to melt away. Notwithstanding the awkward ring episode, I left for Venice feeling madly in love and thinking my world was in temporary conjunction with a passing star.

CHAPTER THREE

Men in White Gloves

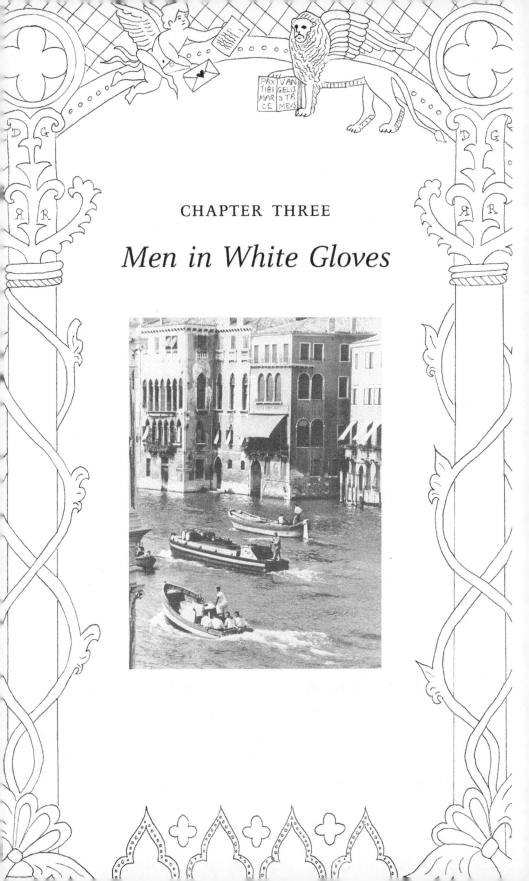

Previous page: *Venice in 1957 was a working city with a rush hour. As there was no riva or walkway, the only way of travelling along the Grand Canal was, and is, by boat. In the background, you can see Palazzo Bolani Erizzo, built in the 13th century; to the left of it, Palazzo Dolfin.*

WHAT AM I doing? I asked myself, as I stood at the window of my compartment on the Orient Express bound for Venice, and watched Paris disappear. Am I looking for something or someone? Or am I running away from someone or something? Am I hunter or hunted? Did David cry, like I'm sure my father cried when the Golden Arrow left Victoria? These and other questions hung in the air like cigarette smoke.

The Orient Express made the Golden Arrow look like the District Line trains that Jean shared her flat with. From my table in the dining car, an air of intrigue and suspense hung about the other passengers. They definitely weren't business people, or holidaymakers. To me, they looked like exiled monarchs, disenfranchised princes, grand dukes, maharajas, notorious American heiresses, coroneted heads, counts, gamblers, spies and money-launderers. Venice was so close to the frontier of Communist Slovenia that even I knew of goings-on and traffickings. On the table before me lay the sealed envelope that David had given me. I opened it, and read, 'Instead of a ring'.

As the train clattered through Burgundy, I dozed off while wondering what to expect of the Brandolini d'Adda. Awakened six times for passports and tickets, I slept little. When I pulled up the blind of my single sleeper compartment the following morning, a postcard scene opened before me: the Swiss Alps looked like a world of enchantment, snow-capped peaks, cattle grazing on high pastures, chalets, lakes and fields ablaze with wild flowers. The purity of the light and the brightness of the colours snapped me out of my morning weariness. Pausing at Brig, I was struck by the sight of the mountain police wearing lederhosen, tricorn hats and feathers, like Renaissance huntsmen. We passed through the Simplon tunnel and, some twenty kilometres later, emerged at Domodossola in Italy.

After Milan, the penultimate stop, the train pulled away for the final charge across the Veneto. I took in scenes of picturesque and pastoral beauty. The countryside looked lovely in the early-summer sunshine, very green and sprayed with the colours of wild flowers, like the English countryside in midsummer. A nervous *tremolo* tingled in my spine. The clackety-clack of the wheels rose into a harangue that seemed to tangle my insides. I cursed the lurching of the train as I tried to apply make-up.

At ten o'clock on 5 June, I arrived at Santa Lucia station. Alighting, I expected to hear a typically Italian urban cacophony, but all I heard was a soundless calm. The place seemed empty. In a rising panic, I was about to ask myself if this was some kind of dream or nightmare, or just a huge mistake that would leave me stranded luggageless in Venice, when a strikingly handsome man in his thirties appeared before me smartly dressed in a summer suit.

'Miss Johnson?' he asked me.

'Yes.'

'Brandolini,' he said, extending a hand. 'Welcome to Venice.'

Something about the man, his bearing, appearance, manner and confident look, made it fairly obvious to me that this was Conte Brando Brandolini d'Adda, but I wasn't absolutely sure. 'You must be . . .'

'Yes, I am,' smiled the Conte. '*Sono . . .*' The Conte then uttered a long line of rapid Italian that was completely unintelligible to me. 'And your name. Is it Gillian or Gill?'

'Gill.'

'Italians find "Gill" a little difficult. Would you mind if we called you Giulietta? It might help you feel more at home.'

I'd never thought of myself as a 'Giulietta', but as soon as the Conte mentioned it, I realised the appeal and saw the opportunity.

'Call me whatever you like,' I said. 'I answer to various names back home.'

The Conte laughed, and as he did so, two men dressed like liveried butlers approached and bowed profoundly in unison. One was about my height, dark, slim and distinguished; the other stood several inches taller and broader, had a blunter appearance and the fair complexion of the northern Italians.

'Giulietta, this is Domenico.' The smaller more distinguished of the two stepped forward. 'He runs everything. If you need anything, ask Domenico. He has a little French.'

'*Buon giorno, Meess Johnson,*' said Domenico, with a smile and a bow.

'And this is Angelo,' said the Conte. The larger of the two men stepped forward, and bowed.

The contrast between Domenico and Angelo, slim and small meets large and broad-shouldered, evoked extreme burlesque. That both wore identical liveries of navy trousers and matching shirts with red beading around the shoulders and pockets seemed to highlight their contrasting physiques. What particularly caught my eye were their spotless white gloves.

'Please, come this way,' said the Conte.

I briefly wondered about my trunk, but before I could say 'lost luggage' or '*bagagli smarriti*', I had emerged into the lemon sunlight of a sparkling Venetian early-summer morning.

We descended broad steps directly to the waters of the Grand Canal. Boarding a *motoscafo*, we travelled the short distance from the railway station to the car park, located by the causeway, an extended bridge that joins Venice to the mainland.

A large, polished, two-tone, cream-coloured Cadillac, doors open, boot agape, awaited us on the quayside. I could have comfortably parked my old Austin 7 in the boot. We set off to the crunching and grinding of gears with the Conte at the wheel, me in the passenger seat, Domenico and Angelo in the back.

'We're not actually going to Venice,' said the Conte. 'At least, not yet. We have taken a seaside villa north-east of the lagoon in Lignano Pineta between Venice and Trieste. It's a so-called modern development . . .' he managed to make 'modern development' sound like 'screaming eyesore' '. . . but it is on the beach and secluded. We will stay there a few days.'

I wondered if I should mention luggage. I had no idea where my trunk was. Gone on ahead? Left behind in Paris? Still standing on the platform at Victoria Station?

'Don't worry about your luggage,' said the Conte, telepathically. 'Everything has been taken care of. En route to Lignano, we will stop for lunch at Vistorta, a little estate we have on *terra firma*. Do you know the town of Sacile?'

'No.'

'I should have said, "Have you *heard* of the town of Sacile?"'

'Erm . . .'

'Few have. It's the nearest town to Vistorta.'

We motored north of the Venetian lagoon, towards the verge

where the Venetian hinterland meets the foothills of the Dolomites: a low, flat, somewhat featureless green countryside of fields, vineyards, pine forests and small rivers. On occasions, we had to brake hard to avoid livestock. Arriving in one piece at Sacile near Udine just across the border where Veneto meets Friuli Venezia Giuli, we swept into the driveway of what looked like a large agricultural estate. A substantial whitewashed colonnaded villa stood in gardens and grounds. Before the car had come fully to a halt outside the front door, Domenico and Angelo leapt out in order to open the passenger door at the very moment the car came to rest.

'Welcome to Vistorta,' said the Conte. 'We like to spend part of the winter here. It gives us almost everything we need, meat, fruit, vegetables, olive oil, wine, flowers, peace and space.' I noticed that when the Conte moved about in direct sunlight the famous Titian red hair of Venice flashed russet-gold.

'In London, the only place you can get olive oil is at the chemist's.'

'I suppose that is appropriate. Olive oil here is the staff of life, as you say in England,' said the Conte.

He led me indoors. The interior came on like an explosion in a fine arts gallery. It was filled with artworks, bibelots and objects doubtless touched by history, many of them (I presumed) of museum quality. You needed eight pairs of eyes to take it all in.

Over lunch of *prosciutto e melone* and pasta, we were waited on by Angelo, who, when not actually serving or removing plates, stood motionless and expressionless, like an immovable statue.

Lunch was over within minutes.

'*Andiamo a Lignano,*' said the Conte, as he led the way outside and back to the Cadillac. As Domenico and Angelo loaded baskets of fresh fruit and vegetables and cases of wine, I noticed that my trunk had miraculously appeared in the boot. We resumed our seats in the car. The Conte fired up the engine and we set off to the crunching of gravel, not gears.

After some forty-five minutes' motoring eastward along the northern fringe of the lagoon, then further eastward still, we turned down a stony wavering track that descended through pines that muted and filtered the afternoon sun. Beyond the trunks and parasol canopies flashed the startling blue of the lagoon.

'Ernest Hemingway came here three years ago,' said the Conte. 'He was friends with the Kechlers who developed this place. He described it as the "Italian Florida".'

'I've never been to Florida,' I said, 'so I don't know if that is a compliment or not.'

'He only stayed a few hours, and was given a plot of land, which he never took up.'

As we crunched along the track, pebbles pinging off the Cadillac's undertray, I glanced into the wing mirror and saw billowing clouds of dust. After making many emergency diagonal manoeuvres to avoid potholes and large rocks, which seemed to constitute more of the track than the track itself, we arrived at a secluded villa set on a hillside a short walk from the water's edge.

'Welcome to Villa Kechler,' said the Conte. 'It is a little simple, but this is the nearest isolated beach to Venice.'

Entering by the front door, we walked through a large white living room, and stepped out on to a raised terrace on which stood a collection of earthenware pots and urns, ranging from knee height to my height, spilling over with brilliant flowers. To one side, beneath a wide orange parasol, a young woman sat at a table, her back angled towards me. At her feet were two young boys. Remaining seated, the woman turned, looked at me and smiled brilliantly.

'*Cara*, this is Miss Johnson, or Giulietta as I now call her,' said the Conte. 'Giulietta, this is my wife Cristiana, and two of our sons Rodrigo and Leonello. We call Rodrigo "Ruy".'

'It is lovely to meet you,' said the Contessa, with only a slight Italian accent. 'I hope you had a good journey. Excuse me for not getting up.' She placed a manicured hand on her bump.

The Contessa can't have been more than a few years older than me, perhaps thirty, very pretty, exquisitely slender and refined-looking. She had tiny hands, and an air of glowing spring freshness. Her blue eyes were set in a clear complexion of vanilla and cream. Not a blonde hair was out of place. Her bone structure had a birdlike quality. She dressed for pregnancy in white shorts, blue top and a broad-brimmed white hat, but these items were the absolute last word in white shorts, blue top and broad-brimmed white hat. She exuded warmth and charm.

The Contessa turned to the two small boys playing at her feet, wearing trousers and matching tops, fit for the beach. 'Ruy is nine, and Leonello, seven. I'm sure, Giulietta, you will get along well with them.'

Two pairs of large eyes, one brown the other blue, met mine. 'Hello,' I said. 'I'm Giulietta.'

'Hello, Giulietta,' they duetted, and shook my hand in turn. 'It is lovely to meet you.'

'You already speak excellent English,' I said.

'Miss Payne has been looking after them,' said the Contessa. 'She was an English governess. Ruy and Leonello have a younger brother, Nuno, who is three. He is in the care of Fräulein Rasch. Do you speak German?'

'My half-German mother made me give instructions to the staff in German.'

'Was it easier to give instructions in German?' asked the Contessa.

'Yes. The staff *were* German,' I said.

A skinny, mousy girl of about twenty-three appeared, with an even younger-looking girl next to her.

'This is Anna, the children's maid,' said the Contessa, 'and her assistant Santina. They will take care of you. Anna and Santina speak only Italian.' The two maids smiled and bowed. Well, I thought, my mother would be in Heaven!

Another maid appeared, looking like a more senior and more assured version of Anna. 'Giulietta, this is Laura. Laura takes care of me. How is your French?'

I moved my head from side to side. '*Le chapeau de la cousine du jardinier.*'

The Contessa laughed.

After their initial greeting, the boys fell silent, and occasionally glanced at each other. After a few minutes, I realised they could communicate by telepathy, and were talking about me.

Set between pines and the lagoon, in a bosky sloping margin where rosemary and thyme grew to the water's edge, Villa Kechler was a modern, elegant three-storey affair of *loggie* and balconies painted white and folded into a restful garden of vines, olives, jasmine, lavender, salvia, agapanthus, orange trees and cascading white bougainvillaea. Directly in front of the villa grew a tall solitary pine. Nearby stood a small villa that housed the staff. During the course of the afternoon, I was introduced to the French chef whose girlfriend-cum-sous-chef Geneveffa was Italian. How curious, I thought, that the Contessa should have a French, not Venetian or Italian, chef. I had always assumed that Italians only ever touched the food their mothers had cooked for them, which could only ever be replicated by an Italian chef.

That evening, on a soft, still, velvet night of inconceivable beauty, as the moon, like a violet lamp, lit the sea with a silver pathway, I walked down to the beach and sat on the sand. With the stars out, the Adriatic lapping in collapsing wavelets, and the fragrance of sage, citrus and eucalyptus hanging in the air, I listened to the sawing of cicadas while I reflected that, for all its ups and downs, life indeed had its moments and this was one of them. Then I looked back on a day of surprises, even shocks, perhaps the greatest of which was that I hadn't thought of David for at least twelve hours.

I embraced the sheer incalculable wonder of the sequence of blind chances that had led me to this spot: dropping in on Universal Aunts on the very day that a letter from Venice had landed on Miss Maclean's desk; meeting Oliver Messel, who happened to know Aunt Ida, who happened to ring on the very evening after my interview with Messel. Happenstance? Transient astral convergence? I wondered at all the other times when Fate might have nodded and beckoned but I, for whatever reason, had ignored or mistaken it, and the gossamer moment passed. So much of life hangs, or falls clattering to the ground, by chance encounters and near misses.

New day, new me.

'All I need from you,' said the Contessa, breakfasting on melon, yoghurt and honey, as the Mediterranean sun burnt through the umbrella pines, which drugged the air, 'is to look after Ruy and Leonello, be there for them, come through for them, and make sure they are happy. Read to them in English, talk to them in English – but only English, please, not Italian or any other language. I would also like you to supervise Nurse Rasch who is looking after Nuno. Meanwhile, I must rest.'

'I will do whatever is necessary to make the boys happy – in English,' I said.

The Contessa asked me about my family. I told her about my sister and two brothers, about my parents and their vast ramified families. 'My mother was one of seven siblings, my father one of ten,' I said.

The Contessa received this with approval. 'It is so important to have a good family life,' she said. 'This is something we care very deeply about.' She stared mistily at the sea, and the sea looked back at her with indifference. She then turned to me. 'It is important to have a proper "mamma" figure, "mamma" being that all-important figure in the lives of every Italian boy and girl.' There was a scarcely detectable note of wistfulness in her voice.

'Of course. May I ask when you are expecting?'.

'In the next three to four weeks.' She placed a hand on her bump. 'I will give birth in Lausanne. All three boys were born in Lausanne.' She looked up, smiled and sighed. 'I am longing for a girl.'

When the subject of boyfriends was delicately touched upon ('And did you stop over long in Paris?'), she asked me about David, and took in what I told her with interest. 'I can see that he makes you happy,' she said. 'That is good. For an unattached foreign girl, Italy can be . . . *distracting*. You say David lives in Paris?'

'Yes.'

'He must come to stay.'

There were no visitors to Villa Kechler. This was a bathing-in-the-sea (no swimming-pool) holiday for the boys, as well as time out for the Contessa. It was as private as private gets.

The peaceful flow of days at Villa Kechler reminded me of my own bucket-spade-and-shrimping-net idylls at my parents' house on Selsey Bill, a phase of my life that came to an abrupt end when the army, answering the threat of German invasion after the fall of Dunkirk in June 1940, mined our beachfront garden rendering the property uninhabitable.

In a letter to my parents, perhaps subconsciously, I drew comparison with my own childhood:

To Mr and Mrs Guy Johnson
6 June 1957

> Villa Kechler
> La Pineta
> Lignano
> P. di Udine

The Contessa is a tiny beautiful person who adores her children. They all talk perfect English which makes it easy for me – but the servants talk Italian or French and the nurse only German. This is a charming little villa on a very exclusive little beach and we are only here for ten days. I think it is just so the Contessa can be on the beach undisturbed. Her baby is due at the end of the month . . . The weather is wonderful, and the children are sweet. We are waited on hand and foot and the food is superb. They must be fantastically rich. They think nothing of flying to New York for a week. The children's clothes are wonderful, mostly English and French. There is every sort of English and French magazine to read and books. The servants all adore the family, which is so nice.

The Contessa spent most of the mornings in bed, visited daily by a nurse who put her through a light exercise regime. She would thereafter spend the day relaxing on the terrace. With immaculate nails and hair, she always looked, even in late pregnancy, very attractive, almost party-ready. She certainly wasn't about to read the boys books in English or help them build sandcastles. That was where I stepped in.

Every morning, I dressed Ruy and Leonello in twin outfits from Rowe of Bond Street, short-sleeved shirts and shorts, usually in green, blue or red. I let them choose the day's colour. If their choices clashed, I would say, 'Since Ruy chose yesterday, I think Leonello should decide today.' That done, we went out to seize the day.

The boys avoided looking like Tweedledum and Tweedledee. Unless you knew them, you would never have put them down as brothers. Ruy, hazel eyes, cinnamon hair, was physically and emotionally robust, outgoing, sometimes naughty, and most certainly a potential future industrial Titan. I found him charming and intelligent. His clothes fitted more snugly than Leonello's. Leonello was handsome in a classic Italian way. He looked more fragile, darker than Ruy. He seemed quite nervous and shy. Curiously, I only caught fleeting glimpses of Nuno, an adorable little boy with blond hair. His nurse, Fräulein Rasch, kept him out of sight. It soon became clear that neither Ruy nor Leonello needed looking after as such: it was more a matter of having fun with them.

Lunch was an unvarying diet of *prosciutto e melone*, then green gnocchi with tomato sauce, followed by meat, then fruit and cheese, all taken on a small parasoled table on the terrace. On the side were Parmesan, olive oil and wine from Vistorta. We ate as a family, outdoors and speaking English.

I read Ruy and Leonello the *Swallows and Amazons* series, as well as A. A. Milne's poem 'Buckingham Palace'. Meanwhile, on the beach, we developed our skills in designing, engineering and constructing sandcastles, which the boys built with a look of intense absorption. In my time off, I deepened my acquaintance with the works of Georgette Heyer.

'Miss Payne was quite strict,' said Ruy to me one day. 'So we are pleased to have you instead.'

'Thank you,' I replied.

'Miss Payne was very good,' said the Contessa. 'Her moral training was forbidding in intent, which was what the boys needed. When they began not to take her seriously, or became clever enough to get around her, I knew it was time to move on to a new phase.'

'Miss Payne clearly did superbly,' I said. 'I'm sure the boys and I will get along well and have fun too.'

'*Bravo!*' cried the Contessa, nodding in agreement. 'The only thing you need to watch carefully is Ruy when there is pasta about.'

How strange, I thought, that the Conte and Contessa had appointed me to look after these two beautiful boys, prized repositories of their dynastic hopes, without ever having met me, never mind interviewed me. Yet they accepted me as a friend or relation. The National Gallery may sprinkle its fairy dust, but together Oliver Messel and Aunt Ida had sprinkled something far more valuable.

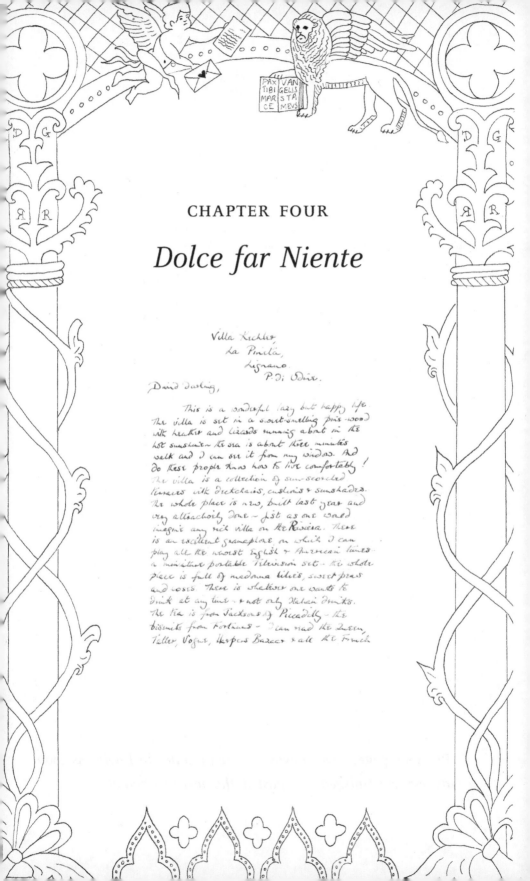

CHAPTER FOUR

Dolce far Niente

Villa Kuchter,
La Pinета,
Lignano.
P. Di Odine.

Dario darling,

This is a wonderful lazy but happy life.
The villa is set in a sweet-smelling pine-wood
with heather and lizards running about in the
hot sunshine. the sea is about three minutes'
walk and I can see it from my window. And
do these people know how to live comfortably!
The villa is a collection of sun-scorched
terraces with deckchairs, cushions & sunshades.
The whole place is new, built last year and
very attractively done — just as one would
imagine any rich villa on the Riviera. There
is an excellent gramophone on which I can
play all the newest English & American tunes.
a miniature portable Television set. the whole
place is full of madonna lilies, sweet peas
and roses. There is whatever one wants to
drink at any time — & not only Italian drinks.
The tea is from Jacksons of Piccadilly — the
biscuits from Fortnums — I can read the Queen,
Tatler, Vogue, Harpers Bazaar & all the French

Previous page: *I was always writing a letter to David. As soon as one was finished and posted, the next one began.*

To David Ross

[11 June 1957]

Villa Kechler

La Pineta

Lignano

P. di Udine

David darling,

This is a wonderful lazy but happy life. The villa is set in a sweet-smelling pine-wood with heather and lizards running about in the hot sunshine. The sea is about three minutes' walk and I can see it from my window. And do these people know how to live comfortably! The villa is a collection of sun-scorched terraces with deckchairs, cushions and sunshades. The whole place is new, built last year and very attractively done – just as one would expect of any rich villa on the Riviera. There is an excellent gramophone on which I can play all the newest English and American tunes, a miniature portable television set – the whole place is full of Madonna lilies, sweet peas and roses. There is whatever one wants to drink at any time and not only Italian drinks. The tea is from Jacksons of Piccadilly – the biscuits from Fortnum's – I can read the Queen, Tatler, Vogue, Harper's Bazaar *and all the French and American journals. All the servants fall over each other to do things for me. The beach is just as 'ritzy'. I go there every day with the Conte and Contessa, children and nurse. We are treated like royalty – they*

75

even sweep the beach for us! Deckchairs, bathing huts, parasols, and even fresh water showers. I'm sure that all this is very bad for my immortal soul (if I have one) and I shall get fat and lazy – the food is so wonderful. But somehow none of it sticks in the gullet (this doesn't refer to the food!!) at all, because they are such a charming and kind-hearted couple – one might almost use the word simple – except that it would be quite wrong – because theirs is a sort of super-sophistication.

My duties, as I suspected, are almost non-existent. I am English and that is enough. I must supervise the nurse and the children's maids, I must play with the children on the beach and read to them occasionally. Rodrigo and Leonello are charming. They even talk English to each other when playing! They are affectionate, easy to please, obedient and yet high-spirited. But of course it is the three-year-old baby Nuno that I have fallen for. He looks exactly like a Bronzino angel with long fair hair in a fringe, blue eyes and black lashes. He hardly speaks at all but can understand perfectly whether spoken to in Italian, German, French or English. The conversations which go on in a mixture of all four the whole time are fantastic.

. . .

I find that the Daily Telegraph *and the* Express *arrive for me every day by post – but everything in them seems rather unreal . . .*

God bless you

A bientôt

Giulietta

(This is what I'm called now)

My job mostly amounted to the application of common sense, something in which I felt quite proficient. However, one person's common sense could be another person's uncommon idiocy. Sensitivities had to be respected. Among the first things I noticed about living with the Brandolini was that, whereas in England people talked of little else,

One.

Did.

Not.

Mention.

The.

War.

That was rule number one. Rule number two was: avoid heavyweight topics, and don't be afraid to retreat behind the safety curtain of the trivial and the obvious. In fact, the more trivial and obvious the better. If delivered correctly, and with the right degree of insouciance, trivia sometimes had the effect of making people think you were talking in code, which could be deemed sophisticated and in-the-know. I never heard the Conte talk to the boys, or anyone else for that matter, about anything *important*, history, politics or the tumult of world affairs. Heaven forbid you should accidentally drop into the conversation anything about communism, socialism or the Cold War. As for the previous year's paroxysms, the Hungarian Revolution, the Suez crisis and the threat of nuclear annihilation, these were but tinkling sideshows. Were I to launch into a conversation about any of the above, I should get a slight, not exactly brush-off, but an ever-so-dismissive back-of-the-hand gesture from the Conte as if to say that he might not be bothered. The Conte took his politics and his world affairs in homeopathic dilution if at all.

Italy had had a difficult war, heroically changing sides

halfway through. At least, that was how British eyes saw it. Perhaps Italian eyes saw it differently. Conflicting loyalties are nothing new in Italy. Throughout Italian history, wars with all their romantic requirements in terms of loyalty, service and duty, were an extreme extension of *La Bella Figura*, the performance art of being Italian. You never knew whose side, or sides, your interlocutor's ancestors had been on, so you avoided the subject.

Of course I couldn't help myself.

'Shall I tell you about the time I was nearly hit by a Doodlebug?' I asked the boys one morning.

'What is a Doodlebug?' asked Ruy.

'It sounds funny,' said Leonello.

'I agree, Leonello,' I said. 'It makes it sound rather fun, doesn't it? Like a toy. But it wasn't a toy. Its real name, if you're interested, was the more sinister-sounding V-1 flying bomb. It was a sort of flying bomb that the Germans launched on southern England from northern France. It made a very frightening noise. I think they called it a Doodlebug to make it seem less frightening.'

'Oh, yes, please!' chorused the boys. 'Tell us what happened.'

'All right, then. It happened one afternoon in July 1944. I was eleven years old and living in the countryside. I'd gone to tea with a friend. We were playing in the garden when we heard this noise, a deep humming, buzzing, throbbing, chugging noise, like a giant mosquito or a car with its silencer removed – the drone of the dreaded Doodlebug.' I stared at the boys with theatrical horror.

'I'd already heard Doodlebugs many times before,' I continued, 'but only distantly. This one was loud. And getting louder. We were always told to hit the ground if we were being bombed. Of course, we did no such thing. We were too interested to see what would happen next. The important thing was that we could *hear* the Doodlebug.'

'Why was that important?' asked Ruy.

'That meant it was still flying. The Doodlebug was designed to fly until it ran out of fuel, at which point it fell to earth and blew up. So if the engine had cut out, that would have been the real danger signal. It meant the Doodlebug was about to strike.'

'So what happened?' said the boys.

'The noise grew louder and louder and louder, until this large metal thing, looking like a rocket with a fireball coming out of the back, streaked over our heads at about tree-height. The noise sounded like something from Hell: a loud, ugly, grinding roar. The rocket shot out flames and smoke. And then, guess what?'

Ruy and Leonello stared at me agog.

'What happened, Giuli? What happened?'

'Just as the Doodlebug passed overhead, it fell silent.'

Ruy and Leonello stood and stared transfixed, in a silence that matched the Doodlebug's.

'Go on. Go on,' urged Ruy.

'The Doodlebug landed in a field about two hundred metres away and blew up, like that.' I imitated a conflagration with my arms. 'Finding ourselves still alive, my friend and I ran screaming into the house. I was wearing my best silk dress. When I looked down it was covered with burn marks.'

'Were you hurt?' asked Ruy.

'Luckily not. But let me tell you,' I said, lowering myself on

79

to my haunches and staring levelly at Ruy, 'having faced down a Doodlebug and heard it screaming towards me, everything else in life has seemed . . . well . . .' I gave a dismissive shrug.

Ruy and Leonello turned and looked at each other but said nothing.

One morning, I stumbled on the Conte doing something to his eyelashes. He turned to me. 'Giulietta, can you help?' He handed me a small twirly metal device. 'I wonder if you can cut my eyelashes.'

The Conte's eyelashes were a striking part of his appearance. They were baroque bordering on rococo. Maybe, they were a metaphor for something.

When I realised he wasn't joking, I set about trimming his eyelashes, the idea being that pruned cilia would regrow to greater lengths. I trimmed Ruy's and Leonello's eyelashes too. Every few days, the Contessa would ask, 'Have you cut the children's eyelashes?'

This, I thought, is what being a Universal Aunt is all about: rolling up one's sleeves, getting hands-on, solving problems and improving lives.

The Conte always looked well cared-for. He had the calm, uncrimped complexion of the international rich. He bore few of the abrasions and marks that a combination of stress, bills, debts and other slings and arrows imprint upon others. His sartorial precision combined with self-sacrifice, ruthless scientific grooming and perfect body shape made him the most immaculate man. I learnt that the Conte was fifteen years older than the Contessa, who was five years older than me. He worked at it; he put in the hours. By the time his nails and hair were done, and he'd decided what to wear, the day was almost half over.

After a week at Lignano, I began to feel *de trop*. I wasn't needed. There were too many staff. I sometimes caught myself thinking, You swapped a decent job in London for glorified baby-sitting. How is that progress? I never successfully answered this question, so I tried to stop asking it.

I would address the Contessa every morning with, 'Is there anything you'd like me to do with the boys?'

'Oh, no,' she'd reply. 'Just be with them during the day. Talk to them in English. Read to them before they go to bed. Take them swimming. Keep an eye on them. Make sure Ruy doesn't eat too much. Where are Nuno and Fräulein Rasch?'

'Have you heard the expression *dolce far niente*?' cut in a voice from over my shoulder one morning. I turned to where the Conte was lying on a sun-lounger.

'Mmm . . . The sweetness of doing nothing?'

'You hear it in Italy. It is about relaxing and letting the world go by. It's not idleness or laziness, although to the untrained or ill-disciplined eye, it can often seem so.'

The Contessa gave me a resigned look, as if to say, 'Here we go . . .'

'It is a way of letting the world tell you what it wants,' continued the Conte, talking to the sky. 'It is about stepping aside, seeing the world differently, and admitting new ideas and thoughts. I've had some of my *idee più dolce* [best ideas] while doing *niente*.'

'Perhaps you should try putting your *idee più dolce* to use, other than creating *idee ancora migliore,*' (even better ideas) called the Contessa towards the sun-lounger. She turned to me conspiratorially. 'I've often thought he should become a museum curator.'

Early one evening, lying on the cool, freshly laundered, ironed and lavender-scented sheets of my bed, idly turning, sometimes two or three at a time, the pages of a Georgette Heyer novel, I heard a knock at the door.

Laura, the Contessa's maid, entered with an envelope.

'*Ceci est arrivé dans le livraison d'aujourd'hui du palazzo.* This arrived in today's delivery from Venice,' she said.

My heart leapt. A letter from David! When I recognised my mother's very regular babyish hand, my heart sank.

I reluctantly opened the envelope. My parents were en route from Yugoslavia and were intending to visit Venice to see that I was having a lovely time. They would arrive on 25 June and stay two nights at the Europa.

That's next week! Oh, no! Their solicitude about my well-being was, of course, greatly appreciated, but . . . wait! I threw aside Georgette Heyer. That's not why they're coming to Venice, I thought. They want to make sure that I'm not with David.

CHAPTER FIVE

'La Meess'

Previous page: *Palazzo Brandolini is among the best examples of late Venetian Gothic architecture, built in the late fifteenth century.*

WE LEFT VILLA KECHLER on Friday, 15 June. Stopping briefly at Vistorta, we proceeded to Venice. Resuming the threads of my debut at Palazzo Brandolini, I shall try to pass them through the eye of a needle.

Anna, my maid, took me by lift to the top floor of the palazzo, where a great marbled salon opened out before us. Less grand and less gilt-stricken than the *piano nobile* but its equal in scale, it covered most of the palazzo's footprint. Through curtainless windows, it overlooked the Grand Canal and the garden. In Venice, this kind of front-to-back room is a *portego*. Howsoever originally purposed, that purpose had been superseded by a children's playroom. Around the edges were clustered sofas, chairs, cupboards filled with toys, table tennis, and a television set. Hanging galactically over the scene, Murano chandeliers of multi-coloured glass looked like an accident in a boiled-sweet factory, proof that beyond vulgarity lies true taste. Shafts of sunlight blessed slowly rotating constellations of motes, while the reflections of the sun on the Grand Canal played kaleidoscopically on the ceiling. The boys' bedrooms, my bedroom and several spare bedrooms opened on to this great space.

In my room, a curtained four-poster stood recessed into a shell-like alcove. A writing table and chair looked out over the garden. A gramophone player stood on a sideboard. My clothes, unpacked and pressed, were hanging behind a curtain (no wardrobe). It was a room for sleeping, listening to music and writing letters on a theme of *Dear So-and-so, I can scarcely believe it. My ascent from restricted circumstances in Victoria to palatial splendour in Venice has left me at something of a loss for words, and yet with plenty of time on my hands to restore that loss . . .*

Although Anna had only Italian, I managed to wrest from her alphabet of gestures, facial expressions, body language and random whispered syllables the intelligence that she came from Vistorta and had worked under Miss Payne, my pre-decessor.

Anna took care of my and the boys' clothes. If, inadvertently, I dropped so much as a sock, within minutes Anna would steal in, gather it up, take it to the laundry and have it cleaned, pressed, ironed, folded, and returned to my room later that day. The speed of turnaround was fortuitous. Being uninterested in clothes, I kept the sparsest summer wardrobe.

The staff in large households illustrate a rider to Parkinson's Law that work expands to fill the time allocated for its completion. In this variant, staff numbers tend to rise exponentially as work expands to fill the time allocated for its completion. The more staff you have, the more staff you need. Staff require understudies, locos, shadows, stand-bys and administrators. If the owner of the house is having a baby, that expansion is further accelerated by the addition of nurses, governesses and people like me who are entrusted with childcare, and who for some reason need maids who themselves need maids.

Everywhere I went in the palazzo, an army of young girls shod in soft-soled shoes passed soundlessly before me like an animated frieze, quiet as mice, neat as pins, busy as bees. Growing up, I had often observed that grand families reserve a formal room for feast days and high holidays. In Palazzo Brandolini, the entire *piano nobile* looked like that room. There was never a question of anything, or anyone, lying carelessly about. I felt one was expected to pose, transforming oneself into human furniture to complement the décor.

My main ally proved to be Laura, the Contessa's maid and shadow. About thirty-five, she had French and Italian, was kind to me and the boys, and was thoroughly decent, polite and helpful.

The French chef and Geneveffa rarely put in appearances, but every morning I visited the kitchens to convey the Contessa's instructions on the day's menu. As the menu rarely changed, my interactions with the French chef and Geneveffa were limited.

The laundry was run by a friendly middle-aged woman who organised the maids. Her office, the ironing room, looked out over the garden. She and her assistant presided over a museum of flat irons arranged on a great heater. Hung throughout with drying and airing clothes, sheets and pillow cases, the ironing room smelt deliciously of freshly laundered, warm cotton and linen.

As the sheets in the palazzo were changed every day, the ironing room was a busy, open-all-hours throbbing turbine of industry, a place in which you were certain to find company and warmth, which was especially welcome if the palazzo grew chilly, as it often did. If the Conte and Contessa were travelling and if the boys were in bed, I would steal into the ironing room, sit by the heater and try to glean Italian from the laundry woman.

I was known by the household as 'La Meess', but no one

thankfully asked me *who* I was: it was taken on trust that I was a credible individual. No one looked over my shoulder or asked, 'Where is Miss Payne?' or 'Is Miss Payne unwell?' except Fräulein Rasch, the baleful Hieronymus-Bosch-visaged nurse, my *bête noire*, sometimes addressed as *Schwester* (Sister). In the land of the hypochondriac, the doctor is king and the nurse queen. Well, in theory. Thankfully, no one had told Nurse Rasch. The antidote to such logic, she was indeed the instant remedy to several maladies. Her very presence spurred one into feeling younger, stronger, fitter and more vigorous.

Maybe it was an English–German thing: I could tell that she detested me. She was a seething cauldron of hatred on a rolling boil. That the Contessa insisted that the family speak English can only have turned up the heat. I doubt that the mirrors in the palazzo detained her. A little over fifty, scraggy, dark-complexioned, Nurse Rasch wore an expression that had congealed into a gargoyle of contempt mixed with stoically born despair. She had terrible teeth: stillborn vampire with added silver. The smell of carbolic hung in the air whenever she was around. Vaguely nunlike, her starched and ironed nurse's uniform bore a full house of medals, betokening years of competent handling of health crises great and small in the war against illness and injury. The medals clanked, so that you could hear her coming. She took every instruction with a forlorn shrug and carried it out with scarcely concealed disgust. Her self-administered middle-of-the-night haircut told the sorry tale of her true state of mind. Not exactly hostile, she was certainly unfriendly. I think she wished I was someone else.

While it was unclear whether Fräulein Rasch was German or Austrian or Swiss-German, I was wary of letting her know of my own roots in Leipzig. That would have complicated matters. So I stuck to English. In one rare exchange, we discussed attitudes towards childcare.

'We are told that certain traits are valuable when looking after children,' she said. 'For example, "in control of emotions", "single-minded" and "aggressive if necessary".'

Our antipathy was more about class than nationality. She clearly thought that the arrival of this young snooty lady (me) had undermined her. She held her position on harder terms than I held mine. However, she trod carefully. She knew that the Contessa and I talked openly. I was part of the family; she was a nurse. She addressed the Contessa as 'Signora'; I, by garbling a few appropriate-sounding syllables, managed to avoid calling the Contessa anything at all.

In the mornings, I would wake to birdsong, the clanking of a dredger and the distant thud of pile-driving, which struck me as a visceral event, rather than as a sound. Or maybe I was hearing Nurse Rasch getting dressed.

While noises wafted in from outside, Palazzo Brandolini was almost ecclesiastical in its hush. Throughout the day, I rarely heard any internal noise coming from either above, below or either side, other than the occasional click-clack of someone wandering about the *piano nobile*, or the distant murmurings of salon conversation, or the sounds of a coloratura soprano coming from the Conte's gramophone. At least I think it was from the Conte's gramophone. It could have been the real thing. Among the Conte's friends, Maria Callas, the World's Most

Expensive Voice, was at the peak of her fame, acclaim and notoriety if not her voice.

'La Fenice, 1949,' the Conte said to me one day. 'She played both Wagner's Brünnhilde and Bellini's Elvira in the same season. It was a turning point in her career. Her vitality and magnetism were astonishing, thrilling to an almost pharmaceutical degree.' The Conte often talked about Callas, and listened to her singing almost every evening. She visited the palazzo as a guest, but I wasn't introduced. Later that summer in Venice, Callas would reach another famous turning point in her life.

I turned my thoughts to Ruy and Leonello. The Contessa was fastidious in the matter of the boys' appearance and dress, in keeping with *La Bella Figura*, the subordination of goodness to beauty, which to the rest of the world seems like an exorbitant fixation with appearances and correct behaviour taken to an extreme that sometimes perverts morality. *Look and behave right; get away with wrong.* And yet Rowe of Bond Street couldn't have been more English. They were distinguished purveyors of sailor suits for small boys, a look that Prince Bertie, later Edward VII, pioneered, or had pioneered for him by his mother, Queen Victoria, in 1846 when England was still important. This Italian attitude to Englishness I found completely charming and, of course, very un-English. The English tend to dress down for comfort and practicality, like the Duchess who arrives for tea in her gardening clothes; I doubt the Contessa had gardening clothes. At least that is how the English like to think of themselves. Perhaps they are deluded.

Washed, dressed and combed, Ruy, Leonello and I would descend to the Contessa's bedroom where she took breakfast in bed, always perfectly turned out. The occasion was really an excuse for the boys to see 'Mummy', and for the Contessa to see the *bambini*. The boys would run in and jump on to the bed where the Contessa would wrap them in absent-minded embraces while she issued polyglottal instructions to staff, and exchanged gossip over the telephone.

This intimate, sacred communion between mother and children was not a private affair. Staff treated the Contessa's bedroom as a thoroughfare, coming and going as they pleased. Maids flitted in and out, unannounced. The door was always open; I'm not sure that there even was a door. Privacy was not a Venetian priority, not when you have an army of staff on manoeuvres. I simply walked in and sat on the edge of the bed.

Like French royalty, the Contessa held daily *levées*. From bowers of plumped-up silk and lace, she would lie in bed while we pondered, plotted and planned the day. Not that there was much to ponder, plot or plan. One day felt much like another.

'What would the boys like to eat?' the Contessa would say.

'PASTA!'

'Apart from pasta.'

The Contessa might ask me to help her with correspondence, writing letters in French or English, and replying to invitations. As there was no typewriter, I wrote by hand. Unlike the Conte, the Contessa kept a busy diary. I became increasingly cast as *de facto* secretary, taking care of the Contessa's 'personal admin', the sort of mission drift I welcomed.

The Conte and Contessa's bedroom overlooked the gardens. The footprint of the room was about twice the size of an average family house in England. The interior continued the theme of the *piano nobile*, all monumental curlicues and flourishes. The walls were lined with sapphire damask edged with frothy gilded plasterwork. Cream silk Austrian blinds were drawn over the windows. An elegant fragrance hung in the air. There were no pictures on the walls, only mirrors. Leading off the bedroom were various bathrooms and dressing rooms. In scale and appearance, the bedroom was not unlike the one pictured in John Singer Sargent's *An Interior in Venice* (1899), which portrays members of the Curtis family of expatriate Americans in Palazzo Barbaro, just beyond the Accademia Bridge, which Henry James fictionalised as Palazzo Leporelli in *The Wings of a Dove.*

Sometimes the children might speak a few words in Italian, only to be reprimanded. *'Inglese!'* the Contessa would say. She didn't mind if I tried out my Italian, but she always ensured that the boys spoke English. This enforced use of the English tongue wasn't the Contessa being polite to me. She was adamant that hers would be an English-speaking family, even when family members were talking privately among themselves.

The Conte, meanwhile, would wander in wearing a silk dressing gown, say a cheery *'Buon giorno, Giulietta,'* then wander off. He would never have plonked himself on the bed as I did.

The Conte and Contessa rarely appeared to have to *juggle.* Their problems were other people's dreams. The stresses, strains and complications that daily pester and blight our lives never seemed to penetrate the Brandolini's untroubled opulence. With great style, they danced on the far purple edge of *dolce far niente.* If they had struggles, the imperatives of *La Bella Figura* suppressed them.

Every morning, flat wicker baskets would arrive overflowing with vegetables, fruit, chicken, beef, pork, wine and fresh flowers. Everything was 'off the estate'. This cornucopia supplied the menu of the day: melon, figs or pears, then green pasta, followed by a course of grilled meat served with artichoke hearts, peas and zucchini slathered in butter. Curiously, fish and seafood never featured. The only item that was bought in was prosciutto San Daniele, which Domenico would pick up every morning from a nearby *salumeria* whose rafters were hung with hams. I have never tasted prosciutto quite like it before or since. The Conte and Contessa lived in a vertically integrated world in which they owned or controlled almost everything they looked at or touched. This was the dream of the super-rich: absolute control with no accountability.

So, the children were raised in this gilded labyrinth within a watery labyrinth, immersed in scroll and curlicue. Everywhere they went, eyes watched, feet followed and white-gloved hands supported. It all made perfect sense, provided you remembered not to look outside for too long. Was I witnessing the final curtain of an old Renaissance, or the dress rehearsal of a new Renaissance, or just a phantom pregnancy?

'Have you mastered the geography of the palazzo?' asked the Contessa, during one of her *levées*. 'It took me months. Have you got to know everyone?'

'I think I know my way around. I've met Anna, Laura, Domenico, Angelo, the French chef, Geneveffa . . .'

'There are fourteen staff, I think. What am I saying? I *know* there are fourteen staff.'

Just the fourteen, I thought. 'Good heavens! Let's see . . .' I went through a pantomime of mental arithmetic. 'Yes, I think that's slightly more than we have at home. Before the war, we rubbed along with just five, including an under-nanny. Can't think how we coped. After the war, we had to rationalise the household even further, so we said goodbye to the cook, house maid, parlour maid, nursery maid, part-time gardener and, improbably, the floor polisher, leaving just Nanny.'

'*Rationalise the household* sounds painful,' said the Contessa. 'Our staff are part of our extended family. To "rationalise" them would be self-mutilation. Now,' she added, changing the subject, 'we must discuss your holiday. You must be exhausted looking after the children.'

'!!!!'

I couldn't have felt less tired. My job was like one long holiday, only better. Perhaps the Contessa wanted the boys to herself for a while. Or perhaps she needed my room. I was dimly aware of traffic in high-season guests, although it was hard to tell who was dropping by and who was staying. I doubt the Contessa wanted to promote her hospitality. She wasn't one to tolerate visitors who just wanted to 'have a look'.

Although David and I had discussed a summer holiday, it always seemed like fantasy. I never dreamt that it might happen, never mind that my job at Palazzo Brandolini might include a holiday.

'Thank you,' I said to the Contessa. 'That is most kind.'

'When would you like to take it?' she asked.

Clueless, I blurted out, 'Early September.'

'*Perfetto!* And most wise. Venice is busiest then. The telephone never stops ringing. My goodness . . . The requests! The demands! The assumptions! Some people expect a state visit. Others seem to think the palazzo is a restaurant, bathroom and telephone booth, and check in and out as they please, as if they own the place. They treat it as an asylum . . . *No questions asked, you're welcome!* I have to turn so many away.'

'If early September is difficult,' I said to the Contessa, 'I can always change the dates.'

'No, no. I insist. If I may, where do you intend to go?'

'David and I were thinking of southern France. David's always had a *thing* about France.'

I felt embarrassed to mention, never mind discuss, David. I was unsure if the Contessa was versed in the unwritten rules in England that frowned on unmarried couples holidaying together, and, if so versed, what she thought of them.

'*Bravo!* How will you travel? Does David have a car?'

'I don't believe he does. He drives a Vespa.'

'Vespa!' The Contessa's eyes lit up and she smiled as if she had never heard of anything so exciting. In those days, Vespas were a commonplace conveyance, but two people touring France on one would have been considered both surprising and adventurous.

'We will be perfectly all right. A Vespa is actually a very good way of seeing the scenery. You travel at the ideal height and speed.'

'Well, er . . . your . . .'

'David.'

'*David* is welcome to stay with us in Venice, if his plans allow it. Consider him invited. Will he come to meet you here?'

'No. I will meet him in Lyon.'

'Then he must come to stay when you return.'

'That would be lovely. That is most kind.'

'*Di niente.* You are welcome.'

I felt quite overcome. To promote David over the queue of would-be guests beating at her door was more than generous.

CHAPTER SIX

The Lido

Previous page: *Ruy Brandolini d'Adda and I pictured hard at work on the Lido beach.*

IF THE WEATHER was fine, which it invariably was, Ruy, Leonello and I headed for the beach on Lido Island south of Venice for swimming and a picnic. At nine thirty sharp, the captain would throw away his cigarette, adjust his cap and fire up the *motoscafo*. As we proceeded slowly down the Grand Canal, it was fun to be stared at from the Accademia Bridge and from *vaporetti* (water buses). I should think the captain got a buzz out of it too. Just as we cleared Santa Maria della Salute, Longhena's masterpiece, and passed the largest collection of striped mooring poles in Venice, the captain would open up, and, for a second or two, all I would be able to see was the peerless blue sky. The gondolas moored alongside the Piazzetta and the Doge's Palace would rise and fall in stately cadence as we passed.

Off we flew with the light of the Adriatic crashing down on us, the bows bouncing on the water, the sunlit spray glittering our faces, and our wake whorling behind us. As we dodged crowded shipping, the only incongruous scenic detail was the matt-grey forms of British and American warships. These structures, driven only by the need to support the purpose for which they were designed, seemed out of place in the lagoon.

Sometimes, we would pick up guests. A few palazzi along from Palazzo Brandolini towards the Rialto, the Conte's younger sister Maria delle Grazie Gonzaga lived in Palazzo Papadopoli, a splendid mid-sixteenth-century pile that belonged to her husband, Conte Leonardo Valenti Arrivabene Gonzaga.

Conte Leonardo's mother, Vera, was a member of the Papadopoli family, merchants from Corfu who had settled in Venice in the early nineteenth century.

Graziella, as she was more succinctly known, would often ring. Her faltering English was good enough for a chat. Classically Italian-looking with dark hair, eyebrows and eyes, she would often be having her immaculate matchstick legs waxed; she was to legs-waxers what I was to hairdressers. She would sometimes join us in the *motoscafo*. Upon learning that I had worked at the National Gallery, she told me that I must visit Palazzo Papadopoli. I failed to spot the knowing look in Graziella's eye or to twig the art-historical significance of Palazzo Papadopoli.

Approaching the Lido, the *motoscafo* throttled back and travelled up a short canal to a small basin behind the Excelsior, the 1920s Gothic hotel where Mussolini stayed when he met Hitler in June 1934. Disembarking to the usual gratifying flurry of white gloves, we mounted low wide steps, and walked through the marbled lobby, a mad-cap Babel of strangely tongued summer-season chimera, reigning and exiled monarchs, bogus barons, middlemen, spies, cheats, women with international hair who'd seen better days, and stateless men whose success was attributable to the alchemy of tax avoidance. I loved the air of excitement, latent danger, sinister rendezvous, assignations, false smiles and raking eyes. There was often a beachrobed man standing in a small puddle at Reception, a Swiss-roll towel under one arm, leaning over the counter while shouting at dictation speed into a telephone (*'What do you mean the claim has been thrown out?'* . . . *'She sold her jewellery? My God! For how much?'* . . . *'He's probably slithering about on this beach somewhere'*). I would always nod hello to the young men behind the desk. Passing through the lobby, we descended a grand flight of some fifteen marble steps to find ourselves in strong sunlight on the beach.

This beach was unlike any other. A line of blue-and-white cabanas ran for a couple of hundred yards to left and right. You could easily have lived in these substantial structures with their loos and showers; perhaps some people did. They were furnished with English-style deckchairs and wooden daybeds. Dividing one cabana from the next, waist-height canvas divisions extended a few yards towards the sea. Each cabana had its own patch of sun-baked beach tempered by canvas awnings leading to a tennis-court-sized oblong of Demerara-like sand that a multitude of labouring hands had cleaned and raked the night before. Some had brightly coloured pillows scattered about in an easy hedonistic manner.

The cabanas were leased to anyone who could afford the quicksand ground rent. If you turned left, you stared at Siberia; turn right and you faced the Gold Coast. We turned right. The first two cabanas were taken by the Cicognas, the pre-eminent Venetian family, and the Brandolini d'Adda respectively.

As we were bowed towards ours, other beach-goers put down their paperbacks, looked up from backgammon duels and drew down their dark glasses. A *corps de ballet* of waiters dressed like *gondolieri* in baggy trousers and straw boaters hovered ready to offer towels, hang up bathing suits, serve drinks and bring canapés and cigarettes. It was a far cry from the sideways rain and soggy sandwiches of my childhood seaside holidays.

This ritual of passing from *motoscafo* to lobby to beach to cabana was a daily pleasure that always gave me a surge of self-confidence. Those Venetians certainly know a thing or two about making you feel welcome and special. I could quite happily have stopped there and returned to the palazzo.

Hungry eyes were upon us. Signs saying *'Privato'* and *'Riservato'* created an understood barrier that, if breached, would have resulted in a pair of white gloves shooing the intruder away or even escorting him to safety. Beyond our segment of the beach, onlookers trolled back and forth like roving predators in an aimless state of ungratifiable desire at the sight of our little colony. I noticed that some English beachcombers had binoculars and, properly curious, would settle down to a thorough examination. Meanwhile, even in this pre-season season, news of our arrival would be diffused among the posse of photographers who patrolled the beach.

These were the first days in which a woman was allowed on to a beach without having to wear a beach-hut-like bathing suit. So I squeezed into last year's costume, and took the boys to play by the water's edge.

'Come on, you two,' I said. 'Today is a perfect day for building sandcastles.'

Like the Contessa, the Conte wasn't the sort to make idle promenades around Venice, check up on the sights or casually drop in on galleries. But he did enjoy the Lido. With unhurried dignity, he would show up at about noon, dressed in fine beachwear – Mediterranean blue shirt and striped cotton shorts – and arrange himself on a daybed. Of course, swimming was out of the question. I don't recall him ever going near the water.

Meanwhile, the *motoscafo*, having spent the morning shuttling back and forth, would finally arrive laden with lunch.

Here, the concept of a beach picnic as traditionally understood ended. Domenico and Angelo would appear staggering under the weight of large boxes of hot and cold food brought from the palazzo. A tablecloth would be spread on a daybed. Seated on small canvas pillows on the sand, we were served *vitello tonnato*, prosciutto, melon, gnocchi, cheese and fruit on crested china, washed down with chilled white wine and iced water. Even when the Conte and Contessa were absent, this routine was rigidly upheld.

I found the idea of white-gloved butlers bowing to me on a beach as they served a four-course picnic lunch slightly ludicrous, but 'Please don't bother' would have been insulting, and might have broken a spell. No wonder the English tourists boggled at us through binoculars. They must have thought we were either mad or play-acting.

After lunch, some people snoozed, while the children played in the sand. Domenico and Angelo would bear away the food boxes. By the time the beach party was ready to go home at about 3 p.m., the heat of the day was beginning to fade.

After one last dip, we boarded the *motoscafo* and sometimes went on cruises into the lagoon, exploring Murano, Burano and Torcello. I particularly liked Torcello. Its forlorn and desolate aspect was the absolute opposite of Venice. Among its treeless meadows and vineyards, the sole landmark was the ancient church of Santa Maria Assunta, founded in 639, modified in 864 and again in 1008.

On the way home, in lavender afternoon light, the indeterminate template of the Venetian skyline slowly resolved itself into pinnacles, *campanili*, domes, crooked towers, television aerials, chimneys leaning at improbable angles, tottering palazzi, weather-vanes and various strange architectural excrescences. Cruising up the Grand Canal, the captain would bring the *motoscafo* in from mid-canal to landing stage by describing an ever more exuberant series of commas written in the water. After a brief rest at the palazzo, the boys and I would take Daisy for a walk around Venice.

A large door in the perimeter wall of the palazzo garden opened on to Campiello dei Squelini, a small square with large shady trees. The hushed Dorsoduro hinterland was made up of a filigree of alleys with a few sotto-voce shops that included the *salumeria* where Domenico bought prosciutto. I loved catching unexpected glimpses of leafy courtyards with plashing fountains. Swerving students from Ca' Foscari university and the occasional nun, we would wend our way towards the Rialto, crossing the Grand Canal and making for Piazza San Marco where the famous basilica stood burnished, glowing and magnificent.

In Venice, a street is a *calle*; small *calli* are *callette* or *calleselle*. Some *calli* lead to other *calli* or to *campi* or *campielli*; others lead to a dead end; a few to a cliff edge. 'Venice has *campi*, "fields", not "squares",' said the Conte. 'There is only one square: Piazza San Marco.'

Walking about, you soon realise Venice has almost no vertical or horizontal lines, and very few absolutely straight lines at all. Almost all of the city either leans or undulates. Gravity, floods and time are in charge; glacially, they are sculpting the city to fit.

Being a quiet city with little greenery, Venice has very distinct acoustics. You can stand in the centre of a *campo* like Santo Stefano and hear with complete clarity every syllable of several conversations taking place at once at various points around the perimeter. I would extend Napoleon's famous quote about Piazza San Marco being the 'drawing room of Europe' by saying that the whole of Venice is like a giant sitting room built in an echo chamber. I wonder if this everyday antiphonal chatter inspired the likes of Giovanni Gabrieli to compose his wonderful canzonas and polychoral works that throw the music to and fro between points of the compass and which reverberate so magnificently when performed in the galleries and lofts of San Marco.

We passed scenes of wild canalside commerce, sprawling food markets of purple artichokes, asparagus, borlotti beans, bitter radicchio and peas grown on Torcello and Sant'Erasmo, and the bounty of the Adriatic laid out on ice, shrimps, octopus, sea bass, scallops, clams, oysters and sardines, while crates of soft-shell crabs tried vainly to claw their way to freedom.

There were few tourists, and those few were either independent travellers on specific cultural or social missions, or ingénues seemingly in a state of deep shock as they trailed about aimlessly and passively. Or they were Americans. You could see Americans a mile off, dressed like frustrated golfers who had missed both the cut and the boat home.

At every step, I breathed, tasted, heard and felt Venice's great age, and often reflected that this preservation was due to the complete absence of motor-cars. The magnificent things about Venice were still magnificent. In the evenings, the sun would ignite the sun-bleached plaster and brickwork to a fiery, almost luminous orange. And when the rays angled low, there was something ineffably and explicitly golden about Venice – not bling, but real gold, trafficked and heaped from the east to supply her pomp and delicacy.

Often these expeditions involved a *gelato*. Seated at one café, I overheard a cravated, monocled tour guide discoursing with great solemnity to some clients over *espressi*.

'. . .Venetians have suffered their share of humiliations . . . Relegated from player to pawn, they put on a brave face and carried on enjoying themselves despite extreme adversity. Some argue that the weaker Venice became, the more she rejoiced in her reputation as the city of "panache and pageantry", that the more "actual" her decline, the more "apparent" her glory. This simply shows how adaptable the Venetians were. When their traditional markets disappeared, they didn't let the grass grow under their feet. They invented new markets and turned to painting, decorating, sculpting and composing. Venice's reputation for great art, prodigal sensuality and for carnival sprang from a combination of political expediency and cold business calculation.'

I caught his eye. He paused. He held a rolled-up copy of *The Times*. I smiled, as if to say, 'Please ignore me and continue.' He continued.

'And they have been vindicated. Only the most Philistine, sententious and Gradgrindian Victorian would say that the Venetians should have spent their money more wisely. The palazzi, monuments, churches, bridges and such bell towers as still stand . . . these and her art and music are what make Venice so fascinating, so impressive, so beautiful and so enduring. History has absolved the Venetians' genius for sensory indulgence. The genesis, rise, fall, rise, fall, atrophy and collapse of Venice are subject to perennial review, but her artistic truths live on, and Venice can probably claim more artistic truths than any other city . . .'

On another occasion at another café as we drank orange juice, I watched as an elegant woman, brunette, her blue eyes and olive skin eye-catchingly made-up, probably in her forties, talked expressively to a girl who listened attentively. They were looking at a book of Giovanni Bellini paintings, and were talking about Bellini's portrait of Doge Leonardo Loredan, one of my favourites. I couldn't help tuning in. '*È il ritratto non solo di un uomo ma anche della struttura di potere della Venezia del Cinquecento: una testa su un triangolo di damasco di seta; prestigio e bellezza, ma niente potere, e neanche tanto spazio ai vertici – haha!* It's a portrait not only of a man but also of the hierarchy of sixteenth-century Venice: a head on a triangle of silk damask; prestige and beauty, but no power, and not much room at the top either – haha!' The bracelets on her wrists clanked musically as she spoke. One thing I missed about the National Gallery were little cameos of art-world life such as this, with their arresting, glamorous, attention-snagging, ear-catching people and their different attitudes towards culture.

If we entered a shop, the boys would be curtsied or bowed to. I was never allowed to pay. Heaven forbid that I should even think of carrying so much as a parcel or a shopping bag back to the palazzo. A bunch of flowers was the maximum payload, or the merchants would cry, '*Non ha bisogno di portarli a casa. Sono per il Conte. Li consegneremo.* There is no need to carry them home. They are for the Conte. We will deliver them.'

We might cross a small humpbacked bridge and plunge into the darkest recesses of the labyrinth, whereupon the shift in atmosphere from enchantment to mean-streets piquancy was instantaneous and almost palpable. The dark, narrow and festering *callette* had small slits of skylight running overhead, but the daylight was usually partly obscured by lines of washing, while the usual sounds of Venice were drowned by transistor radios and television sets. I felt busy eyes upon us. Although some Venetians were clearly living in poverty, they seemed to feel neither resentment nor animosity. On the rare occasions that the Conte and Contessa stepped out in public, the proverbial man on the *vaporetto* would have recognised them. I also discerned a knowing but proud look in the faces of Venetians, 'honour pick'd from the chaff and ruin of the times', as Shakespeare put it: even the most humble Venetian can look you in the eye, knowing that his ancestors not only built this city from scratch, but also saw off kings, emperors, popes and sultans, and even had sovereigns and pontiffs bow to the Doge.

Back at the palazzo, the routine was supper then bathtime. If guests were invited, I sometimes joined them in the Palma Vecchio frescoed dining room. Usually I preferred to dine with the boys in a small pantry, waited on by Domenico and Angelo, still white-gloved. The white-glove routine was never taken absolutely seriously. With a smile, a slight bow, and a twinkle, there was an element of theatre and amusement to it, and if the boys fooled around, Domenico and Angelo joined in.

Later, when the boys were put to bed, Domenico sometimes asked if I'd like to join him on a *gran passeggiata* and take coffee. Just before we stepped outside, he would look me up and down.

'*A Venezia, ci vestiamo quando usciamo.* Sempre. *Conosco persone che si lavano, si radono, si stirano la camicia, si stirano i pantalone e lucidano le scarpe solo per comprare una pagnotta o un limone.* In Venice, we dress up when we go out. *Always.*

I know people who will wash, shave, iron their shirt, press their trousers, and polish their shoes just to buy a loaf of bread or a lemon.'

Once we'd finally made it outside the front door, we set off. Nodded to by locals, Domenico would respond with a casual 'Ciao' from the side of his mouth.

'*Venezia è una vita intima, organizzata, come un formicaio o un alveare di costumi, religioni e politiche diverse. Quindi andiamo tutti d'accordo; siamo sempre educati e rispettosi.* Venice is an intimate, organised sort of life, like an ant heap or beehive of differing manners, religions and politics. So we all get on; we are always polite and respectful.'

Over *espressi* at a café near the Rialto, we chatted pointlessly in Italian and French. I always wanted to ask Domenico what he had done in the war, but felt it would seem invasive and rude. As with all Italians, a discreet but firmly affixed veil was drawn over the subject.

If I was left alone in the palazzo, I would go to the *piano nobile*, fling open the doors overlooking the Grand Canal, walk out on to the balcony and exult in the day's last rays while taking in the inexhaustible sight of Il Canalazzo, a scene unchanged in six hundred years. Padded hangings were draped over the balustrades so that you could lean on them in comfort, drop your eyes to the canal and while away a few minutes watching traffic and perhaps saluting a passing gondola. The altitude of this lofty perch precluded anyone at water level successfully tossing flowers, or even holding a conversation with one. One definitely looked down on proceedings.

On this balcony, Cecil Beaton photographed the Conte dressed as a Venetian *magnifico* for the famous Beistegui Ball of

September 1951: Carlos 'Charlie' de Beistegui, French-born, Eton-educated Spanish-Mexican heir to a silver fortune, threw a costumed palazzo-warming party at Palazzo Labia, for which Oliver Messel designed the hostess Lady Diana Cooper's Cleopatra dress of silver-blue with panniers of old rose in the style of Tiepolo, to complement Tiepolo's frescoes in Palazzo Labia that depict the career of Cleopatra. The ball was described as 'party of the century', partly because no hostess dared compete with it.

It is a curiosity of the Grand Canal that it has no walkway or *riva*. Without miraculous powers, you cannot walk *along* the canal. It remains, as it were, a private thoroughfare for owners of palazzi.

There was always activity of some sort going on on the Grand Canal. The marine air was usually further salted with newly enfranchised noises that resolved themselves into the guttural cries and nautical oaths of bargees and the caterwauling of gondoliers exchanging insults. Having abandoned the main subject of their dispute, they often took up the quarrel laterally and reflected lengthily, profanely and in detail on each other's parentage, while making operatic claims of impending bankruptcy, social ruin, family shame, incurable disease and violent death. The raillery was pitiless, especially when focused on aspects of personal appearance, hair colour, skin colour, height, girth and so on. You don't need much Italian to find the language of the canals perfectly comprehensible.

As the velvet gloaming descended, great flotillas of candle-lit gondolas would drift along to dissonant arias by rival minstrels. Gondoliers who had spent much of the day settling scores, avenging insults and exchanging 'compliments' would sing to each other, mainly for tourist consumption. (I doubt for one minute these vocalists sang because they thought the other chap was a splendid fellow.) Through the guttering candlelight, lungfuls of contending Puccini and Verdi filtered up to the balcony, bouncing off the walls of the opposing palazzi. It wasn't exactly romantic (these gondolas were filled with tourists), but it was a madeleine of romantic thoughts and feelings.

During lulls in traffic on the Grand Canal, I would listen to the many sounds of water lapping against stone: a smacking, slapping, gurgling, splashing noise. My daily fix of the Grand Canal satisfied, I would sweep back indoors.

At night, Venice fell silent but for the sounds of moored boats scraping the walls and bumping into each other, the slap of water against stone, and the occasional echo of footsteps, while out in the lagoon a navigation bell tolled watery laments.

It is easy to understand why, in May 1797, while Venice was dissolved in luxury and Napoleon and his troops simply walked in, the Venetian Association of Hairdressers still had 852 members. Whatever else is happening in the world, hair needs dressing, especially in Venice which for centuries was prized for its mirrors, and especially if you spend your days on the Lido. I felt I needed, if not actually to compete with the Contessa in the hair department, at least to look like I was trying. Besides, I felt on-show. One never knew who might drop in. And I didn't want to frighten the boys. So I went on an unconscionable number of trips to the hairdresser, same chap as the Contessa, but whereas he came to the palazzo for her hair, I went to him for mine. Fortunately, I lacked the Italian to partic-ipate in the usual hairdresser gossip beyond a few enquiries about London.

'*Là!*' cried the hairdresser finally. '*Sono le estremità che sono importanti. Capelli e scarpe, ma soprattutto capelli. Dicono tanto sul carattere di qualcuno, no?* It's the extremities that are impor-tant. Hair and shoes, but mostly hair. They say so much about someone's character, no?'

'*Sì, sì!*'

'*Tante donne sono tenute in ostaggio dai capelli e dai scarpe, ma poche se ne rendono conto.* Women are held hostage by their hair and shoes, but few of them realise it.'

Looking like a mistake in a candy-floss factory, I walked back to the palazzo wondering if I were being held hostage by my hair and was experiencing what would later be termed Stockholm Syndrome.

Applauding the confectioner's art, the Contessa said, 'When *dolce far niente* meets *La Bella Figura* by the seaside, hair-dressers go . . . *like that!*' She imitated a conflagration using her entire upper body.

'With me, it goes deeper,' I said. 'My hair would be the last thing to go. Even dressed in rags, living under bridges and eating out of tins, I'd still go to the hairdresser.'

'You know, Giulietta, you could almost be Italian,' breathed the Contessa.

Later, as she left for her *accouchement* in Lausanne, taking with her Nuno and Nurse Rasch, the Contessa said, 'If you want to go out in the evening, don't go out alone. Ask Domenico to escort you. He can find his way around Venice blindfolded.'

Although the Contessa never gave explicit reasons for her

injunction, I could imagine several. Tracing your way home among the haphazard and shadowy back canals and narrow passageways, guided by the often baffling signposts and the curious Venetian dialect, stared at by cats, one could easily become disoriented and perhaps frightened. It was common to find two signposts indicating 'Piazza San Marco' pointing in opposite directions. Ambiguous signposts were part of the thrilling gamble of walking through Venice. Even in daylight, those parts of Venice that were not golden or at least gilded could be dark and faintly sinister. They often played tricks on your internal compass.

'Actually, Venice is one of the safest cities,' the Contessa assured me. 'An intruder could never escape. The police can seal it off within minutes. And if anyone tried to escape by water . . . *ooh!* . . . they'd need to know the lagoon . . . And on the Excelsior beach, if there was the slightest doubt about someone, a concierge would soon be at his or her elbow. Venice is safe. Why do so many people like to come here?'

CHAPTER SEVEN

Palazzo Brandolini

Previous page: *On the* piano nobile *of Palazzo Brandolini, I felt I was expected to pose like a piece of furniture or musical instrument. I neither saw nor heard anyone play the harp in the background.*

THE PALAZZO WAS a labyrinth in three dimensions, with doubtless hidden doors for swift entry and exit. The ground floor seemed to consist of great empty marble spaces. The first floor remained something of a mystery. It housed the kitchens, the laundry and the staff quarters, but I only ever visited the kitchens and the laundry. The rest of the floor remained *terra incognita.* The *piano nobile* was the great setpiece: one very impressive salon overlooked the Grand Canal via full-length windows framed by Gothic arches sustained by slender columns.

'Would you like to know more about the palazzo?' asked the Conte, turning the full light of his gaze upon me.

'I should love to.'

'Historically, this is Palazzo Giustiniani dalle Zogie meaning "Palazzo Giustiniani of the Jewels", so-called because of the splendour of the dress of that branch of the Giustiniani family,' said the Conte, as he showed me round. 'The twin palazzo next door was Palazzo Giustiniani dei Vescovi, which means "of the Bishops": one of the Giustiniani family, Lorenzo, became the first Patriarch of Venice in 1451. Gentile Bellini's portrait of Lorenzo in 1445 hangs in the Accademia. My ancestors bought Palazzo Giustiniani dalle Zogie in 1876. Today people refer to it as Palazzo Brandolini, according to the Venetian custom of naming palazzi after their owners.'

As we strolled through baroque conceit piled on to baroque conceit, the Conte related the story of the palazzo.

The Giustiniani were one of the great Venetian families, allegedly descended from Emperor Justinian. During the twelfth century, thanks to war and plague, the family was wiped out bar one, a monk sequestered in the convent of San Nicolò on the Lido. As the Giustiniani line teetered on extinction, the Venetians petitioned the Pope to release the young monk from his vows. After a suitable negotiation, His Holiness agreed. The young Giustiniani married the daughter of the Doge. Their prodigious offspring of twelve included nine boys. Not only was the line restored but also glorified. A century later three Gothic palaces bore the name Giustiniani, all on prime sites. The present Palazzo Brandolini was one of twin adjoining palazzi that housed different wings of the Giustiniani family. The slightly larger twin now houses part of Ca' Foscari University. In an earlier incarnation, Ca' Foscari lodged Henry III of France on his famous visit of 1574, when it is said that the warmth of his reception left an indelible mark on the mind of the twenty-three-year-old king.

The Giustiniani name popped up again in May 1797: Angelo Giustiniani, Governor of Treviso on behalf of the Venetian Senate, confronted Napoleon in an inn, just as Bonaparte and his army were trampling towards Venice. After a fierce argument, Giustiniani offered Napoleon his life rather than grant the Corsican passage. Perhaps Giustiniani felt that he owed Venice, which six hundred years earlier had saved his line, a debt of honour. Napoleon tried to tempt Giustiniani: 'In the destruction of Venice that I have devised, I shall spare Giustiniani,' he said. This earned Bonaparte the rebuke that Giustiniani would 'blush for his wealth were it to remain intact amid the ruin of his countrymen'.

'I doubt Giustiniani's stand made much difference,' said the Conte. 'At least he showed resolution and defiance.' The Conte led the way as we entered the main *salone*. 'On a far more important matter,' he said changing the subject, 'in this palazzo, Richard Wagner spent several months between 1858 and 1859 writing the second act of *Tristan and Isolde*.'

'It's all a real composer needs, isn't it?'

'We keep quiet about Wagner,' continued the Conte.

'Why?'

'Have you met a Wagner fan?' The Conte stared in mock-horror. 'They would be queueing outside all day and night. Time stands still for Wagner fans.'

'I'm sure he was inspired by the romance of Venice.'

In the ectoplasmic wake of Wagner, we walked out on to the balcony and watched the late afternoon stilling of the Grand Canal. Palazzo Brandolini indeed held an enviable, inspiring position. Look right, and you saw the Accademia Bridge; look left, and you almost saw the Rialto.

'Richard Wagner stood on this very balcony and saw the same scene,' said the Conte. 'And after him, Princess Louise d'Artois, niece of King Louis XVIII of France, who died in this palazzo in 1864. It wasn't so long ago that in August and September the canal became a municipal swimming-pool. Boys would jump from bridges or wait by the marble statues on the ground floor of the palazzi while they prepared to dive in. You'd be mad to do that now.'

Whichever eye had sumptuously re-edified Palazzo Bran-dolini, it had created a stage on which the Conte and Contessa could play out a role that perpetuated a narrative about Venetian opulence. Palazzo Brandolini was an exception to the general dilapidation and crepuscular air that hung about its peers. It out-gleamed all. All it lacked was a motor-racing circuit on the roof, to match the one on top of the Fiat factory in Turin.

To David Ross
Wednesday, 19 June 1957

Palazzo Brandolini

S. Barnaba-Venezia

David darling –

This is an ancient palazzo done in the Grand Manner on the big bend between the Accademia and Rialto bridges. Until about 150 years ago it was called Palazzo Giustiniani and was built in the late fifteenth century by one of the Doges of that name. It is Gothic in style. The Brandolini themselves date back to 539 AD!! But the old Palazzo Brandolini is not on the Grand Canal altho' still called by their name. It is a wonderful combination of three rich periods – fifteenth century, early Victorian (very sumptuous) and present-day riches belonging to the Contessa, so that everything is newly decorated and furnished. The state apartments are beautiful – they all have lovely original wood Venetian ceilings all painted and gilded (sixteenth century). The dining room has a fresco by Palma Vecchio and opens out on to a balcony covered with wisteria where we eat when it's hot. At the back there is a wonderful courtyard with a well in the centre and a formal garden, all of which is floodlit every night. It must have always been a very rich palazzo, as gardens of this size are most unusual in Venice.

I can't start to tell you all about the drawing rooms – but they are lovely and all the hangings and covers were new for

Princess Ira [von Fürstenberg]'s wedding, eighteen months ago. In every room there is a lovely Venetian glass chandelier – very ornate and highly coloured – which would look vulgar anywhere else, but wonderful here. There is a lift which is lined with silk brocade, gilded mirrors and velvet!

The suite which I have with the two boys was new last year and is lovely. Three bedrooms, bathroom (all mod cons) and an enormous hall in the grand manner. My bedroom is charming with mauve Chinese wallpaper and curtains (which go round the bed too!) and pale olive green and gilt furniture all en suite (I think you'd call it empire style), but it is all brand new! My bedroom looks over the garden and on the other side there is another room where at night I can watch the processions of gondolas following to music – it is a wonderful sight and being on the bend in the canal, it is the best view one can get. The front door steps go down into the canal and there are lots of enormous red and white striped gondola posts.

The Contessa has gone to Lausanne for the baby with the nurse and little boy so I am left with the Conte – as there is no housekeeper, I am in charge! I have three immediate servants of my own, but altho' charming, they are all peasants and a bit dim. There is Domenico the manservant who will do anything and is helpful as he can speak a little French and then Anna and Santina who are really 'ladies' maids' for me and the two boys. I can just step out of my clothes and leave them lying on the floor if I feel like it! Clean dresses every day! I have a little trouble with the maids who can only speak unintelligible Italian. The chef speaks French luckily. Here in Venice the men all wear white and gold uniforms.

Every morning at about 9.30 the Conte's motor launch (which is brand new and v. smooth) arrives at the steps and another uniformed flunkey takes us out to the Lido. Whew! The plage *at Lignano had nothing on this. We walk thro' a super luxury hotel à la Monte Carlo and down wonderful marble steps on to a private beach – where I'm sure they would wash your feet if you asked them to! I have had my photograph taken every day walking down the steps and I can have as many free copies as I want but I haven't been to look at them yet. There is everything on the beach – huts, sun blinds, deckchairs, cushions, Lilos, pier, diving boards, boats, and even beds to lie on for sun bathing (at least I suppose that's what they're for!). The boys are both very good-looking, particularly Leonello the second one, who is really a beautiful child. They have masses of lovely clothes and are always dressed alike. They cause quite a sensation in Venice and I have several times been stopped and told how beautiful Leonello is and they then ask their names and when the children say Brandolini everyone bows and scrapes. In Italy all the children of a Conte are Conte too at birth, so both boys are called 'Signor Conte' all the time. Venetians are enormous snobs. The only English I have yet seen here are* <u>ghastly</u> *– in fact all the tourists look terrible. I count myself a native and just pray and try to look like one.*

The Contessa has already taken me to a hairdresser and I've had my hair cut shorter and it's got bleached in the sun already. I am very brown – in fact my arms are dark brown! I am very 'one-up' at the Lido, because this is the very beginning of the season and everyone's white, while I'm dark brown from Lignano. I have never seen such a tiny expectant mum as the Contessa – she wore a bathing suit and bathed up to the moment she left. Fascinating. All the money comes from her – she is an

Agnelli and besides being one of the oldest families in Europe, they own Fiat. This letter is beginning to ramble. I will stop now and maybe write more anon.

On Sunday, I went to the Frari church with the two boys – it is quite near here. I expect you have been in this church as it is the next most important after S. Marco and I think it has lovely proportions. It has two glorious colourful Titians in it and is very light and airy and more like an English cathedral. As it was Trinity Sunday it was full of people and there was a majestic procession with all the paraphernalia. It was all very impressive and romantic with the smell of incense and Madonna lilies everywhere and people kneeling all over the stone floor.

I bought a really good guide book and adore just wandering around looking at all the wonderful buildings and quiet corners. Luckily the tourists all seem to stick to the Piazza S. Marco. It is a very expensive city – but then I don't really have to buy anything. The Conte is going to pay me mostly in dollars – which is wonderful as I can use them anywhere.

I hope all this doesn't make you too restless and envious – it really is a dream-like life and I often have to pinch myself to make sure I'm still me. Sometimes I spare a thought for poor David sweltering in the heat of Paris, because I have read in the papers that there is a heatwave all over northern Europe. Don't make yourself ill by doing too much in the hot weather. Venice is very peaceful in that respect as there is no rush and bustle.

. . .

The Brandolini seem to know everyone in Europe who is anyone – so the season, which isn't really in full spate until August, will be fascinating.

The fruit and vegetables in this country are wonderful – I have never seen or tasted such gorgeous fraises du bois.

I am very happy and hope you are too, <u>you idiot</u>!

Love and xxx

Giulietta

Bbbbrrr . . . bbbbbbrrrrr . . . bbbrrrr . . . The gentle throb of the *motoscafo*'s engine came across as half sound, half vibration as I and my parents cruised slowly down the Grand Canal from the station. I was explaining to them the *dramatis personae* of the palazzo.

'And then there's the French chef, who is tactile and covered with blood,' I said, 'but not as aggressive as most people who are tactile and covered with blood. The only person whom I prefer not to get on with is Fräulein Rasch, whose sense of humour seems to be clouded over by an icy and toxic rage that she holds towards me. Thank goodness she doesn't know that I'm part-German.'

I'd scarcely had time to find my bearings when my parents showed up, looking relaxed from their holiday in Yugoslavia. As we thrummed past the palazzi, I could see their expressions struggling adequately to comprehend feelings of awe and wonder at Venice, and probable nostalgia at the thought of their honeymoon spent here some thirty-four years earlier. I dropped them off at the Europa Hotel by Piazza San Marco.

That evening, the captain and I took the *motoscafo* over to the Europa, picked up my parents and idled the short distance back to Palazzo Brandolini. As the *motoscafo* pirouetted around and came alongside, immaculately attired staff reached out to help us ashore. Bowed into the sedan chair, my parents were wobbled up to the *piano nobile*. My mother was momentarily stunned to unaccustomed silence as her eyes feasted on the splendour.

'I see what you mean,' was all she could manage as she pivoted around. It hurt her to say anything overtly complimentary.

There were just the four of us – the Conte, me and my parents – that evening in the dining room with the Palma Vecchio fresco. I was not at all embarrassed about having my parents there. They knew Venice, had a little Italian, and my father at least could be relied upon to provide civilised company.

Their visit would have shown to the Conte and therefore to the Contessa, who would have had it conveyed to her in Lausanne, that I had parents who were still married and who apparently thought nothing of crossing Europe to see how their daughter was getting on. That would have gone down well, I felt.

As I said goodnight to them when they boarded the *motoscafo* back to the Europa, my father mumbled, 'The visitors' book probably reads like a *Who's Who* of European history.'

The following day, I took time off from looking after the boys and lunched with my parents at a small ristorante on Calle Lunga San Barnaba, a short walk into the Dorsoduro hinterland behind the palazzo. The tiny restaurant was dimly lit and had about a dozen tables in two rooms, with a small courtyard at the back. We took a table inside. I asked the waitress what pastas they served.

'I ask,' she said. A few moments later, she returned. 'We don't do pasta.'

'Pizza?'

'No pizza. *Carne. Solo carne.* Meat. Only meat.' The waitress went away. Moments later, the owner came along, a smiling man with intelligent eyes, slight girth and broad shoulders over which he wore a lightweight tweed sports jacket.

'You ask for pasta and pizza, yes? Haha. This is some English joke, yes?'

'No, no, I . . .'

''Ere we are in Venice, okay? So you need to understand something about Venice, okay? Unlike other parts of Italy, Venice never 'ad *contadine*, people who worked the land, because there was no land to work. We only 'ave traders and merchants. They 'ave a different mentality.' He tapped his temple. ''So we don't have the *contadine* food, like pasta, or maybe pizza if you are from Napoli. *Pasta e pizze* are not Venetian food. *Questo sono il cibo degli oppressi.* These are the food of the oppressed. Here we serve meat, *ossobucco*, which is veal shin, *fegato alla Veneziana* which is calves' liver, *porchetta* which is pig, okay?'

He probably made the same speech umpteen times a day. It tasted like the *specialità della casa*.

I ordered artichoke salad and then *fegato alla Veneziana* to my mother's tomato *burrata* confit. My father chose *caprese* salad and *porchetta*.

My mother then gave me a rapid-fire catechism on what I was doing in Venice. *What is the work like? What do you wear? How much do you get paid? Do you have time off? What are the boys like? What is the family like?* She seemed surprisingly interested. I hardly had time to begin each answer when she fired off the next round. I wondered if she was trying to confuse me into letting slip something about David.

My aim throughout my parents' stay was to avoid talking

about David. I didn't want my parents to know that I'd stayed with him in Paris. And they certainly weren't about to know that David and I planned a fortnight's holiday later that summer.

'And did you see David in Paris?' asked my mother.

Here we go, I thought. 'Who? Oh, him. Er, very briefly. He met me at the Gare du Nord and put me on the train to Venice.'

That seemed to shut them up. I could tell that my mother didn't believe me. My father preferred less contentious topics.

'Have you worked out where you fit into the pecking order of the household?' he asked.

'Technically, I'm not part of the household,' I replied grandly. 'I'm more a member of the family. I answer to Ruy and Leonello. They excuse me from household politics.'

My parents took the hint about 'household politics'. For the rest of their stay, David was never mentioned, although my father couldn't resist asking, 'When are you coming home?'

When I arrived back at the palazzo, the Conte, noticing a shift in my mood, took me aside. 'As long as you have a half-decent relationship with your parents, try to savour your time with them. There'll be days when you'd love to sit down and talk to them, but they won't be there.'

My parents left two days later. As Ruy, Leonello and I passed their hotel on our daily commute to the Lido, we hooted and waved at what we hoped was their room. Sadness stole over me. My father, less so my mother, wanted me home. Mentally and emotionally, however, I had already moved on to a place of happiness beyond anything he could provide. Of course he was happy that I was happy, but in his eyes was written sadness that our close relationship was changing.

A few days later, as the Conte left Venice to join the Contessa in Lausanne, his last words to me were, 'Giulietta, you are in charge, okay? *Arrivederci!*'

'Haha!' I laughed as I joined the rest of the household in waving the Conte off. I was standing in the front row as we crowded on to the small quay. When the *motoscafo* growled off down the Grand Canal, I stopped waving, turned and saw fourteen pairs of eyes staring at me expectantly.

Me? In charge? Of a fifteenth-century Gothic Renaissance palazzo? Was I missing a joke? Miss Maclean had never asked if I could run a Venetian palazzo. It was a surreal notion but, then, what could be more surreal than Venice?

My authority was more doge-like than actual. Domenico, the only member of the household with whom I felt fully able to communicate, was the one who knew and understood above all the complex internal mechanisms, relationships and protocols of the palazzo. Agile, omnipresent, he and Angelo maintained their dawn-to-dusk marathon of vigilance. Meanwhile, the Conte rang every evening to ask after the children. Everyone seemed relaxed, even happy, about my precipitous promotion, except, that is, Fräulein Rasch. Cloudily and moodily, she seemed worried, worried that I might *not* trip up.

I set myself the task of teaching Leonello to swim. Having taught my brothers, I knew roughly how. Ruy and I would load Leonello on to an inflatable dinghy and tow him gently out to sea. Amid yelps of pleasurable terror, Ruy and I would lower him gently into the water. While I held him by the chin, Leonello began to swim. After much encouragement and several days' work, we got there. Soon, he was swimming by himself, and out of his depth, still yelping with pleasurable terror.

It struck me what blind faith the Conte and Contessa must

have placed in me to entrust not only their eldest two sons to my care, but also their palazzo, staff and *motoscafo*. They'd met me only three weeks earlier. I still wasn't allowed out unchaperoned in the evenings.

The only beachless day was Sunday. To the marvellous tintinnabulation of bells, the boys and I would walk to Santa Maria Gloriosa dei Frari, resting place of Titian and Claudio Monteverdi. The Frari vied with Santi Giovanni e Paolo for the honour of Venice's second most important church after San Marco, although, despite several attempts, I had yet to locate Santi Giovanni e Paolo.

It always amused me that, while the priest mumbled and droned his way through the service, often pausing for what seemed an eternity while he collected himself from some reverie, members of the congregation would produce transistor radios and newspapers, only to look up for the five minutes that elapsed during the elevation of the Host. Miraculously, the priest would get through the service without mishap. I spent most of the service staring at Titian's *Assumption of the Virgin*, which hangs behind the altar.

On some Sundays I would devolve the boys' supervision to Anna, and head off on an ecclesiastical safari, dropping in on other churches. For church-lovers who struggle in heat, Venice is close to heaven. I'm not looking for an epiphany, I would say to myself, as I leant into a west door, just a little time to myself and, who knows, enlightenment.

Music, especially choral, emanating from a west door hit my mind like a summons. I would steal in, take a pew, and let the voices or the organ recital waft about me while, lost in thought, I took in the monuments, memorials and marbles. In that twilight world of words, voices and ecclesiastical space, daily doubts seemed to dissolve into the eternal. Human tribulation put firmly in its place, I would step outside feeling a soul-refreshing sense of solace and uplift, comfort and excitement.

If there was a service on, so much the better. I love formal church services with their traditions, history and the reassuring language and phrases of the liturgy. Venice, however, takes the religion thing off in a different direction. You only have to put your head around the doors of any two or three of Venice's alleged 365 churches to realise that the true religion of Venice is the worship of beauty.

To Mr and Mrs Guy Johnson
Monday, 1 July 1957

Palazzo Brandolini
Venezia

My darling Mummie and Daddy,

I hope that you will not mind me typing this letter, but it is very hot indeed again here, and somehow it is cooler to type than to write as my hand seems to stick to the paper when I hold a pen. However, I read that there is another heatwave in England and 200 people fainted at Wimbledon.

I am all alone here in charge of the children and I am really enjoying it very much. The Count telephones every evening from Lausanne, but so far there is no news from the Countess about the baby.

Leonello swam yesterday for the first time, twenty strokes without stopping, and to-day he swam out of his depth so I really feel that it is a great victory as he is such a nervous little boy.

Yesterday I went church sightseeing and went to the Carmine Church, which is a fourteenth-century edifice and has a lovely altarpiece by Cima, who is very well represented in the National Gallery. The maid takes the children to church every Sunday and feast day, of which there seem to be many, and while they are thus employed, I wander round and look at all the churches clutching my guide book.

Now that the Count is away, the motorboat is at my disposal, but so far I have had no cause to use it.

There is really no more news, but life goes on in its quiet luxurious way and I am very content if somewhat lonely – so do write to me occasionally.

With much love xxx

Gill

CHAPTER EIGHT

Heatwave

Previous page: *My favourite moment of the day was descending from the Excelsior Hotel on to the Lido beach in the mornings. The posse of photographers always gave one a psychological lift.*

L'ONDATA DI CALDO infernale was on everyone's lips. People were watching the mercury rise, feeling the drag, and praying for rain. A smothering pale haze drained all colour from the city and reduced the sun to a partial opacity, like a pale yellow cataract, so that it appeared to have no connection either to the daylight or to the heat. A heatwave of biblical proportions that was roasting northern Europe had reached Venice.

One morning, I peered out from an upper-floor window. Silently, the great coruscating palazzi basked magnificently, quivering in the refractional air that hung thickly and appeared to turn the façades into liquid versions of themselves. I stared at the windows and immemorial masonry of the opposing palazzi, and they stared back at me, waiting, watching, wise, inscrutable. A solitary water-taxi glided across the water's face. The cry of a bargee briefly shattered the silence with an explosion of sound.

Opening the windows didn't help. There was no breeze. Without air-conditioning, the only cool was an imaginary one provided by fresh flowers from Vistorta. Venturing out of the palazzo wasn't much help either.

In the midday torpor, the *calletti* felt airless and suffocating. Gondolas idled at their moorings. The motionless, stagnating waters of the canals that interlaced the city bore a powdery bloom on the meniscus. As there is neither grass nor vegetation in Venice to absorb the heat, the sun radiated off walls and polished flagstones, and hit me in the face. Men, stripped to the waist, dozed in the shade. Dogs and cats suspended hostilities and spatchcocked themselves on whatever cool surfaces they could find. In the food markets, sides of beef and pork swarmed with flies. Beyond the rooftops and the outer limits of Venice, far out in the indeterminate shallow-prone wetland of the lagoon, autumn came early to the island of Torcello as the pomegranate trees shed their leaves.

To escape the heat, we hastened to the Lido and stayed until the evening. I would launch myself on a Lilo and let Ruy and Leonello try to tip me into the water.

At nights, we crawled from our beds and slept on the marble floor. When the marble grew too hot, the boys suggested we go downstairs and sleep in the Conte and Contessa's high-ceilinged bedroom. 'Of course,' laughed the Conte, when I rang him for permission. I felt grateful for the ice packs and cold water that the staff provided, not so much for the relief they gave us as from knowing that the staff were 'on my side'. This seemed to chime with the Contessa's rules on chaperonage: women were to be guarded and looked after.

Meanwhile, the season was beginning to liven up. In Venice, you soon get to recognise every face you meet so I was able mentally to tick off new arrivals one by one as I wandered about . . . *American couple with daughter . . . British probable aristocrat with wife . . . Possible film star; can't put name to face . . . Two women, tweeds, polished brogues. Radclyffe Hall Appreciation Society? . . . Honeymoon couple from Spain . . . Three sailors in uniform, British . . .* At rush hour on the Lido, international accents wafted about, like expensive perfume. Various unattached women hung around. I watched one young man smartly dressed in shorts and polo shirt, carrying a beach bag. As he trawled the

cabanas, his walk now quick and again slow, he looked periscop-
ically about him. I expect he wanted somewhere to change into
his bathing suit.

It was indeed prescient of Aunt Ida to insist that I pack cigarettes when I left London. A summons from the police was
delivered to Palazzo Brandolini one morning. It was something
to do with my failing to alert the immigration authorities about
my presence in Venice, and something else to do with my international driving licence, which I had mislaid. So I stuffed as many
packets of cigarettes as I could into my handbag, and set off for
the police station near Riva degli Schiavoni, the waterfront prom-
enade near the piazza. Expecting a terrifying, sinister, arbitrary,
faceless and unaccountable labyrinth of bureaucracy every bit as
mind-bending as Venice itself, I found half a dozen idling young
carabinieri who could not have seemed happier to find a young
Englishwoman walking in, especially one with a bit of Italian and
some cigarettes. A couple of hours later, I emerged from a cloud
of blue smoke not only with my visa extended but also with a
new international driving licence. The *carabinieri* assured me that
I could always count on them for help.

To David Ross
2 July 1957

Palazzo Brandolini
Venezia

David darling,

*The whole of Europe is sizzling and I feel very sorry for you in
Paris. Altho' it is terrifically hot here, we are very well equipped
to cope with it – for instance at the moment, I am lying on my*

bed quite nude, altho' actually I'm so brown that I look as though I'm wearing a white bathing suit permanently, with an enormous electric fan giving me goose-flesh and bottles of iced water, fruit, etc., but it is phenomenal weather even for Venice and one does not attempt to go out of doors between 1 o'clock and 5.30. Even at the Lido, the sand is so hot that it hurts thro' shoes. The only answer is to bathe all the morning – which I do – just lying on a Lilo in the sea for an hour or so. The extraordinary thing is that I feel bursting with health . . .We [Ruy, Leonello and I] spend the whole of every day roaring with laughter! But at least I've taught the younger one to swim – by the simple expedient of dropping him off a boat and all he did was shriek, 'But, Julie, I don't touch!' and then proceeded to swim.

And life continues in its fabulous way – I find Venice quite fascinating and all the Gothic architecture most attractive but I don't like the seventeenth–eighteenth century stuff much, like the Scuola and Chiesa of S. Rocco. The Church of the Carmine is lovely* and there is a lovely* altarpiece by Giov. Bellini and in the sacristy there is the remains of a fourteenth-century fresco depicting the Annunciation and lovely* ceilings and ceramics of the same period – the whole place was very much used and I was fascinated to see amid all this antiquity, a tray with a modern espresso coffee machine for the priests. Roman Catholics are nothing if not practical. Gone are all my growing enthusiasms for Catholicism and I no longer accompany the boys to mass – last time I went I was surrounded by slick-looking Italians who were discussing television all thro' the service while the priest mumbled completely inaudibly and when they processed past me there was a strong aroma of alcohol and unwashed humanity, urgh!

*Sorry about this – I always run out of adjectives

. . .

My parents turned up for two days last week on their way back from Yugoslavia. They came and dined at the palazzo and were enormously impressed. Inexplicably I was miserable when they were here and immediately after they'd gone – not homesickness – quite the opposite – a sort of sadness that I know I have outgrown them and will never live at home again.

David, it really is enormously funny suddenly to be left in charge of a palace. I have to approve the menus every day and say whether I want the servants to do anything in particular – three of them present themselves every morning and then I have to instruct the boatman as well. All this is done in French, which is very good for me, and where essential in Italian. I can make myself understood on the telephone in Italian now, which I think is quite an achievement. The baby hasn't arrived yet and the Conte and Contessa are stewing in Lausanne. They ring me up every morning!

. . .

The people on the Lido are mostly ghastly –from all parts of the world and mostly awful bulging old females suffering from a surfeit of eating, drinking, babies, make-up, dye, etc., etc. – so there is little competition apart from the odd floosy, which is quite fun. Do you know that a glass of mineral water on the plage costs 2/6? If there's anything I or the children want, I just order it and give the cabin number.

I have only found two nice English people on the plage and they're charming – otherwise my usual ploy is to speak either

French or German when I see 'Les Anglais', because otherwise they pester me. There is a very nice French family two cabins away and I talk them quite a lot – I have several times heard English people discussing my probable nationality!

I have been in trouble with the police on two counts! A) for not registering my presence in Venice, which I forgot about, and B) I lost my International Driving Permit. However I spent a cheerful hour at the Police Headquarters with six lovely carabinieri and I plied them with English cigarettes, which they gleefully told me were 'contrabbando', and in the end everything was satisfactorily accomplished – apart from the fact that I must write a letter in Italian to the Minister of the Interior! Haha! The only answer to that is 'non capito'.

By the way, Sir Laurence Olivier and his lady stayed here with the Brandolini last summer! In a way all this luxury is rather a waste when there is no one to gloat over it all with. I just have to behave as though this is exactly what I'm used to, and who could possibly exist without a lady's maid anyway?

. . .

The other night I dreamt that you were drowning – but my little maid assures me that dreams of drowning are 'molto fortunato' – I hope so.

Buona notte caro mio

Giulietta

CHAPTER NINE

The Woman on the Beach

Previous page: *Alone in Venice, Nancy Mitford joined us on the Lido beach almost every day for three weeks. I felt privileged that someone as 'unimportant' as me should spend so much time chatting to her.*

IT WAS AT this time, while the Conte and Contessa were in Lausanne, that a woman arrived at the Cicogna cabana next to the Brandolini's. I saw her one morning sitting on a deckchair on the beach, watching two dogs tumble over each other in the margin where the Adriatic laps the sand. I hadn't seen her before. She must have been a guest of the Cicognas. Whereas most people who went to the Lido were part of a group or couple, this woman seemed unattached and sitting in pointed isolation, as if the tide had brought her in and plonked her on the beach. She clearly wasn't Italian. It was mid-morning, pre-season. No Italian woman would be seen dead on the Lido beach before twelve thirty, even in high season. I walked past her a couple of times. I recognised her but couldn't put my finger on why. She was about my mother's age, early fifties: clear smooth pale skin, high forehead, sad emerald eyes with eyelids that draped like curtains, making her look intelligent and difficult. Her scimitar-shaped eyebrows, elegantly angular bone structure described a face that seemed both of-its-day and timeless. She looked like an eternal type of beauty that I'd seen in paintings. She wore a tight pearl necklace, a pale blue sleeveless knee-length dress and a narrow-brimmed straw hat. On her lap was a book. As I passed by her, our eyes momentarily met. I kept asking myself, Why is she sitting on the beach alone so early in the day? Was this a mark of individualism or possible symptom of sociopathy? I expect she was asking similar questions of me. After half an hour, she stood up. Tall and elegant, she walked off the beach and up the steps to the lobby of the Excelsior.

The next day, she was there again, this time sitting next to an overweight man. They were talking. Sound travels quite well over sand. What entered my ear was an *obbligato* of throttled and tourniqueted vowels. Instead of the short *o*s and *a*s of Italian, I picked up the elongated and elevated *eewh*s and *urrh*s of cut-glass gold-standard upper received pronunciation English, the accent of the ruling classes, the intonation of my parents' era, such as a female *cherecter* in an Oscar Wilde play might have.

'So we ended up winning the *waa-aar*,' she was saying to her companion, 'but losing the Emp*iiiir*e and finding ourselves in hock to A*meeeer*ica. That's civilisation for you! So never mind the Bright Young *Thiiiings*. This is a time of pulling in, dressing down and not looking rich . . .' She spoke with an up-and-down cadence, as if singing a recitative.

It was then that I realised I was eavesdropping on Nancy Mitford.

Everyone had read *The Pursuit of Love*, which came out just after the war when people craved colour and wit. Most people had read its sequel *Love in a Cold Climate.* Some had read *The Blessing*, and a few, her biography of Madame de Pompadour. Nancy was considered the pre-eminent English woman of letters, the peer of Evelyn Waugh and Anthony Powell. I was in the presence of a literary lioness.

Her companion sounded like he had failed to master the art of breath-control. He spoke in sentences of one word only.

'Egg! Timers!' he wheezed. 'That's. What. They. Should. Bloody. Well. Make. With. This. Sand. And. Hour. Glasses.' It

144

was as if he began each word without enough air in his lungs, so that he had to wheeze out the final syllable.

'This is Venice, not Bournemouth,' answered the woman I took as Nancy. 'I'm sure that if they wanted to do something with their sand other than lie on it, the Venetians would come up with something far more imaginative and original than egg timers.'

I couldn't quite believe my eyes. Or ears.

With the Conte and Contessa away in Lausanne, I was feeling lonely, and welcomed the chance of grown-up company. However, before I did anything so stupid as introduce myself, I needed to make sure that the person in front of me really was *the* Nancy Mitford.

The boys were happily playing on the beach with some other boys. So, leaving them for a few minutes, I closed my Heyer using my finger as a bookmark, stood up and walked briskly towards the steps that cascaded down from the Excelsior lobby. Stationed in his customary position at the foot of the stairs was the paparazzo. I marched up to him.

'Excuse me, can you tell me who the Englishwoman is in the Cicogna cabana?'

'*Mi dispiace, non la conosco.* She come 'ere often. Maybe you ask at Reception.'

To enter the lobby after the solar glare of the beach was to plunge momentarily into darkness. After my eyes had adjusted to the light, I found myself standing next to what looked like a promising stand-up row between a man dressed in a festive shirt, dark glasses and sombrero, and one of the managers.

Bypassing this altercation, and moving swiftly past the usual man standing in a puddle of Adriatic while wearing a damp beachrobe and shouting down the telephone, I aimed for Reception.

'Excuse me,' I told the young man at the desk. 'The English woman in the Cicogna cabana . . . I forget her name. It *is* Miss Mitford, isn't it?'

The young man gave me a knowing look. 'Yes, that is correct, and the gentleman is Lord Portland, I think.'

'Thank you.'

My thoughts scattering in all directions, I retraced the balustrade steps leading down to the beach, taking two at a time and at an oblique angle. Brushing past the paparazzo, I walked a few paces out on to the beach and called, 'Ruy! Leonello! Would you like something to drink?'

'No!' they cried in unison, with a leave-us-alone tone.

I turned. Nancy was eyeing me. 'Are you the new girl, or are you Miss Payne's understudy?' she said, from her deckchair. 'I heard that Cristiana was thinking of auditioning.'

'I'm the new girl. Miss Payne has left.'

'Good for you. And Cristiana and Brando . . . where are they?' Nancy placed her forearms on the armrests of her deckchair.

'They're in Lausanne.'

'So you're superintending Ruy and Leonello, are you?'

'If you can call it that. My official job is to teach them English, but they already speak it perfectly.' As I stood before Nancy, who remained seated, I felt like a naughty schoolgirl hauled in for questioning.

Nancy raised a hand in a slightly dismissive gesture. 'Clearly your real job is not to teach them English but to do something else,' she said, sitting still like a graven image, 'Have you worked out what that something is yet?'

'Erm, no. Keep them company while the Contessa is away? Raise their game? Solve the riddle to unlocking their potential? Turn them into young gentlemen of the world?'

Nancy gave me a shrewd look that I could have sworn meant, Really? Why have they employed *you* then?

'Or perhaps just add the common touch,' I added pre-emptively.

Nancy smiled. 'I see,' she said. 'Teach them to organise State occasions, that sort of thing. I'm surprised they haven't gone to boarding school in England, somewhere *cherecter*-building. I'm Nancy.' She made no indication she wanted to shake hands, but simply sat back and stretched out her legs.

Her accent! Her intonation! Her speech had a sing-song, high-low pitch, but the final word of each sentence came out as a long, slow drawl. There had been no vowel shift in her diction since I should think the early nineteenth century. Before I could do anything about it, her voice and accent were already in my head, pulling strings, throwing switches and yanking levers. The prejudice attached to accent really is most insistent and pernicious.

"I'm Giulietta or Gill. My job description seems to be under-stood but not spelt out or even stated.'

'Keeping things as vague as possible is precisely how they should be,' she said. She hung her hands limply over the armrests of her deckchair, her fingertips pointing towards the beach. Far from using her hands to articulate her speech, Nancy only made the occasional cavilling gesture.

'I'm neither governess nor au pair nor nanny. The staff call me La Meess.'

'I expect Cristiana just wants someone educated and sensible to keep the boys amused. I'm sure that a young English person adds a certain cachet, don't you think? *La Bella Figura* and all that.'

'I've never thought of myself as an ornament,' I said, as a waiter unfolded a deckchair and placed it next to Nancy's. Nancy faintly gestured for me to sit. 'Thank you.' I glanced at Nancy's elliptical companion. He was asleep.

As I sat down, her eyes fixed on the Georgette Heyer novel that I held, still bookmarked with a finger. 'What do you like about her?'

'I'm hoping that someone can tell me! That's why I keep reading them – to try to find out. I was introduced to her novels in 1949, my last year at school. I've been addicted ever since. It has grown into a vicious habit that needs continual feeding. Most of my values come from her books.'

'How marvellous.' Nancy laughed, her shoulders shaking. Her laugh took fifteen years off her. It was also, I thought, a nervous laugh.

'I buy first editions of her books from a bookshop on the King's Road,' I continued, looking down at the book cover. 'It's run by two old women. One of them told me that one day Georgette Heyer will be famous.'

'I think every woman should read Georgette Heyer before being allowed to vote, marry or open a bank account,' said Nancy.

'Or look after other people's children,' I chimed in. Nancy's emerald gaze rested upon me, briefly.

In those days, everything 'about' other people was instantly recognisable. You didn't need to ask questions to establish who you were talking to; all you had to do was note their dress and speech. It would have been obvious to Nancy that it was obvious to me that she was an impoverished aristocrat, just as it was obvious to me that it would have been obvious to her that I was well brought-up, but . . . irrelevant. We had so many shared touchstones that what more need be said? But what was she doing on her own?

'How did you get the job?' asked Nancy.

'I was working at the National Gallery when my fiancé decided to move to Paris.'

A wariness stole into Nancy's eyes. 'Odd thing for a fiancé to do. Trying to escape?'

'No, no.' I laughed. 'We weren't engaged then. We are now, I think. Instead of festering in London,' I said, turning my body slightly towards Nancy, 'I thought I'd better show some initiative and go abroad too.'

'Where in Paris?'

'Rue Jacob. Hôtel Danube.'

Once again, I felt emeralds X-raying me. Nancy had been living in Paris for eleven years. Her address, rue Monsieur, was a ten-minute walk from rue Jacob. I suspect that as soon as she learnt that 'my fiancé' was living in Paris, she became cautious. She almost certainly would have disapproved of my seeing David. In those days, girls 'like me' (well brought-up, sort-of educated) didn't do things like go off to Paris to see their 'fiancés', a term which could cover a range of sins. That the Hôtel Danube was located so close to rue Monsieur, and that I appeared to be familiar with that part of Paris, would have made her even more wary. She might have thought that I might gossip about her, an unwelcome idea, being a very private person, so private that she was happy to sit alone on the Lido beach in the morning. Anyway, she certainly wasn't about to become best friends with a girl less than half her age.

'What were you doing at the National Gallery?'

'Selling postcards, posters, calendars, things like that.'

'Endless *Hay Wains* and *Fighting Temeraires*.'

'Ha! Yes. I think a lot of people went to the Gallery just to say they'd seen *The Hay Wain*.' In order to try to re-establish credibility, I added, 'I used to work with Sir Philip Hendy.'

'Venice is Venice, but why did you leave the National Gallery?' asked Nancy, suspicious.

I inhaled, then exhaled. 'I got promoted to assistant manager of Publications, so I knew it was time to leave.'

'Your backstory is beginning to sound intriguingly complicated.'

Her emerald eyes gave nothing away. I realised this wasn't a friendly chat but a trial of strength. 'Promotion meant I had to behave,' I said, 'be responsible and try to take things seriously.'

'Frightful thought!'

'It wasn't *me*. I didn't want to risk becoming part of the furniture. But obviously I've no idea what I really want to do, except . . .' I tailed off, unsure of what to say.

'So you took a different turning in the labyrinth of life,' said Nancy, helping me along. 'Understandable. Delusional happiness and confidence based on almost complete ignorance are far more useful, effective and persuasive forces, and have achieved far more in history, than doubt based on knowledge ever will. Congratulations. How did Cristiana and Brando find you?'

'I was introduced by Oliver Messel, a family friend.'

'Oh, good Lord! Of all people to help find childcare!'

'Quite,' I said.

'You said he was a family friend?'

'More of a distant acquaintance.' I felt nervous that Nancy was seeing through me.

'I expect he was disappointed that your past isn't a bit murkier.'

'He never really asked me about who I was. It was all a bit strange.'

'Anyway, good for Oliver. Who needs references when you have Oliver?' She began brushing grains of sand off her dress, then leant back in her chair, and asked the sky, 'How is he?'

'Very well. Busy.'

'I expect he's here somewhere, designing a ball or soaking up *la dolce vita*. Venice is his second home.'

I daren't reciprocate by asking how Nancy knew the Cicognas or the Brandolini or Oliver Messel. On my lips, that risked sounding like 'How come they let you in here?' or more likely, 'How come they let me in here?' Nancy was part of *that* world, the glittering jet set, the cosmopolitan rich and their friends on their Grand European Tour, that invisible club for footloose, super-elite nomads.

She seemed in no rush to break off and get back to Lord Blimp or whoever 'Lord Portland' was. Despite her initial stiffness and wariness, she began to relax. I began to sense that she was almost as pleased to see me as I her.

'I saw you yesterday,' I said. 'Do you spend much time on the Lido?'

Nancy took a deep breath, and stared down at the beach for slightly longer than seemed comfortable. 'Only most of the time, but not intentionally so. I come here every year for a holiday. It's lovely to see friends, swim, drift about, take in the architecture, that sort of thing. But this is pre-season.

The stampeding hordes arrive in late August. Not *me* at all. Know-nothing tourists over for the party. "Super-sewerage and a ball every night," as my father would say. But I love the place to bits at other times of the year. It's a better class of gutter, slightly falling to pieces, but aren't we all?'

A blue-shirted waiter, who was doing the rounds with a silver tray, stopped and asked us if we would like iced water with lemon.

'*Thenk* you.'

'Thank you.'

'I expect you know Venice quite well under the Brandolini dispensation,' said Nancy, holding a glass of iced water to her lips.

'A little. I like the churches and the art.'

'Hate Titian and loathe Tintoretto,' she said, taking a sip, putting her glass down, sitting back and crossing her feet. 'Palette scrapings and paint samples. Just can't get interested. It's probably a psychological defect. I'll bet that a lot of Venetian painting was a way of promoting Venetian merchandise. All those gorgeous silks, brocades and damasks were early soft-furnishings catalogues with a bit of fashion-show thrown in. Clever, really. By the time Canaletto arrived, the perspective broadened out to Venice itself, rather than what Venice sold.'

'I'm with you on Titian.' I felt relieved to be able to talk about something I knew. 'In my mind's eye, I can see the Titians and the Tintoretti hanging in the National Gallery: great in scale more than quality, which is partly what I dislike about them.'

'Although Titian was head, shoulders and torso above Tintoretto,' said Nancy. 'It's funny,' she added, going off on a tangent. 'The Venetians created a political system that prevented personality cults and concentrations of power and influence, but when it came to the arts, the complete opposite applied.'

I was wondering what she meant by this but I was distracted by her accent. I couldn't take my ears off it: it was Aunt Ida's only more so. Never mind 'cut glass', her voice could have engraved Murano at fifty paces. I ate into my stock of small-talk simply to prolong the conversation, while trying not to bore her or sound over-curious. *The food here is awfully good, isn't it? . . . How do you find Venetian coffee?*

'You mentioned "school",' said Nancy, clutching her hands at chest height.

'Yes. St Mary's Calne,' I said. 'Before that I was herded around, dodging bombs and Doodlebugs.'

'You obviously survived the bombs and Doodlebugs, but what about school? President of the Debating Society? Captain of hockey?'

'Strangely, I wasn't picked for the hockey team,' I said. I sensed a Mitford tease. In *The Pursuit of Love*, Uncle Matthew, a portrayal of Nancy's father Baron Redesdale, dismissed hockey girls as having 'legs like gateposts'. 'Anyway,' I continued, crossing my legs, 'I was too busy being naughty, and I haven't finished yet.'

Nancy's body shook with laughter, which seemed genuine as well as nervous, as if she were laughing to relieve tension. She rested her forearms on the armrests of her chair.

'*Thet* sounds promising.'

'Each girl's behaviour was graded into "wholes", "halves" and "nothings",' I said. 'Everyone began as "nothing". I never got beyond "half". There were too many rules. 'You weren't allowed to run down corridors. St Mary's has a lot of corridors, and I was always in a hurry.'

'At least the school persisted with you.' Nancy regarded me coolly.

I sensed that I was more fished than fishing, but I chose to play along. 'The school thought I was clever,' I said. 'I wasn't really, but I worked out how to pretend to be.'

'Mm-hm,' Nancy prompted, interested.

'Revising for exams,' I continued, 'I would work out the questions that might come up, write down the answers, and learn them by heart by torchlight under the bedclothes.'

'Very sensible.' Nancy gave a mildly dismissive gesture and turned to the sea. I detected a wistful twinge. I later learnt that, besides a few months at Francis Holland School in London, Nancy was either home-educated, self-educated or not educated at all.

'The most important things I learnt at school,' I added, 'were strategic thinking and resourcefulness, not what I was taught.'

'Quite. Quite,' said Nancy. 'Why bother to be good at something when you can pretend?' She closed her eyes and held her face towards the sun. 'Still, it probably doesn't pay to show too much strategic thinking and resourcefulness. People might get strange ideas, especially in Italy. *La Bella Figura* means playing dumb, to a certain extent. They don't have the same freedoms here as in England.'

'Huh! I'm not allowed out of the palazzo in the evenings unchaperoned,' I said. 'I'm sensible enough to baby-sit a palazzo, but not to look after myself after dark.'

'Cristiana's idea of chaperonage sounds medieval but it's probably wise,' replied Nancy, freighting the words 'probably wise' with an irony that invited the suffix, 'in your case'. 'I expect you'd live to tell the tale, but you wouldn't want to risk it. I'm sure Domenico can garrotte people with a rubber band.'

'Actually, I'm happy to go along with the Contessa,' I said. 'I don't know anyone here and I hardly know my way around.'

'The cunning city beguiles you street by street,' said Nancy. 'Venice is bewildering enough even in broad daylight. Didn't Shakespeare write something about indirections and misdirections in *The Merchant of Venice*? You need a prayer book to get around, not a map. "Oh, just turn off the street at San Bartolomeo – or is it San Giacomo? – walk two hundred or four hundred metres to the Casanova Café. No, there isn't a signpost any more. Have a grappa at the bar, turn half right, and the correct *calletta* to Rialto will appear on the next turning to your left. If you get lost, don't ask a local! They will confuse you even more."'

'Several times I have set out on missions to find a church or gallery or shop, only to discover that, after winding my way for hours, my destination was right next to the spot I set out from.'

'Mmm, whose barmy idea was it to build palaces and churches on bits of wood in a lagoon?' said Nancy. 'Close your eyes for a moment and imagine the planning meetings that came up with the idea of building palazzi on wooden piles driven into the sand. The more one thinks about it, the madder Venice seems.'

She asked what the boys and I did all day.

'Every morning the *motoscafo* meets us at the water gate and takes us to the Lido,' I said. 'We have a picnic lunch and return home in the mid-afternoon or a little later.'

An emerald flash. 'That's more or less what I do,' she said. 'I come here to read and think.'

'If you'd like a lift . . .? But I expect you have your own boat.'

Nancy's lips tightened. She gave me a detaining look. 'A lift? What a *térréblé* good idea.' She lightened. 'That would be awfully kind. I should love that. *Thenk* you very much. I'm staying with Anna-Maria.'

Nancy had entered Venice at the very top. Contessa Anna Maria Cicogna Mozzoni Volpi di Misurata was the daughter of Count Giuseppe Volpi di Misurata, the 'last Doge of Venice'. Count Volpi brought electric power to Venice, developed utilities across northern Italy and the Balkans, and backed the mainland port of Marghera during the 1920s so that local industry could flourish without spoiling the lagoon. He widened the causeway, and restored a palazzo, which became the Gritti Hotel. He negotiated the Turkish-Italian peace treaty of 1912, which gave Libya and Rhodes to Italy. He attended the Versailles Peace Conference in 1919. As Mussolini's finance minister, he negotiated the redemption of Italian war debt. He was the antidote to *dolce far niente* and was rewarded with a final resting place in the Frari. Perhaps Volpi's most prescient stroke was to found the Venice Film Festival in 1932, the first ever such festival. It ensured a regular stream of Hollywood stars. It was hard to have a conversation in Venice without Volpi's name being dropped. He was the ghost at every *Bella Figura* gathering.

That evening, I rang the Conte for permission to give Nancy a lift in the *motoscafo*.

'Bravo,' he said. 'Send her our love.'

Then I rang Nancy at Anna-Maria Cicogna's. 'We can pick you up at ten o'clock tomorrow,' I said.

'I'll wait outside Peggy Guggenheim's palazzo,' said Nancy. 'Can I bring anything? Shrimp net? Bucket? Spade?'

'No, no.'

'I'm painting my toenails already,' she deadpanned. 'You

should see my outfit.' That Nancy accepted a lift shows how
few people there were in Venice during that pre-season season;
I also felt that it showed she had accepted me.

On 3 July, the Contessa rang. Brandolini had a new heir,
Brandino. 'Please tell everyone at the palazzo. Send them my
best wishes. Celebrate with champagne. Domenico will sort it
out.'

The nativity had been the source of great excitement and
the subject of much speculation and conjecture within the
household. Many shared the Contessa's hopes for a daughter,
but it wasn't to be. That evening everyone gathered in the
cantina to toast Brandino with champagne.

The following morning, the captain flamboyantly and skilfully curved the *motoscafo* into the landing stage at Palazzo
Venier dei Leoni, the 'unfinished palazzo', which Peggy
Guggenheim had bought nine years earlier. Nancy stood there
wearing a pale green dress, her chestnut hair held by a band.

'Morning,' she said, as the captain helped her aboard. She
was holding a book. I could see the author's surname, 'Driberg'.

I peered over the top of dark glasses.

'Oh . . . Boy or girl?' she said.

'Boy.'

Pushing off, we proceeded slowly down what remained of
the Grand Canal before it debouched into St Mark's Basin. As
we drew level with the Doge's Palace, the bows lifted and off
we sped round the outside of San Giorgio Maggiore, slamming
over the waves towards the Lido.

Arriving at the Excelsior, Nancy resumed the conversation exactly where we had left it when we pushed off.

'Hmm, I'm sure Cristiana will get over it.'

We got far more than my usual greeting. The staff stiffened as we entered. I felt pairs of eyes lock on to us. The general manager bowed at Nancy with a *'Buon giorno, signora.'* Nancy responded with an awkward smile. We pressed on through the lobby and descended to the beach.

'Glad to see they've got a new chap,' said Nancy, nodding at the photographer who at that moment was moving into position. 'Previous one gave everyone triple chins.' Somewhere in an archive of the Excelsior there must be dozens of photographs of Nancy stepping down that marble cataract.

'The way I'm looking,' I said, 'I'd be amazed if he didn't give me red-eye, even in broad daylight and in black and white.'

We turned right and arrived at the Brandolini cabana. Many hands offered towels and water. Settling into deckchairs, we chatted while I kept an eye on Ruy and Leonello.

'I wonder why the Conte and Contessa's children are born in Switzerland and not in Italy,' I said.

'I suppose it allows the children to make jokes about the Swiss and get away with it,' she said, with a straight face, adding, 'I don't know. I'm sure there are all sorts of reasons. You won't find a more patriotic family, but I'd imagine that some intelligent and far-sighted people can see risks in being caught Italian if another war breaks out.'

Not an iota of Parisian-ness seemed to have rubbed off on Nancy. Besides her occasional habit of dropping French words for that *mot juste,* her appearance, dress, speech and attitude came across as an improbable satire of an Englishwoman abroad.

Take her attitude to seaside holidays. She regarded a seaside holiday as literally a holiday *by the sea*. She wanted to get to the beach early, not to beat the crowds (there weren't any) but because getting to the beach early is what any sensible English person would do on a seaside holiday. Why stay in bed when there are beaches to be sat on? Mitford genes would never have tolerated *dolce far niente*.

Neither highbrow nor voluptuous, Nancy came across as *vereh* well-bred and intelligent. Women then were naïve by default, suppressed into a state of emotional and intellectual deprivation. We weren't supposed to talk about anything worth talking about. Of course, I didn't fully grasp the extent of this syndrome. But I sensed it and so did Nancy.

'I've never talked about anything interesting to my parents or grandparents,' I said. 'I don't recall my father ever talking to me about politics until after the war. My headmistress at St Mary's told me the facts of life. Even then, in the school library, certain books had pages torn out. If I wanted to bring a book from home, it had to be signed by the headmistress.'

'Perhaps you're the victim of an overprotected upbringing.' I detected an emerald flash of irony, and simply smiled.

Domenico and Angelo arrived and laid out lunch: *prosciutto e melone*, and the usual meditations on pasta with tomato sauce.

'This really is most kind of Cristiana and Brando,' said Nancy, fanning herself with her book. 'Have you seen the prices in the bar?' Nancy nodded towards the Excelsior as she held a piece of prosciutto as fine as a burst balloon.

'I haven't actually. I've scarcely looked at a price in two months.'

'Let's say the waiters know how to keep a straight face.' Using her fingers, Nancy used the prosciutto to pick up a piece of melon, and then put them both into her mouth. 'Mmm.' She nodded, chewing, towards the terrace where lunch was being served. 'And the food . . . the food at Palazzo Brandolini knocks the food up there into a doggy bag.'

'You mentioned yesterday that the Venetian aversion to self-aggrandisement and personality cults was built into the political system, but the opposite applied in the world of art . . .'

'Yes, thank goodness!' she said. 'They built a political system that was so complicated that only a Venetian would be able to understand it, but the brilliance of Venetian art was immediately obvious to everyone who saw it. Artists were celebrated and venerated, as Emperor Charles V did when Titian allowed him to pick up his paintbrush. Dynasties of artists reigned supreme, Bellini, Vivarini, Tintoretto, Bassano, Longhi, Tiepolo, Palma Vecchio, Palma Giovane, Canaletto . . . complete inverse to the political system. Without that lot, Venice would be a fishing village on stilts. So the moral of my story is . . . Actually – haha – I forgot.' Once again, laughter took years off her. 'But I still prefer the Florentines, Raphael, Botticelli and especially Andrea del Sarto.'

Over the pasta course, I told Nancy about my bumbling Florentine debut. Seven years earlier, travelling in Italy with a friend, I had no idea that 'Florence' was 'Firenze'. 'When our train stopped at "Firenze",' I said, 'it was only when a fellow passenger pointed out to us that we'd arrived at Florence that we managed to scramble out just as the train was pulling away.'

'Mmm,' Nancy regarded me, 'and they put you in charge of

the palazzo? Just as well that Cristiana doesn't let you out at night.'

Domenico handed round bowls full of mint ice cream. 'Ah, the ultimate toothpaste,' said Nancy. Turning to me, she asked, 'How long are you staying in Venice?'

'At least until the end of the year.'

'How do you find the palazzo?'

'It's so beautiful, especially the Palma Vecchio frescos.'

'It's beyond reach of any estate agent's glossary, isn't it? But one could never accuse it of being *troppo* cosy.'

'You wouldn't want to pass out in there, not with all that marble.'

'As I pointed out to Brando, his palazzo needs about twenty years of being lived in. I do like a bit of shabbiness.'

As the sun dipped, the shadows lozenged. It was time to go.

'Thank you for letting me join you,' said Nancy.

'It's not my beach to prevent you.' I smiled. 'Same time tomorrow?'

Once again, a wistful look filled her eyes. 'I should be delighted. *Thenk* you.' She paused, then said, 'I jolly well hope they tore plenty of pages out of *my* books.'

Nancy seemed relieved not only to have a lift to and from the Lido, but also to have someone likewise unattached – or semi-detached – for company. She joined our daily commute. After swimming, we would run chicken-skinned to our towels, sit in deckchairs, talk and read, while I looked after the boys.

She was a recluse. Why else sit next to me on a beach almost every day for three weeks? She wanted to lie low, not be seen, not be reached. Perhaps she saw in me a useful idiot:

respectable enough to hold a civilised conversation with, but anonymous enough not to arouse curiosity. That I was almost completely ignorant of the jet set would have further assured her: I *didn't matter.* She could say what she liked knowing it would go no further. Meanwhile, I was someone who deferred and deflected her horror of being unattached in Venice.

CHAPTER TEN

Destiny's Darlings

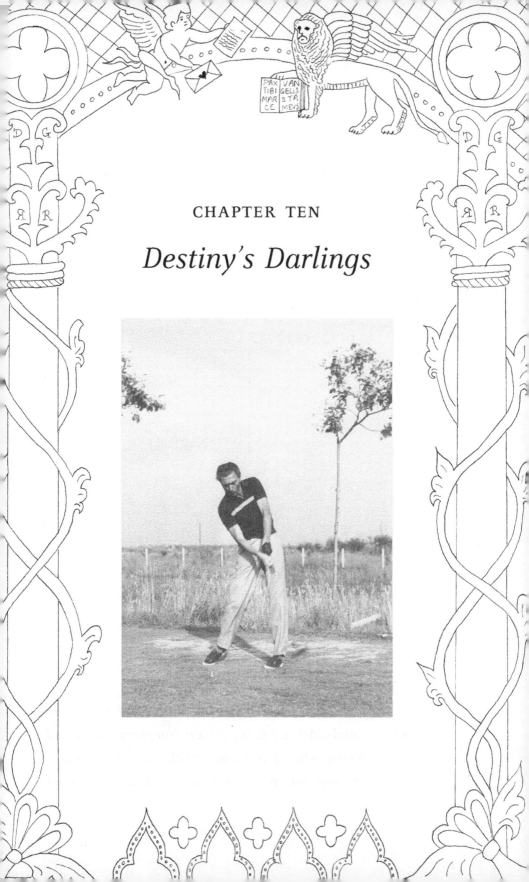

Previous page: *I don't care for golf, but I did admire the Conte Brando Brandolini d'Adda. I found it surprising that a man could be so charming and kind to a woman neither family nor friend, when to do so meant 'nothing' to him. He used to play me music.*

THE CONTE'S FAMILY tree wasn't so much a tree as a sizeable tract of forest that dated from the sixth century, and took the form of an epic catalogue of sonorous titles – conti, contesse, principi and principesse. The Venetian branch was admitted to the Patriarchate of Venice in 1686, which gave them the right to sit on the Great Council, the highest governing body of the city. Among the numerous men-at-arms, soldiers of fortune and mercenaries, the family included the wife of one Holy Roman Emperor (Francis I) who was the mother of another Holy Roman Emperor (Joseph II). There's a Brandolini in the footnotes of every other page of the history of Venice.

Although his title dated from the time of the Holy Roman Emperor and was hard-won on the battlefield, titles in 1957 had dissolved into Italian make-believe. Italy had officially dispensed with heraldry, legitimacy and precedence when it abolished the monarchy and became a republic in June 1946. Titles were thenceforward baubles unsubstantiated by legal writ, unlike in the England where strict rules governed who could inherit what. That didn't stop some people flourishing titles, or others respecting them for it; a few flaunted several, the more the better. This gaily titled pageant was an *Alice in Wonderland* element of Venice that people found amusing and jolly, unless of course they maintained hard Communist principles and were utterly devoid of any sense of humour, irony or romance.

The exotic big-spenders who converged on Venice in summer

in the 1950s thought this was all simply splendid, and played along. Rival shipping tycoons Stavros Niarchos and Aristotle Onassis enjoyed joining in. An aphorism of Nancy's kept resonating in my mind: 'The nouveaux riches are jealous of the penniless aristos, and the penniless aristos are jealous of the nouveaux riches.'

Despite not being Communist or, I hope, lacking a sense of humour, I found it faintly ludicrous that Ruy, Leonello, Nuno and baby Brandino were addressed as 'Conte', and that their cousins the zu Fürstenbergs were hailed as 'Principi' and 'Principessa'. Whenever I spoke to the Conte and Contessa, or the zu Fürstenbergs, I shunned the Uriah Heap-ish title-cringe in favour of the imaginative use of redundant preambles and creative throat-clearing: *'By the way . . . I was wondering if . . .? Do you think it would be sensible if we . . .?'*

The Contessa's family was even more exotic. She was one of seven children by Edoardo Agnelli, whose father Giovanni Agnelli founded Fiat in 1899, and Virginia Bourbon del Monte, whose mother, Kentucky-born redhead Jane Campbell, was quite a character. After Jane Campbell's aunt, Baroness de Westberg, wife of the Netherlands ambassador to Rome, introduced her niece to the Eternal City at the age of thirty-one, Campbell married Carlo Bourbon del Monte Santa Maria, 4th Principe di San Faustino, a direct descendant of Henry IV of France. The newly ennobled Princess Jane outraged, charmed and delighted Roman society, to which she introduced bridge and backgammon. When Mabel Stimson, wife of Henry L. Stimson, the United States Secretary of State, visited Rome and took tea with Princess Jane, she drawled, 'Oh, Princess, how lovely to live in the shadow of the Colosseum where Nero fiddled while Rome burned.'

'It's difficult,' replied Princess Jane. 'Now the men fiddle while the women burn.'

A motor-racing friend Shelagh Cooper knew the Contessa's elder brother Gianni from Formula One Grands Prix. 'He's full of charm,' she said, adding, 'He very intelligent, vain and always interested in motor-racing and racing drivers.' Of the Contessa's six siblings, I only met Clara, the eldest. In looks and character, she and Cristiana were most unalike. Clara was large, dark and only wore black. Pitying, lofty and condescending, she wasn't bothered to be friendly. Without being deliberately rude, she managed to be astronomically remote, and if she ever had to greet me, only did so with stratospherically impassive patronage.

In 1938, at eighteen, Clara had married the Austro-German Prince Tassilo zu Fürstenberg, Knight of Malta, twice her age. The wedding caused a stir on the Fürstenberg side, not because of the age disparity but because Clara had no title. This would drive a fleet of Fiat 1400s through their children's chances of making it into the *Almanach de Gotha*, the authoritative directory and classification of European royalty and higher nobility; meanwhile Tassilo's sons would not be grand enough to be received into the Knights of Malta. They had three children: Egon, Ira and Sebastien. However, by 1957, Clara's affair with Giovanni Nuvoletti, the writer and actor, was well under way. She had run off with him in 1948 when adultery was a crime in Italy. Gianni had to confront them in Switzerland and bring them home.

Not to be outdone by her mother in marrying so young, Princess Ira, at just fourteen, became engaged to Prince Alfonso of Hohenlohe-Langenburg, a thirty-one-year-old car salesman and millionaire. Approval of the marriage had required three family conclaves: two sets of Fürstenberg/Agnelli deliberations and one Hohenlohe family council held in southern Spain. The wedding, which took place in Venice in September 1955, represented the fusing of two great automotive empires, Fiat (Ira) and Volkswagen (Alfonso). Given the geopolitical symbolism, the marriage ranked as a world event.

If any family in Venice could out-host Carlos de Beistegui, it was the Agnelli. The wedding of Princess Ira and Prince Alfonso saw what was reported as the 'biggest assembly of Central European nobility since the war', including three hundred members of the royal houses of Europe. Uncle Gianni gifted pearls and emeralds acquired from the Maharaja of Jaipur. Clara gave an emerald piece believed to have dated from the Crusades, as well as two diamond rings that she had received upon her own wedding seventeen years earlier. The ceremony itself was delayed by one hour after Princess Ira took her time getting dressed, and when Alexandre of Paris, a hugely important hairdresser, fell into the Grand Canal along with another guest just as Princess Ira and Prince Tassilo were boarding a gondola outside Palazzo Brandolini. The waterways were clogged not only with Parisian hairdresser but also with a Venetian navy of gondolas, water-taxis, *vaporetti* and *sandoli* (rowing boats). The drying laundry that hung off balconies along the Grand Canal was replaced with banners and flags – partly to hide the crumbling masonry – and thronged with well-wishers and sightseers as in a Canaletto painting.

The hub of the celebrations was Palazzo Brandolini, refurbished especially for the occasion. Oliver Messel decorated the wedding. 'Scarcely has a cup of coffee been drunk in Venice without involving Oliver,' said the Conte. The 1950s were a golden age both for Venice and for Messel.

Two years later, the waves that this sensational marriage had stirred up had subsided into ripples, but were still large enough to be talked about. Indeed, the family still seemed shaken.

As dusk fell on Wednesday, 10 July, a wind rose, stippling the Grand Canal. Rain perforated the surface with a million pinpricks. That night a great storm seemed to mark the breaking of the heatwave.

The following morning, under clear skies, Venice's architectural largesse hit me with startling clarity, as if my eyeballs had been newly polished. The sun bathed the city in a flawless light that revealed the most incidental minutiae of the morphology of masonry, tracery, quatrefoil openings, mosaics, marble inlays, Islamic arches, ornamental coping, latticework, finials, vermicular stonework, crockets, cusps, shields, scrolls and mottoes engraved over archways and doorways, most of it showing signs of decay. I celebrated with a trip to the hairdresser.

Meanwhile I had forgotten my father's birthday. In order not to hurt his feelings, I needed to invent a reason for my not having written. I concocted a legend about a malady brought on by the rigours of chatelaining a Gothic Renaissance palazzo during a heatwave.

On 12 July, the Conte returned to Venice from Lausanne. 'We have decided to change our plans for the summer,' he said. 'We expect the heatwave to return, so we will go to the mountains for a few weeks where my wife will meet us. Do you know Badrutt's Palace in St Moritz?'

'Erm . . .'

'It's . . . You'll see. There's tennis and golf.'

The Conte seemed almost a father-figure to me. Unlike other Italian men I'd met, he was terribly sweet, in the best possible way. Sometimes I found him in his velvet-muffled damask-lined emerald chamber, dissolved in luxury, lying like a *principe* on a silk moiré daybed, propped up on coroneted white linen pillows, while taking a pedicure and reading a Russian novel.

He lent style and refinement to *dolce far niente*, a mode of living that he made his own. He would idly wander with slow delectation about the palazzo with an exquisite imperturbable languor, while hosts of cherubim hosannaed him, and archangels dished out manna washed down with ambrosia.

He seemed exorbitantly fascinated by his appearance, as if he had skipped a phase of vanity and self-love, and transcended to a higher plane of sophisticated exhibitionism. The only approbation he needed was his own. There was no need for other dependencies, publicity agents, standing ovations, column inches, public acclaim, never mind his own mugshot in the papers . . . All these were either beneath him or superfluous. He was attractive to others but didn't seem to *need* them. He had nothing to prove. Who needs friends and admirers when you have mirrors? He could easily have been misinterpreted as a preposterous specialised figure dedicated to beauty and pleasure, but his charm, civility and sensibility exonerated his vanity.

I expect that now and then he strolled into an office to throw a few papers into the air and run an eye over a column of figures, but he never appeared to stoop to the ruder cares of husbandry and the management of his family's estate. Actually to lift a finger and do anything practical would have been considered *déclassé* anathema. A few sotto-voce instructions whispered into Domenico's ear were enough. Perhaps that was part of his genius: sustainable, seamless, no-hinterland *dolce far niente*.

Notwithstanding every material comfort, the Conte and Contessa were intangibly blessed. They seemed to love one another; they were kind, civilised, cultivated and caring. Above all, they seemed happy. They had met at a party in Cortina when she was a nineteen-year-old drawing student living in Rome. They seemed blissfully, but not excruciatingly, married. They cooed, *'Tesoro . . .'* to each other, meaning 'Treasure', but used in such a way as to mean 'Darling'. *That*, I thought, is how I would like my marriage to be: happy but not unctuously coupled-up. I made a vow that when I married David I would never have rows or say anything nasty. I even began a letter to my father 'It is so lovely to live with a family that has a happy marriage . . .' I never got beyond the first line.

The Conte had an inflexible maxim never to talk to more than eight people in Venice. 'It's one thing to risk having a chunk of cornice or piece of marble crashing down on your head,' he said of the general dilapidation of palazzi, 'quite another to have a hard-up member of the gently fallen nobility come crashing down on top of you.'

In marrying Cristiana Agnelli and restoring Palazzo Brandolini, the Conte was living out the Venetian dream: money, flawless taste, and his place at the topmost layer of the Venetian *mille-feuille* confirmed. The Brandolini outshone their Venetian peers. Many were silently suffering the slow annihilation of time and, fed up with fighting cold, draughts and damp, were capitulating to the demands of economy and leasing the main floors of their palazzi to hotel chains while they retired to top-floor apartments. It must have come as a huge relief.

'I can well understand their motivation,' said the Conte, one day, on one of his walkabouts. 'I expect they justify leasing whole floors to hotels by thinking, I live here for three months of the year, and only in two rooms. Why not turn the rest into a hotel?'

The Conte never appeared to see his role as part of a larger mission to glorify aspects of himself, his family, his pedigree or any particular cause, but his family was well placed to hold out the longest. *Job done. Back to the opera.*

'Think what Venetians have given the world,' he continued. 'Street lighting, casinos, ghettos, the first national health service in Europe, statistical science, carpaccio, the Bellini cocktail, the floating of governmental stock, commercialisation of the mirror, easel-painting, the organ, the violin, the madrigal, the discovery of iris expansion . . . I could add income tax, state censorship and anonymous denunciations, but I won't. After such selfless largesse, perhaps the world will be moved to bring succour to Venice in her darkest hour.'

The straws of that succour were already in the wind. Venice was shifting from the stopover of Grand Tourists bound for Rome, to a mass tourist destination preparing to embrace the throng. That thin plume on the horizon was the first cruise ship bearing down. That crocodile of tourists led by the man with the megaphone in the piazza was the season's first package-tour millipede. That vendor selling postcards that out-Canalettoed Canaletto in their unblushing misrepresentation of Venice was about to spawn thousands of kitsch shops around the world that prostitute and peddle the name and image of Venice. That faint sound of thundering hooves in the distance was the first herd of away-day, trip-of-a-lifetime humanity shouting, 'Let me in!' That hapless tourist about to have his wallet lifted was part of the fodder needed to complete the new evolving ecosystem. As the Grand Tour began its last hurrah, the hunt for the Tourist Dollar in all its variants – the Cultural Aspiration Dollar, the Romance Dollar, the Honeymoon Dollar, the Kiss and Make Up Dollar, the Look At Me Dollar, the Lapsed Puritanical American Dollar, the Memorabilia Dollar, the Connoisseur Dollar, the Credulous Dollar and the Byronic Dollar (evenings only) – was well and truly on. 'Sewerage' hardly begins to cover what was about to hit Venice. The battle for the soul of La Serenissima had already begun.

Nancy seemed noticeably *piano* when the *motoscafo* swerved and bobbed towards Palazzo Venier dei Leoni to pick her up on Saturday, 13 July. Throughout her stay, her default facial expression was one of haunted sadness. It was partly that in repose her features were naturally – *nairturally* – like that, but on this day I noticed her staring at the confused waters of the lagoon as we hurtled towards the Lido. Several times I caught her gazing out to sea, lost in severest contemplation, and only occasionally forcing a smile. Something had rattled her. Within certain strata of English society, it was well known at the time that her marriage to Peter Rodd had long since faded; meanwhile, from friends, newspapers and her best-selling novels, it wasn't hard to join the dots about her complicated relationship with Gaston 'The Colonel' Palewski, the French politician, diplomat and de Gaulle loyalist whom she had met in London during the war. The intensity of her feelings for 'the Col.' can be gleaned from her portrayal of him as Fabrice, Duc de Sauveterre, the love of the heroine Linda Radlett's life in *The Pursuit of Love* who reappears in *Love in a Cold Climate*.

The anguished periods of tantalising deferral that followed her *coup de foudre* were written in the subtitles of Nancy's gaze. While the sea breeze frolicked in her hair as we sat on the beach, Nancy unburdened none of this to me. She told me nothing about her family and she kept her love life close to her chest. The only thing she said, under her breath, was, 'Sometimes the unexpected really does take one by surprise.'

Unknown to me, she had received news from the Colonel that he was to leave Paris for the post of French ambassador in Rome, if not ending their relationship at least putting several hundred miles between them. In a telegram she sent from Venice on this day, she replied:

O DESESPOIR. O RAGE. O FELICITATIONS! NANCY

I can well imagine how she felt.

This was also the year when, in December, her long-awaited divorce from Peter Rodd was settled. In those days, divorce, even loveless ones, was upsetting. Nancy was, in effect, losing both of her men at once. The following March, she would lose her father.

Like some women of her age and class, Nancy was probably intelligent enough to know that she had been brought up in a vanishing milieu, and therefore likely energetic and determined enough to do something about it. And yet, despite her apparent worldly sophistication, and her haughty manner, I noticed a simplicity and ingenuousness about her. A romantic sensibility coloured her outlook as if she led the life of a heroine of a novel, superimposing her own images on the world as she saw it. Unkind though it may seem, I saw Nancy less as a successful writer and wit, more as an incomplete person who had made some brave and difficult choices, but had failed to find happiness.

One morning on the Lido, towards the end of her holiday, I plucked up courage and asked her about her life. She turned and cast her emerald eyes towards the sea; there on the white-flecked cobalt horizon, a flotilla of yachts consulted prior to a regatta. There was a long silence, a silence that left me dangling.

Oh dear, I thought. Have I struck a chord or hit a nerve? Hmm . . . That's blown it. I've really gone and upset her now.

The silence ended when Nancy took a deep breath and declared, '"Princess fed up with Prince seeks frog!" How about that?'

She managed a smile. I laughed. Then she laughed too.

'I saw an advertisement for a package tour to Venice the other day,' said Nancy, out of nothing. 'I was horrified.'

'Let me guess,' I said. 'A sprint through St Mark's, the Doge's Palace, the Frari, and then a masked and caped gondola ride to *O Sole Mio*, with loo breaks every half-hour.'

'Not at all. What horrified me was that I was actually tempted! Just shows that life can be beautiful so long as you don't try to overanalyse it or be too clever or sophisticated.'

It crossed my mind that I might be being eyed up as literary pabulum, or sized up for a cameo appearance in a Mitford novel. Then I remembered that I was too boring, and that Nancy mainly wrote about family and friends. I was beige, vanilla, neutral, nothing, a social figment. Besides, there was a super-abundance of raw material right here in Venice, the beauty, the history, the exquisite – and not so exquisite – summer-season sybarites, the holidaying grotesques, the personages, the egos, the 'super-sewerage', the feuds, the playing off of one interloper against another, and the blunders of the uninitiated.

Nancy kept quiet about work-in-progress, but she mentioned something about a book, 'for anyone who wants to sleep better, prop open doors, light fires or who has an outdoor loo with an untenanted nail'.

A distant mournful wail from the railway station announced the arrival of the first trainload of the high-season visitors. Nancy bowed out of Venice just as the season was about to get going.

The Conte hosted a lunch to honour Conte Brandino Brandolini. Among the guests was the Prince zu Fürstenberg, a friendly fellow somewhat unkempt with wild hair, who looked like he'd just dropped in from hunting in the Tirolean Alps. I had just enough French, Italian and German to make it to the petits fours without everyone shrieking with laughter.

To Mr and Mrs Guy Johnson
Monday, 14 July 1957

Palazzo Brandolini
S. Barnaba-Venezia

Darling Mummie and Daddy,

I am sorry I haven't written sooner, but I have had a slight attack of something – don't quite know what, but it manifested

itself with a temperature, aches and pains and a sore throat.
Now I feel better.

. . .

The heatwave really was pretty terrible – I think that was the
only reason I was ill. It ended with a storm last Thursday night.
Some people said it was the hottest and most humid weather
in Venice for eighty years! Hundreds of old people died here.
The boys and I moved downstairs into the state apartments
where it was a little cooler – not much. The boys slept in the
big bedroom and I slept in the Count's room (if you remember
it). I had to do this on my own initiative because it was unbear-
able upstairs, and then I rang up the Count and told him and
he was very pleased. Actually it was rather fun being ill lying
in state in that gorgeous room waited on hand and foot with
ice packs, etc., and they made much more fuss than was neces-
sary. They are curiously informal people – everyone in the
household wandered into my bedroom at one time or another,
including all the menservants! Just to see how I was getting on.

During the very hot weather we started going to the Lido for
the whole day, because Venice was so unbearable – we left here
at about 9 a.m. and didn't come back until 7.30 p.m. We have
a picnic lunch on the beach – if you can call it a picnic lunch
with tables, chairs, and all the paraphernalia and two man-
servants to wait on us. Some of the English tourists just stood
and stared at the proceedings.

The Count has returned now, and yesterday our lunch party
included the Prince zu Fürstenberg, apart from many other
notables.

I told you on the postcard that the Countess has had another boy, didn't I? I think that everyone has now recovered from the disappointment. She is still in Lausanne and now plans are slightly altered and we are going to St Moritz for four weeks on 24 July to stay at the Palace Hotel. Evidently the summer enter-tainments at S Moritz are tennis and golf.

. . .

I have had two dresses made by the Countess's dressmaker – they are a great success, particularly the one made with that blue and white spotted shantung. All I did was cut out the pictures from Vogue *and she came for one fitting. I am thrilled. They are so beautifully made and finished off.*

. . .

Lots of love and XXX
Gill

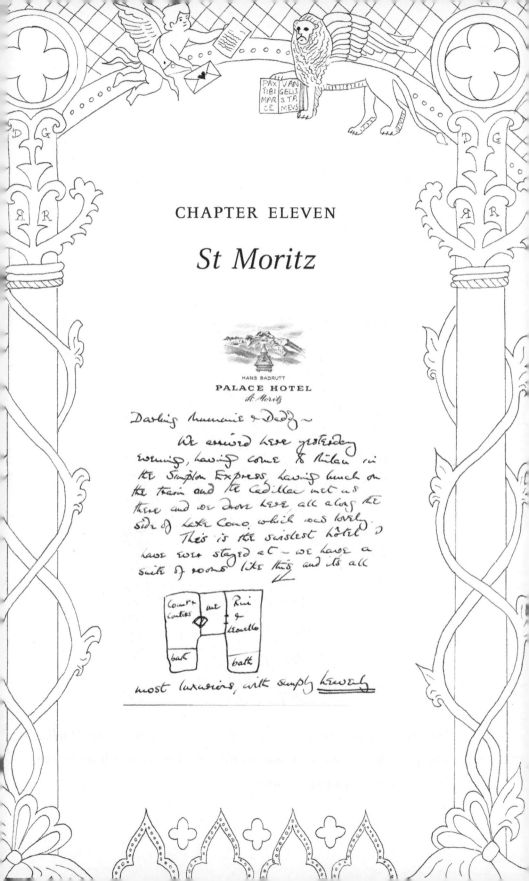

CHAPTER ELEVEN

St Moritz

HANS BADRUTT
PALACE HOTEL
St Moritz

Darling Mummie & Dadg~

We arrived here yesterday evening, having come to Milan in the Simplon Express, having lunch on the train and the Cadillac met us there and we drove here all along the side of Lake Como which was lovely.

This is the swishest hotel I have ever stayed at ~ we have a suite of rooms like this and its all

Count & Contess	me	Rui & Isabella
bath		bath

most luxurious, with simply heavenly

Previous page: *The letterhead of Badrutt's Palace, St Moritz. The breathless tone was due to the altitude as much as to the hotel's luxurious appointments.*

THE THIRD SUNDAY of July traditionally marks the festival of the *Redentore* (Redeemer), the most important historic event in the Venetian calendar. It celebrates the end of the plague of 1576, which claimed, among its fifty thousand Venetian victims, the life of Titian. In 1957, the celebrations had an edge. I read in *Corriere della Sera* that the heatwave had claimed more than eight hundred Venetian lives.

We packed the balconies of Palazzo Brandolini as this ancient nautical pageant glided the length of the great S of the Grand Canal. Gondolas and floating pavilions dominated, leaving just enough room for the *Bucentaur*, the largest most magnificent waterborne palace of them all. It is descended from the State barge of the old doges, hung with scarlet damask, the golden lion of St Mark glowing on the poop, and the oarsmen's jackets picked out with golden thread. Three hundred and eighty-one years after the first Redentore, the festival left me with a powerful sense of Venice as a golden city.

After more rain, the return of the heatwave that the Conte had forecast turned our thoughts to the cool mountain air in the Alps to the north-west.

One joy of living with the Brandolini was being able to whizz off here and there on a whim with minimal planning, little fuss and no stress. The household machinery that handled all logistics invisibly took care of all arrangements, reservations and packing. All that remained for me to do was to get my hair done and nails painted.

The Conte, Ruy, Leonello, Laura, Domenico and I set off from Palazzo Brandolini in the *motoscafo*. Disembarking at the railway terminus, we boarded the Simplon Express to Milan.

As the train clattered across the Veneto, the Conte turned to me and said, as quietly as the noise of the train allowed, 'Giulietta, I wonder if I might ask a favour. When we arrive at Milan, we will continue by car to St Moritz. Unfortunately Domenico has a problem with his driving licence . . . An unfortunate accident in Sacile. A drunkard stepped into the road . . . Most tragic. His licence is suspended. I wonder if you would like to drive us.'

Hmm, I thought, Milan to St Moritz, now there's a challenge, like a long-distance Cresta Run done back-to-front and on wheels, the kind of trip that a reckless daredevil would race for a wager. Being one who has an unshakeable belief in their own abilities, including exploring the outer edges of the handling envelope of a fully laden Cadillac on Alpine roads, I said, 'Of course.'

'Are you sure it is not a problem?' said the Conte, a stern look in his gaze.

'Not at all. I have no fear of driving any sort of car.'

'*Bravissima!*'

The Conte never asked if I held a driving licence. But we'd already talked cars. I'd already bored him rigid with high-octane tales of riding with Stirling Moss and Mike Hawthorn. Maybe from those breathless legends, he had deduced my proficiency at the wheel. On his part, I assumed his reluctance to drive stemmed from a deep-seated Venetian wariness of dry land,

and a preference for the amphibious life at La Serenissima. So, arriving in Milan station, we were greeted by the family Cadillac.

As I folded myself into the driving seat, savouring the heavy but satisfying and complex clunk of the door, I asked myself, Why does the family that owns Fiat drive an American car? I never found a satisfactory answer. Overflowing with expensive and probably superfluous luggage, trunks, hatboxes, the Conte's golf clubs and important items of furniture, such as the Conte's gramophone and a pile of records, which Laura held on her lap, we set off, bouncing and surfing our way to St Moritz.

In automotive design terms, the 1950s was the era of tail-fins and white-wall tyres; Cadillacs in particular were vehicles of status, escapism, the freedom of the road and the American Dream. They were the smartest cars of the age. I thought, The Brandolini Cadillac puts my old Austin in its place. You've got to hand it to those Americans, they know how to build cars.

We motored north, passing Monza at a stately pace. After skirting Lake Como, we began to climb. Being American, the Cadillac is designed to drive on man-made roads built especially for cars, roads that are predominantly straight. In Europe, however, most roads were originally built by or for animals, and in the Swiss Alps, roads probably derive from the tracks of nimble-footed ibex and chamois. So while the Cadillac was fine driving across the plains around Milan, it was quite a different matter winding up through the Alps. With its generous suspension, I felt as if I was driving a waterbed.

Reaching high into the Engadine Valley in south-east

Switzerland, the journey to St Moritz is every bit as dramatic as the destination. The farming villages and cow-rich soft Alpine pastures soon gave way to more precipitous terrain as we squeezed through Alpine defiles, tiptoed along corniches, crossed bold arches thrown over mighty torrents in plunging chasms, careered around hairpins and spiralled upwards towards Engadine. Meanwhile, the Conte told stories about the lengths to which people go to reach St Moritz.

'In Switzerland, access to the slopes and peaks is considered a human right,' he said. 'In that way, the Swiss Alps are ironically a great leveller. But St Moritz tilts the playing field. It takes a certain determination to get there. A few brave souls try to fly to Samedan airport just next to St Moritz, but the weather is unpredictable. The outcome lies in God's hands, not the pilot's. Sometimes, pilots can mistake the frozen St Moritzersee, the lake that St Moritz overlooks, for the runway. Landing at Samedan can be like trying to get a hole-in-one at the golf course, which is perhaps why they built the golf course next to the runway, as a reminder. Really if you saw the crazy things that some people get up to here in winter, you'd think evolution had taken a wrong turn. You often see minor deities hobbling around on crutches.'

'Don't worry,' I said, as I threw her around a particularly sharp hairpin in a too-high gear, 'I've alerted next-of-kin.'

The air felt noticeably thin as we arrived at the cloud-capped citadel of St Moritz. Stillness enveloped the upper reaches of the Engadine, a rarefied world that more than redeemed the tourist brochure promises of sapphire skies, glamorous peaks, plunging slopes and placid lakes.

St Moritz sits penned just below the tree line between

Corviglia Mountain and the St Moritzersee. Among the sprinkling of pine chalets overhung with shallow-pitched roofs that
looked like a miniature man-made mountain range, there towers
the unmistakable form of Badrutt's Palace, an imposing if
unconvincing attempt at crossing a mountain *Schloss* with a
fairy-tale castle, complete with mock turrets and bogus castel-
lations built against an imaginary foe. The palace, which opened
in 1896, is the heart of St Moritz, and was owned by the
founding Badrutt dynasty.

As we drew up, Andrea and Hansjurg Badrutt were waiting
for us at the door. Stepping into the antique lobby, I took in
the baroque ceiling, Gobelin tapestries, silk-covered Renaissance
chairs, ecclesiastical fixtures and the sixteenth-century
Assumption of the Madonna. It looked more like the sacristy
of a Gothic cathedral than a resort hotel. Perhaps it was a
spiritual home of sorts. A pianist, a ubiquitous figure in the
bars and restaurants of St Moritz, was tinkling away in an
adjoining room.

We were bowed towards a large suite that gave on to a
magnificent panorama of the St Moritzersee and the Engadine
valley. It was decorated in rococo style with cream and gilt
bedsteads, marble-topped chests of drawers with bronze
handles, a chunky writing table with gilded curving-legged feet
of lions, gilded consoles and gondola-shaped chaises longues
– the everyday aesthetic of the European jet set. Repro classic
French was the favoured style, studded and slathered with gold
and marble, historic emblems of money and power. The thing
that caught my eye, however, was a small bell in my bathroom
that, if rung, summoned not one of the hotel staff but Laura,
the Contessa's maid.

Some say that grand hotels are wonderful places to escape the tyranny of the mundane. They allow you to live like a pampered princess whose every whim is gratified by the push of a button or the tug of a cord or a few words whispered into a telephone. However, having escaped the tyranny of the mundane, the Renaissance man and woman of the Engadine, who are hoping to blend in with their peers, face a number of tough challenges. In winter, they must be proficient in skiing, tobogganing, bobsledding and ice polo; in summer, they must know their way around a golf course and feel completely at home on a tennis court. Indoors, an insatiable appetite for, and stamina at, bridge or backgammon is essential. I, of course, was proficient in none of these activities, and could scarcely tell a golf racket from a tennis club.

The Contessa and baby Brandino arrived from Lausanne, she looking as radiant as ever, and seemingly bearing no signs that she had just given birth.

'No girl,' she said, with a slightly strained smile. 'Maybe there will be another chance, maybe not.'

Nurse Rasch was put in charge of Brandino, much to everyone's relief since it kept her busy. I bumped into her in a corridor of the hotel. She gave me a look of finely chiselled loathing complete with silver inlay. I never asked, but I suspected that her hopes of seeing me fail in my stewardship of the palazzo had been crushed. She disappeared to her own room somewhere in the bowels of the hotel leaving a lingering waft of carbolic. I didn't see her for several days thereafter.

One morning, I found the Conte about to set forth dressed for golf. 'I'm only as bad as my last game, if not worse,' he smiled. 'Terrible golfers like me are happy golfers. If you try to improve, you just get depressed. It will almost certainly go wrong. I, on the other hand, have no such expectations. Do you play?'

'Only if necessary. I haven't addressed a golf ball in years. I used to play with my father, but gave up.'

'You prefer the good walk unspoilt?'

'Not just that,' I said. 'I can't bear cruelty to golf balls and golf courses.'

'*Brava!*' cried the Conte, with a grin, and headed for Samedan golf course.

Dinner in the main restaurant of the Palace was pure theatre. As you enter the giant room overlooking the St Moritzersee, you find yourself standing on a raised platform, like a stage, where everyone can see you, and where you are expected to make a dramatic entrance. Really, you needed to be a newly varnished Barbara Hutton wearing black lipstick and nail polish, or a turbaned Coco Chanel, or a Marchesa Luisa Casati flanked by cheetahs to make an impact – if that's what you wanted, which I didn't. As it was, being accompanied by two young Brandolini, descended from a pre-Louis XV Bourbon on their mother's side and a Holy Roman Emperor or two on their father's, was statement enough, for those who knew.

We were led to a circular table in the middle of the room, radiantly dressed in white linen cloth. Cutlery and glasses gleamed. A small bouquet of flowers stood in the centre. At the far end of the room, a mariachi band played. I felt the eyes of the other guests boring into us as we took our seats. Waiters immediately seized our folded napkins and, with a flourish, flicked them open and draped them over us as if we were about to be hairdressed. Once installed, I could take in most of the room, including the door, in one slow pan. The men wore dinner jackets, the women gowns and jewels. The head waiter gravely presented leather-bound menus that opened like a book. I looked at my menu and saw a blizzard of '*Velouté de . . .*', '*Soufflé de . . .*', and '*Filet de . . .*'

Every course arrived in trolleys on which the plates were domed with great shining silver cloches. Choreographing the occasion, the head waiter looked on sternly as the waiters placed the cloched plates before us. At a signal, the domes were lifted in unison. With expressions of relief that all was to order, the head waiter and his assistants then bowed a profound retreat. Finally came the pudding trolley, which meant an exam in trifles, Pavlovas, tarts, ice creams, cheesecakes, soufflés and crêpes. Just looking at them made me feel like a Dickensian urchin gone to Heaven. When we rose to leave, seemingly the entire waiting staff rushed forward to help, and saluted us as we made for the door.

After that ordeal, we mostly dined in our suite. A caravan of silver 'chariots' wheeled in breakfast, lunch and dinner. At dinner, a priestly hierarchy of waiters pushed in their little methylated-spirit trolleys and synchronistically and flamboyantly began flambéing. The boys and I were fascinated. It was like jet-set trainspotting. If David's day job doesn't work out, I thought, I can easily see him as a waiter; all those miles pushing my Austin 7 would be put to good use. The waiters asked if we wanted a pair of butlers to stay and serve (we didn't). I was staggered at the level of physical idleness that the staff were trained to indulge. If I'd asked nicely, they'd probably have cut up my food and spoon-fed me.

On the gramophone, our favourite record was the soundtrack of *High Society*, the musical romantic comedy that had come out a year earlier starring Bing Crosby, Grace Kelly and Frank Sinatra, set in the mansions of Newport, Rhode Island, whose neglect in the film echoed that of the palazzi in Venice. The Conte was particularly fond of the song 'Who Wants To Be A Millionaire?'.

Nodding towards the boys, he told me, 'You can't start them on Cole Porter early enough.'

One morning the Conte announced that Gianni, the Contessa's elder brother, was giving a party in Monaco that week and had invited him and the Contessa to stay at Villa La Leopolda in Villefranche-sur-Mer. Gianni's private aeroplane would pick them up from Samedan airport, 'Assuming, that is, his pilot can put her down,' said the Conte. 'Giulietta, would you mind if we left you in charge? We will be a few days.'

Gianni, who was altogether a bigger hamster on an altogether bigger wheel than any other member of the jet set, was, at thirty-six, a figure of myth and legend. Even then he was known as the uncrowned 'King of Italy' and a style icon. He travelled by zephyr and trailed fairy dust as he flitted from one 'charming' little airport to another.

As the Contessa waved goodbye, she told me I was to do as I pleased, 'And help yourself to the car.'

Bliss!

To Mr and Mrs Guy Johnson
Monday 29 July 1957

Hans Badrutt
Palace Hotel
St Moritz

Darling Mummie and Daddy –

We arrived here having come to Milan in the Simplon Express, and had lunch on the train. The Cadillac met us and we drove here all along the side of Lake Como, which was lovely.

This is the swishest hotel I have ever stayed at – we have a suite of rooms and it's all most luxurious, with simply <u>heavenly</u> food. The Countess has her maid with her, who looks after all one's clothes and unpacks, etc. The hotel looks straight on to the lake and has tennis courts and all other amenities. Today is a lovely day and it really looks beautiful – blue sky, black mountains with snow on the peaks, which are all reflected in the lake. It is so high that it is very cold at night, and although all the windows are double, the central heating was going full blast and I was not too hot in bed with an eiderdown. But the sun is very hot.

My fountain pen has diarrhoea. I suppose it's the altitude, so excuse this scratchy biro.

Today the Count and Countess are leaving in her brother's private aeroplane for Monte Carlo for five days so I am left here in charge, complete with ladies' maid and Cadillac. I am driving them to the airstrip not far from here.

(Later) I have just returned from seeing them off in a lovely de Havilland Heron – brand new, which is quite a big, four-engined plane.

The Countess has left me her gramophone and a lot of records, which is lovely.

It is much hotter today and you can sunbathe on the balcony.

There are mostly Americans and Italians in this hotel, but all the staff speak any language at all.

Tomorrow we are going to start playing tennis in earnest. They have hired a racquet for me.

I really don't know how long we are staying here for, but anyway until about 15 August.

I hope all is well – I look forward to a letter.

Much love xxx

Gill

Ah, hotel life, so easy, so carefree! So many maids, valets and waiters ready to pop out like the cuckoo in a Swiss clock! No housekeeping problems, no dinner parties to plan, no grocery shopping, and no laundry to send out!

All I had to say to the head waiter at breakfast was, 'Please could we have the car ready at such-and-such a time with a picnic for X people', and the Cadillac would be brought round with a boot full of lunch.

We motored high into the mountains, exploring remote valleys and cresting the Bernina, Aprica and Tirano passes. We peered down ski runs and had snowball fights. The picnics were always lavish affairs.

Among the guests at the hotel was a charming American family, a mother and two girls of about eight and ten, Poo and Tweedy. They were on holiday. I expect someone told them that the Palace Hotel was the finest. As they had no car, I invited them to join us. They seemed thrilled to be driven around the mountains cocooned in a Cadillac.

I almost wept when on Thursday, 15 August, we said goodbye to the Badrutts. However, keeping on the move is a jet-set imperative. Never present an easy target! Having consumed three weeks in the mountains, I drove the party back to Venice via Brescia, Verona, Vincenza and Padua, to find La Serenissima mercifully cooler than before.

CHAPTER TWELVE

The Greatest Show on Earth

Previous page: *This photograph of the Grand Canal viewed from Palazzo Brandolini looking towards the Rialto illustrates why Venice has scarcely changed in hundreds of years. With the facades of the palazzi plunging directly into the water, you couldn't possibly open a shop, bar or trattoria on the waterfront.*

SHE MAY HAVE been meteorologically cooler than before, but in all other respects Venice was hotter than ever. If late August in the Venetian lagoon was the greatest show on earth, the summer of 1957 was its command performance. As I wandered about the city, I could feel the atmosphere changing by the hour. It was as if a barrage of money bombs – or credit bombs – was blitzing her. The hotels were filling, the palazzi were coming to life, and the cafés, bars and restaurants were spilling out on to the *campi*. Meanwhile, the photographers were stubbing out their cigarettes and preparing to stalk their prey. The Grand Canal and St Mark's Basin looked like an animated Canaletto painting only without the special effects (I doubt the Grand Canal ever looked exactly as Canaletto had depicted it). The piazza was a phantasmagoria of people. I joined the queue to have hair and nails done, legs waxed.

From bars, trattorias, hotel lobbies, *vaporetti*, bridges, gondolas, from the piazza and from cabanas on the Lido, broken fragments of strange and fascinating conversations and colloquy would occasionally pierce the white noise of high-season Venice, and fill my ears like an opinionated and censorious Greek chorus offering a purple running commentary of explanation, advice, sermons and speculation on what might or ought to happen.

'What I need is three hundred and fifty thousand dollars to round out my social personality . . .'

'So I told her, "If you're going to be rude, lose weight". . .'

'No one who witnessed his impersonation of Byron could possibly forget it' . . . 'Yeah, no matter how much counselling they have . . .'

'So I told my pilot that I had to have peonies wherever I land . . .'

'He's not stupid. I mean he doesn't sit there reading the *Beano*. He's just infinitely more pompous than people infinitely more important than him . . .'

'It would help our relationship if you never complained . . .'

'Do you think enough people recognised me at Harry's Bar?'

'Hmm, the pills seem to be working . . .'

'They've got to be blonde, rich, stupid and grateful . . .'

'The only person who recognised me at Cipriani was the sommelier, which I took as a personal insult . . .'

'She has a personality like sparkling mineral water: bubbly, but nothing there . . .'

'So I pointed out to him that really important people buy their own beaches . . .'

'I once pitched for business in the shallow end of the Excelsior pool' . . . 'Yes, and you were still out of your depth.'

'He went from flirtation via agonised desire to pathological jealousy in between the antipasti and the primi piatti . . .'

'Chit-chat and high heels all day long . . .'

'She loves herself so much'. . . 'Well, she's easy to please, and doesn't get bored . . .'

'We had all eight courses and we're all still alive . . .'

As the lights came on in Europe, people wanted new kinds of fun. Desiring sparkle and gaiety, the jet set, especially the American branch, had the resources to lead the way, and where else than to Venice, with its beauty, beach, food, security, tolerance and exclusivity? In some ways, Venice in 1957 represented an encounter between New World innocence and cash, and Old World wiles.

The jet set liked to stay within its charmed circle, but was always alive to fresh faces and new blood. Recognising that some social barriers were collapsing, they saluted catalysts of change. If you had what it takes – three or more of either looks, glamour, charm, wealth, flawless taste, sporting prowess, wit, grandeur, grandiosity or ineffable pizzazz – you were invited to audition at a cocktail party or lunch party and – who knew? – become one of destiny's darlings. I watched it all unfold, and couldn't help listening in while keeping an eye on the boys.

The golden rules were unwritten: never talk to the press but do pose for photographers; avoid asking questions if you can help it, or risk being asked questions in return; keep it gay and frivolous, anything to divert the chit-chat from weighty and sensitive topics; be kind to, but never befriend, staff; don't waste time with the wrong sort; keep moving; keep smiling; always be pleased to see people; and always stick with the rich – they are less likely to exploit you.

Jet-set semiotics were sharply defined and instantly recognisable within the set, but could easily appear hazy and indistinct to outsiders. In dress, table, homes and manners, members of the set shared couturiers, interior designers and, in some cases, hairdressers. They spent much of their time restlessly flitting between social hives in Europe and the United

States, according to a carefully observed calendar of seasons. Late August and early September could mean only one thing: Venice. All roads, shipping lanes, railways and airways became thoroughfares for jet-set stars bound for La Serenissima.

The scene was further enchanted by the 18th Venice International Film Festival. Henry Fonda appeared on the Lido with Baroness Afdera Franchetti, his fourth and latest wife, who descended from a distinguished Jewish family in Venice. They had met via Audrey Hepburn. At twenty-six, Afdera was half Henry's age. With them was Henry's daughter Jane by Henry's second wife Frances Ford Seymour.

Even the Royal Navy showed up. Sailing home from exercises in the Turkish Black Sea, HMS *Birmingham* docked alongside the Piazzetta by the Doge's Palace. Rear Admiral Sir Christopher Bonham-Carter invited the Conte and Contessa, the Conte's brother Tiberto and me aboard for cocktails.

I remember the wonderful perspective that the upper deck afforded on the Doge's Palace, as well as the view to San Marco. The lower ranks served drinks while the officers looked immaculate in their tropical uniforms, and one by one asked what I was doing in Venice. Good question!

Afterwards, the Conte and Contessa invited Sir Christopher to dine at the palazzo, while I hit the town with the officers. I reckoned that a squadron of officers from the Royal Navy was sufficient chaperonage to clear the Contessa's strict injunction on such matters.

Naturally, if you owned a historic gingerbread palazzo, you were in demand and sought out by default. However, the Conte and Contessa never seemed bothered. With an air of mild bemusement, they were happy to observe the swirl of events from their eyrie above the fray. They were the still turning point of the social maelstrom, and stood at the centre of all theories, emotions and moral attitudes towards high-season Venice. But they preferred to spend time picnicking with their children on the Lido and listening to opera.

'There are only so many fun people before they get horribly tacky,' the Conte told me, as he prepared to go on a three-day fishing trip in Cortina with Sir Christopher, 'and only so many rich people before they get horribly boring. Tight-rope walking the *zeitgeist* is exhausting, so I leave it to others.'

Occasionally, the Conte and Contessa amused themselves by hosting exotic aliens and minor deities (whom I dimly recognised, but couldn't name) seasonally removed from their accustomed fastnesses, whose summer was incomplete without paying homage to La Serenissima. You would sometimes see them wandering about the piazza, or brooding vacantly over coffee at Caffè Florian, or staking out tables at Cipriani on Torcello Island: tottering dukes wearing crumpled linens, spindly countesses, distinguished personages, loud-mouthed two-fisted belly-up-to-the-bar Americans, who could often be found chugging the authoritative Bellini in Harry's Bar, and, occasionally, Byronic romantics who emerged at dusk. Venice put even the greatest egos into their place. She may have been poor but she was never unfashionable. She was beyond fashionable: she was exclusive. Venice was on the itinerary of the Chantilly of society, the grand, the super-rich, the great, the near-great and the few who were doomed to succeed. 'Love' is not too strong a word for the irresistible allure that these people felt. Visitors who caught the Venice bug could scarcely wait to return, especially if they had friends who owned a palazzo.

'Sooner or later,' said the Contessa, 'everyone comes to Venice.'

The *motoscafo* was busy all day ferrying guests between the palazzo, the railway station and the Lido. Among them, Oliver Messel arrived with his nephew, the pre-Princess-Margaret Tony Armstrong-Jones on whose arm was his girlfriend, Jacqui Chan. Armstrong-Jones was heading for Bellerive in Switzerland for the wedding later in August of Prince Sadruddin Aga Khan (son of Sir Sultan Mahomed Shah, Aga Khan, who had died the month before, and Andrée Carron) to Nina Dyer, Sri-Lankan-born daughter of a tea-plantation owner and his Indian wife. Nina's previous husband was Baron Hans Heinrich Thyssen-Bornemisza.

'I'm here pretending to look professional,' said Oliver, when we met in the palazzo, 'so I left the canvas and oils at home. How are you?'

'Very well. Thank you for introducing me to the Brandolini.'

'Fate seems determined to bring our families together! I trust you are flowering in Venice.'

Before I had time to respond, Oliver added conspiratorially, 'One golden rule: always be in the right place at the right time with the right people . . .'

'Wearing the right shoes, speaking the right slang, and seeing the right shows . . .' threw in Armstrong-Jones over Messel's shoulder.

'Have you been to the Lido yet? It's a glorious Darwinian struggle with rules that most people don't understand. And there is no one clever enough, subtle enough and determined enough to play the game properly who is stupid enough to play it at all . . .'

'Except Aristotle, Stavros and Gianni,' interjected Armstrong-Jones.

'Quite. Gill, this is my nephew Tony.'

'Hello,' I said, smiling at the dapper, trim figure, who looked at me with lively blue eyes. I knew *of* Armstrong-Jones. He had read architecture at Cambridge at the same time as David, who had mentioned him as a promising photographer.

'The jet set is like a time-and-motion study,' continued Oliver, still in conspiratorial mode, his lively dark eyes darting everywhere. 'As soon as anything like a consensus emerges, something else happens and, at a mysterious tom-tom, the set moves on, trailing from one beautiful resort to the next, without a worry or care in the world.'

'Or so it seems,' inserted Armstrong-Jones.

'Thank you, Tony. It's one of the wonders of the natural world.'

Accompanying Messel was a tall, heavily built man with a square head on which his blond hair had been swept back and flattened smooth against his skull. A cigarette dangled from an elegant hand.

'Gill, this is Vagn Riis-Hansen.'

'Hello.'

'Gill embodies Universal Aunts' finest hour.'

'Ah, yes,' said Vagn Riis-Hansen, and, turning to me, practically clicked his heels in salute. And then the Messel-Armstrong-Jones party drifted off.

Later, I came across Oliver walking around the *piano nobile*, holding up a large mirror. 'Just checking how the interior looks from every angle,' he said, when he saw my reflection. 'In my line, one is forever striving for a kind of aesthetic melange. I don't mean "Excommunicated bishop meets Frederick Barbarossa's catamite in Byzantium". It's gentler than that. I'm interested in the grandiloquence and wide embrace of the baroque. Décor should be entertainment as much as decoration.'

'If you don't mind me asking, Mr Messel, can you tell me a little of what you do? Your name seems to crop up everywhere.'

'I'm in the colour, romance and wit business, *dahling*, otherwise known as theatrical design: stage sets and costumes for ballets and operas, and the odd ball. It's a Sisyphean struggle. The wastepaper basket is full well before lunchtime. If I like an idea, I'll try it out on a few friends. If the friends survive the ordeal with health and sanity intact, I carry on. The trick is to conjure a look of richness, romance, evanescence and glamour from the most improbable paraphernalia – the sort of stuff that respectable housewives wouldn't give attic space to. Every rubbish dump is an opportunity. It is amazing what effects one can create with sweet wrappers, bits of chicken wire and Sellotape. Gauze and effect, my dear!'

'The Restoration Department of the National Gallery could really do with someone like you.'

'Oh, that's only half of it,' continued Messel. 'Other important ingredients and catalysts of my work include black coffee, paranoia, panic and insomnia. That's the fun bit out of the way. Then a few weeks later, after a few hoped-for curtain calls, ovations and rave reviews, *pfft*! Everything returns to its previous state. Debris to debris. Set design is the most unstable and reversible alchemy.' A momentary wistfulness dimmed Messel's expression. 'Few things have a shorter shelf-life – it leaves nothing but expenses, a few frayed friendships, and the fading memory of a certain glamour.'

If you were a special guest of the Brandolini, the Conte might pick you up or bid you farewell in person from the station, if he wasn't busy listening to Maria Callas or fly fishing with the Royal Navy. One morning, the Conte, Ruy, Leonello and I went to Venice station to meet a particularly cherished personage. While we were standing on the platform, a train arrived – not ours, another – and disgorged its passengers. The train then stood at the platform, as trains do. I was chatting to the Conte when I noticed Ruy and Leonello squatting down and talking to each other excitedly while pointing at something beneath the train. Whatever it was, it was clearly an object of fascination. The Conte and I carried on chatting when Ruy turned to us. 'Papa! Giuly! There is a man under the train. Look!'

Ruy indicated one of the bogies. I followed his gaze and made out a large organic-shaped object in the metal under-carriage. The object moved, and, like a pile of wet laundry, fell out on to the track. It resolved itself into two young men, unshaven, dark and wearing clothes of fantastic shoddiness in sizes too large so that the garments hung from their thin frames. They were definitely not in Venice on holiday, they certainly fell short of *La Bella Figura*, and they most emphatically were not the guests we had come to meet.

Picking themselves up, one of them shot us a fierce look and shouted a few primitively expressive syllables. Both men then ran vigorously and forcefully away from us over the railway tracks, as if their lives depended on it. Perhaps their lives did indeed depend on it. A cry went up. Two *carabinieri* gave chase. But, *just like that*, the men were gone.

Ruy and Leonello thought this was great fun.

I felt shocked, and unable to hide it. I knew precisely what I had witnessed. One medieval chronicler observed that 'All the gold in Christendom passes through the hands of the Venetians,' but so do many other things. The frontier with Yugoslavia was a few kilometres away. These men were fleeing not just the police but Communism; they were collateral in a broader political struggle that was rending Europe. The episode dramatised the weird and grotesque juxtaposition of the gilded and perma-tanned flotsam of capitalism that washed up in Venice to play, and the very different foreigners who were fleeing the Iron Curtain. 'Twas ever thus: some fifteen hundred years earlier, when Goths, Huns, Avars and Lombards descended from the north and tore into the Roman Empire, Venice was born on a lonely margin of the Adriatic. She began her life as a glorified refugee camp.

I felt guilty that Ruy and Leonello had unwittingly exposed the men. The Contessa's injunction on my going out unaccompanied after dark resonated loudly. Was there a risk of encountering desperadoes on the run?

'Who are those men?' asked Ruy. 'What were they doing under the train? Why did they run away?'

'Good questions, Ruy,' I said. 'I wonder . . . Who knows? I should think they fell asleep and missed their station. I've often done that. In future, if you see someone hiding under a train, try to ignore them.'

I turned to the Conte, who bore an impassive expression. He betrayed no indication that he wished to contribute to the situation. '*Ogni giornata*. It happens every day,' he shrugged. 'Another Gothic invasion. Some people want to go to Geneva rather than to parties, the beach and the fun.'

Outwardly, he and those two men were polar opposites;

inwardly they had similar motives. As one who looked to Switzerland for his family's security, the Conte probably sympathised with those refugees. But he wasn't one to encourage talk of such matters. He seemed to want his children kept innocent of the tides and shifting sands of geopolitics, at least for the time being.

Looking back on this incident nearly 67 years later, I realise that even if the Conte had felt shocked, I doubt he would have reacted any differently. In those days, the elder generation didn't. They never showed anxiety, especially not to young children. On the contrary, they carried on as normal, pretending that everything was safe, even if they knew it wasn't. Just as my father never betrayed any concern as he dandled me on his knee one night in early June 1940 in our house on Selsey Bill while we watched anti-aircraft fire and listened to the distant thud of artillery and the wail of air raid sirens during the fall of Dunkirk, so the Conte would never have betrayed his inner feelings about a couple of refugees tumbling out from beneath a train in front of his children. Besides, *La Bella Figura* dictated that if you are a Conte, you do not react like a headless chicken at the first sign of danger.

Although Switzerland was never brutalised by the war, it wasn't considered 'free'. However, if you were on the run from behind the Iron Curtain, almost anything else looks like freedom. The conflicts of the war hadn't ended: they had simply shifted shape.

It was interesting to observe the psychological effect that the combination of the palazzo and the Conte had on visitors. Most guests appeared so reverentially awed by the place that many fell into a state of meek compliance. Such was the Conte's mysterious skill and mastery of small forces that he seemed able to use that awe to diffuse order, discipline and tranquillity, and, without mentioning anything, never mind laying down hard rules, he magically induced in everyone who crossed his threshold a keen sense of decorum and respect. And he did all this remotely. He was psychic, telepathic, and kept a kind of suspended presence about the palazzo. One felt that were one to breach an invisible red line of behaviour, manners, etiquette or propriety, no matter how seemingly slight, or should you ever offend a member of his staff, the Conte would very soon hear of it or even see it by some panopticon that could peer around corners, so that, upon a minute signal to Domenico, that guest would be removed and despatched via oubliette. The Conte and Contessa were not ones to tolerate poor behaviour by anyone, including themselves. In Palazzo Brandolini, I never saw or heard flamboyant mood swings. Although in his mischievous moments the Conte loved a good fracas, he generally preferred his drama taken sitting down and in three acts.

Meanwhile, the character of the Lido beach shifted. The staff at the Excelsior, normally smiling and engaging, became supercilious and high-handed with their '*Mi dispiace signore, siamo pieni . . . Ah, Altezza, non vi aspettavamo. Farò sparecchiare il tuo solito tavolo.* I'm sorry, sir, we are full . . . Ah, Your Highness, we weren't expecting you. I'll have your usual table cleared.'

Descending the steps from the Excelsior on our daily visit

to the beach, we were greeted by one of the most narcissistic and competitive playgrounds: the Lido beach in season, where exotic social creatures gathered for shimmering matinees beneath a sky of heavenly azure while yachts glissaded along the horizon.

As we stared at the sunburnt bodies basting themselves in their own urbanity with the sun-glitter on the Adriatic beyond, all I saw was a mass of convexities and concavities.

'I see the tourists are out in force,' dismissed the Contessa, as we stood surveying what looked like a festival of body types, the breeze riffling her silky golden hair. She added, 'It's like happy hour at a seal colony.' Always looking *à point*, the Contessa wore her bathing suit under a voluminous maternity blouse, and was shod in talking-point wedges.

We picked through the sunbathers' paraphernalia, paperback books, sun-tan lotion, towels, beach bags and cameras as we made our way towards the cabana.

I could probably have made up an entire sub-oeuvre of once-upon-a-time stories for the children simply by basing them on the characters we saw: here was the Prince whom the Fairy had turned into the Ugly Toad; there was the Queen of Vampires, and the Evil Dwarf; that surely was the Wolf in Sheep's Clothing; are those the Three Little Pigs?; and – look! - here comes the Troll Bride; and there goes the Handsome Prince; but what is he doing with the Damsel-in-Distress? Quick, run! Here comes the Wicked Witch! Or is she the Cruel Stepmother? Has anyone spotted the Happily-Ever-After Couple yet?

Some 'names' cast considerable glare. The Lido in September 1957 was the end of the rainbow for certain multi-millionaires, who had got there by breaking away from history, proving everyone wrong, escaping predestination and getting on. For others still seeking a rainbow, a strategic week spent on this narrow littoral could literally add a new dimension to the address book of any presentable man or woman armed with a beach ball for bouncing into picnics and parties, whose retrieval was an excuse to strike up conversation.

In this conclave of the transient, not every interloper was famous or achieved or glamorous or even simply rich. There were a few colourful types who seemed to have given up on life's struggles and surrendered to hedonism for as long as their trust funds, allowances, dowries and settlements permitted. And then there was the occasional bore and buffoon.

To some, the fun, the partying and the games were a means, not an end. The shinier parts of Venice attracted a mix of dispossessed, displaced and distressed playboys, playgirls, black sheep and titled satyrs all brazenly vying to charm anyone into picking up the tab at the right places, and perhaps retrieve their extravagance by a glittering marriage. Then there were the clingers-on, the bottom-feeders, the limpets, the defaulters, the high-end charlatans, the operators and sundry social lepidoptera, all neurotically feeding on the fringes of the jet set, trying to sustain their precarious lives. Perhaps some had arrived hanging on to the underside of train carriages.

The Lido was the only part of Venice that had managed the extraordinary feat of making the visitors themselves the bona-fide attraction or, if not attraction, object of horrified fascination. As an art dealer scrutinises portraits for authenticity, I found myself focusing on brows, eyes, chins and noses, trying to discern veracity and provenance beneath the layers of artfully applied paint. If I were to liken the people to pictures,

I'd have said one or two were over-restored, over-cleaned and over-varnished. Some women had botched later additions; others had definitely been touched up, re-stretched and re-framed. A few were obvious fakes.

'You can be a huge personage on the Lido,' laughed the Conte, as he stretched out on a daybed, 'but back in Venice, you are just another strange little nonentity with a laminated face and tortured hair. Venice in high season is proof, or illustration, that in order to survive on this planet, you have to be either incredibly ugly or incredibly beautiful. Anything in between gets eaten.'

While the Conte celebrated the sun, the Contessa, who found sunbathing pointless, would swim with the boys.

Jewellery wasn't normally worn on the Lido. To do so was considered vulgar. Rules are there to be broken, however, and some fine merchandise of one sort or another was on show, pearls, bracelets, brooches, rings, glinty glittery things and other signs of life.

One day in late August there was a stir of impending arrival on the Lido beach. Amid the glitter, the gold and the tarnished emerged the thin, fragile figure of Barbara Hutton. The Woolworth heiress, America's Dollar Princess, the original Poor Little Rich Girl, made her entrance like Cleopatra, surrounded by five hand-kissing courtiers and Baron von Cramm, her prince-consort husband, the German tennis ace and twice French Open champion. Pallidly beautiful and looking like Dresden china in pearls, her tiny feet peeping from Chinese silk pyjamas, Barbara lay down on a daybed while her 'vultures' formed a protective palisade. It was said of this over-dressed gypsy queen that she reigned over a retinue of forty trunks and a train of auxiliaries. Every year she summered at the Excelsior. (Curiously, she had been my parents' neighbour at home in Winfield House, Regent's Park, London, a property she later bestowed on the United States.)

In the post-war recovery, Americans had a head start on Europeans in almost every walk of life, being generally richer. In coming to Venice to discover the arts of *la dolce vita, dolce far niente* and *La Bella Figura*, they craved to be less inhibited, less puritanical and less, well, American. I met several, usually women, who were recovering from immersion courses in the furniture and art of eighteenth-century France in which their husbands had enrolled them to keep up with the rage for Aubusson rugs, ormolu clocks, Louis XV and Louis XVI side tables, cloisonné birds, Sèvres porcelain and other accoutrements that gripped the Upper East Side as essential backdrops and 'conversation pieces' to gracious living and flawless taste in the States. It was said that rich American women who wanted to live like aristocratic Frenchwomen were helping lift Paris from the detritus of war. Some didn't stop there. Instead of learning about aristocratic furniture, why not marry a real aristocrat with a historic name and background?

Take Barbara Hutton. Her personal life was as familiar to the world as Greta Garbo's or Rita Hayworth's. Perpetually and alternately besieged and caressed by renowned suitors, she could tolerate only fresh-minted flattery. She was the Venice of heiresses. Baron von Cramm was husband number six. His predecessors in that dubious office were Alexis Mdivani, a Georgian playboy; Count Kurt von Haugwitz-Reventlow, a scheming Dane; Cary Grant, the film star; Prince Igor Troubetzkoy, a French-Russian sportsman; and Porfirio

Rubirosa, a Dominican diplomat and alleged assassin. Von Cramm was no Antony. After fewer than two years, his tenure was up for review, and everyone knew it. Penniless princes, dukes, counts and viscounts crawled from distant cabanas to compete in fawning over Barbara and kissing her hand. Her great, wounded, vulnerable blue eyes looked out mistily through thick black eyelashes, while her praetorian guard of 'vultures' diligently repulsed undesirables with barbed-wire stares and sometimes sharp elbows. I couldn't pretend that I cared, or that I didn't notice.

That summer, Barbara gave a dinner party for forty on Torcello, which she had lit with thousands of candles. There was no *placement*. 'It wasn't so much a game of lottery as to who you sat next to,' said one guest, 'as Russian roulette.'

The Conte told me about how Princess Jane, the Contessa's grandmother, had had a hand in Barbara's entrée to Venice.

'Jane was known as the "eccentric Princess of the Lido",' he said. 'Every summer, she took an apartment in the Excelsior.' The Conte told me how, dressed in full-length white, Princess Jane played backgammon and sipped Amaretto and cream while she held court in her cabana. In the 1930s, she was a widow in her seventies when she met Barbara Hutton, then trying to wriggle free from her family while fleeing bad press in the States. 'Princess Jane was still a formidable presence,' said the Conte. 'Her judgements on who did and did not matter, delivered from beneath a white parasol on her sandy assize, were held in highest esteem. She took Barbara under her wing.'

'For Barbara, that must have been like opening a door to an alternative universe.'

'Yes and no. When Venice was founded in the early Middle

Ages, the Republic was the New World of the Old World. She was built by merchant princes. Barbara is the granddaughter of Frank Winfield Woolworth of the five-and-ten-cent retail empire, one of the greatest merchant princes of the newer New World across the Atlantic.'

'So she fits in perfectly.'

'I expect she thinks she does. With that and the nod from my grandmother-in-law, who wouldn't?'

In fact Barbara Hutton stuck out like a bejewelled thumb.

While the jet set, with their courtiers, satellites, front-men and hangers-on, cavorted about the Lido, I industriously busied myself with Ruy and Leonello, taking them swimming and giving anxious care to re-reading them *Swallows and Amazons*.

CHAPTER THIRTEEN

Greek Gods

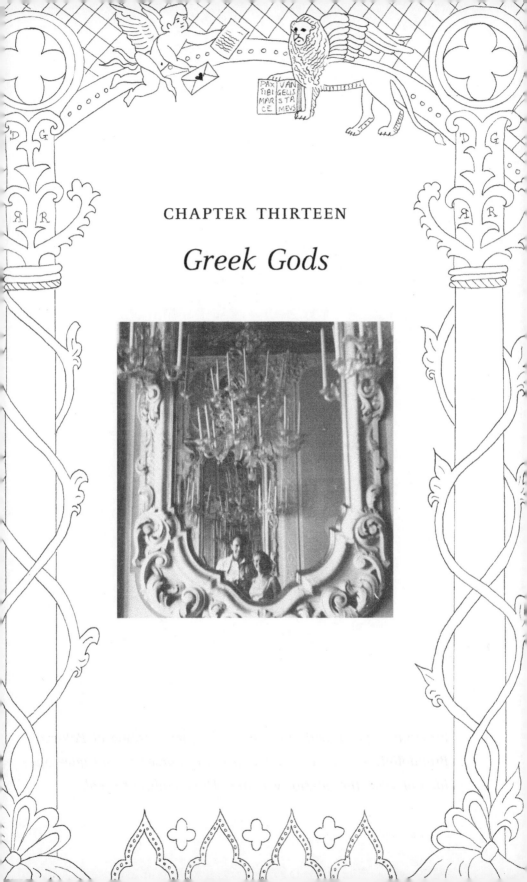

Previous page: *David and me on the* piano nobile *of Palazzo Brandolini: we wanted a photograph of ourselves that gave an idea of what the interior was like. The candles are real.*

THE PEAK OF high season was marked by the Regatta Storica on 1 September. It was celebrated with every circumstance of cost and dazzle. Along the Grand Canal, balconies were dressed with banners, flags, draperies, cushions and the occasional bedspread, to go alongside the drying laundry.

Princess Ira von Fürstenberg, the Contessa's niece, came to lunch with her husband Prince Alfonso of Hohenlohe-Langenburg. Slim and pretty, she had an imperious manner and wore a lot of make-up. Eight years my junior, she looked the same age, if not older. I found the Prince charming and friendly.

After lunch, the party swelled. Various members of the family turned up, along with friends and highlights of the Venetian *Who's Who*. Among them was Lord Lambton, his wife Bindy and two of their children. Lambton was a neighbour of my family in Darlington. My paternal grandfather even worked for Lambton & Co., 'the bank of the coal trade', as it was known. Lambton told me how, as a boy, he'd met Arthur Conan Doyle.

The boys and I watched the Regatta Storica from the balcony. The *Bucentaur* led the flotilla, filling the canal with a blaze of colour and music. If you urgently needed to cross the canal from one side to the other, now was the time to do it; you could probably have used the slow flotilla as stepping stones.

Meanwhile, new arrivals continued to pile in. Heading the pack, Elsa Maxwell, the legendary party host, cut a striking figure.

Five feet one inch in all directions, she was born in a theatre box during the performance of an opera in Keokuk in Iowa. She exploded on to the scene like a tornado with a glass of champagne in one hand and a press release in the other. The reputed Queen of International Party Making, she put the Lido on the social map in the 1920s by inviting over Noël Coward, Cole Porter and Tallulah Bankhead, the actress. Her raucous laugh and perennial high spirits could have navigated local shipping through fog. At anything closer than thirty feet, I should think the effect was quite frightening, especially if it was late and the last *vaporetto* had left. However, almost everyone prized her connections. With her bubbling sociability, her quaint jollity and her polished button eyes glinting with potential hysteria, she became, as one friend put it, a 'brilliant conduit between dissimilar people'. On 3 September, she put on a carefully choreographed Greek Ball for 160 at the Danieli Hotel in honour of Maria Callas.

Summer 1957 marked an unfortunate turning point in the diva's career. Callas's famous cancellations, walk-outs, rows and lawsuits were beginning to wear out people's patience. The final straw came during La Scala's season at the Edinburgh Festival that summer. Close to breakdown, Callas cancelled her fifth and final performance in *La Sonnambula*. (Her doctor had advised her to cancel Edinburgh altogether.) Her contract stipulated four performances; the fifth was sprung on her by the manager of La Scala. Disinclined to save the manager's face, Callas left for Venice to attend Elsa's ball in her honour. While fans queued in Edinburgh, Maria was photographed dancing at the Danieli. She had 'betrayed' her public for the jet set.

Callas was past her peak. Her voice was in decline. She was suffering nervous exhaustion, insomnia, sinus trouble and swollen legs. Increasingly, her stage entrances were met with boos and hisses alongside the usual rapturous applause. Her arrival on the social scene of Venice was met with a more muted response, except from one quarter.

The Greek Ball marked the first encounter between Callas and Aristotle Onassis, the telephone engineer turned shipping tycoon. They met again, two days later, aboard *Christina O*, Onassis's yacht, which was moored on the Zattere, the water-front pavement that runs along the southern edge of Venice. Callas was accompanied by her husband Giovanni Meneghini, twenty-nine years her senior (Onassis would later refer to him as an 'undertaker').

When an invitation arrived to take tea aboard *Christina O*, it was with a heightened sense of curiosity that we set out for the Zattere.

'So, we've seen the Royal Navy,' said the Conte as we wended our way through Dorsoduro. 'Now let's inspect the Greek Navy.'

Onassis and his wife Tina greeted us at the top of the *passarella*. By their side were their children Alexander, nine, and Christina nearly seven. A third boy, also called Alexander, seemed shy and spoke perfect English.

While Tina looked coolly on, the Conte and Aristotle greeted one another like old friends, exchanging warm words.

'Haha, indeed, Brando,' said Onassis, wringing the Conte's hand, 'nothing like positive cash flow to lift the spirits . . . How is the family?'

The Suez Crisis of 1956 combined with soaring oil prices had buoyed the shipping industry, which was already booming following a surge in demand after the war. When you are on a high, where better to enjoy the view than Venice?

Looking like an exaggeration of how I imagined he would based on photographs, Onassis evoked an eroded hieroglyph. His small frame, scarcely taller than mine, seemed at odds with his large, sun-lamped and pomaded head, with its great intelligent panda eyes, which were almost always hidden by sunglasses. I found him ugly, but charismatic and witty. I was surprised when, eleven years later, Jackie Kennedy married him.

His similarly panda-eyed children, Alexander and Christina, lacked their father's charm. The idea was that Ruy and Leonello should get on with Alexander and Christina. Things began well as the children ran up and down the deck, but deteriorated when the Onassis children were unfriendly to Ruy and Leonello, which I considered a personal slight. As their champion and mentor, I felt protective towards my charges and stoutly defended them against injustice. The shy Alexander, however, could not have been more delightful.

'Alexander is the son of Peter the Second of Yugoslavia,' whispered the Conte, as Onassis waltzed us around the upper deck. 'Born in a suite at Claridge's.'

While Onassis flung open doors like an estate agent and showed off the dolphin-shaped gold taps, the hospital, the laundry, the air-conditioning system, and the telephones in every state room, I thought, So much taste, and all of it . . . well. Arriving at the salon, we perched on whale-foreskin-covered bar stools while sipping orange juice. I noted an El Greco painting hanging above a white leather sofa.

Tina asked me, 'So what do you do at Palazzo Brandolini?'

'I look after Ruy and Leonello.'

'Ah, a very important job,' interjected Onassis, as he beamed at Ruy and Leonello. Turning to me, he said, 'I hope you have told them the elements of success.'

'Erm . . . well . . .'

'Rise early. If you rise early you will have more time to be successful. And always have a tan; a tan is most important.'

'And if you don't sunbathe, you will have even more time,' I said.

'True! But appearances count. It is important to *look* successful, to *look* like you have come from a sunny country.'

'Do you work on this yacht?' I asked Onassis.

'Of course!' He smiled. 'I run the engine room, I man the bridge, I scrub the decks, I cook in the galley, I operate the bar, I even do my own therapy . . . I wear many hats. I try to do as much as I can by myself. I don't like to have people around me, especially people doing nothing.'

'I meant do you use the yacht as your office?' I asked.

'Haha, no, it is all pleasure.' He laughed, then was theatrically serious: 'But don't tell the taxman. They say the most enjoyable two days on a yacht are the day you buy it and the day you sell it. My rule in life is never to sell, so I may be denying myself half of its pleasure. Come, let me show you something.' We slipped off the bar stools and followed Onassis aft.

A converted Canadian frigate that had seen action on Atlantic convoys, the Normandy landings of 1944 and more recently in the film *Triangle of Sadness* (2022), *Christina O* was like a small liner. The term 'yacht' hardly applied: she had no sails. My uncle Eric owned a sizeable yacht, but very different from *Christina O*, which I rather resented being called a 'yacht'.

'Now, watch,' said Onassis, as we arrived at the ballroom, whose dance floor was mosaicked with a minotaur. At the press of a button, the floor lowered, water sloshed in and within a few minutes, the ballroom had been converted into a swimming-pool.

Onassis turned to face us, his dark glasses making him look insect-like. 'I hope you brought your bathing suits as well as your ball gowns,' he said.

As we prepared to disembark, Onassis stood at the top of the *passarella*, the Zattere filling his lenses. 'When you are rich,' he said, with gravity, addressing me and the boys, one hand on Ruy's shoulder, 'you can do a lot of things that to other people look like excitement and pleasure. But after a while . . . *pah*! They become boring, nonsense, just killing time, trying to pretend that it is cosmically important or that it all means something. It doesn't. What matters is the game, but to play the game you need a prize worth winning or seducing, and a competitor smart enough to be worth beating.'

And with that we said goodbye.

Onassis's great rival, Stavros Niarchos, was also in Venice ('Rich Greeks have been coming to Venice ever since the fall of Constantinople,' said Onassis). *Creole*, Niarchos's black, three-masted 63-metre wooden schooner, was considered the most beautiful yacht in the world, and a proper one too, with sails, not a motorised bathroom appliance or a floating caravan. I expect he'd heard we'd visited *Christina O* and, not wishing to miss out, wanted us to inspect *Creole*. Niarchos was absent when we were invited on board. *Creole*'s beautiful art-hung drawing room felt like someone's home; I heard that Niarchos often lived on board. If *Christina O* was all about money, *Creole* was all about taste, although, ever since it had taken three goes to break the magnum of champagne at her launch in Gosport in 1927, when she was named *Vira*, she was considered unlucky.

Ah, the dance of the shipping leviathans as they disputed the prize of superior wealth, taste, power and women! Their outrageous toys, relationships, marriages, fabulous wealth and the tragedy that seemed to stalk them captivated the world. Just over fourteen years later, both Alexander and Tina Onassis would be dead, he of a plane crash in 1973, she of an overdose in 1974 when she was married to Stavros Niarchos. Meanwhile one of Niarchos's children, Konstantin, died of a cocaine overdose in 1999. The competitive attention-seeking struck me as symptoms of, or attempts to compensate for, something else.

'I suppose Mr Niarchos was out and about in Venice taking in the sights,' I said to the Conte, as we walked away from *Creole*.

'Haha! I doubt it,' he said. 'I should think a better invitation or a more exciting opportunity came his way. People like Stavros, Barbara and Aristotle aren't here to see Venice and pay homage. Goodness, no! They are here because it is the place everyone wants to be seen. It is one of the great ironies of Venice today that, having deliberately suppressed and humiliated powerful personalities throughout most of her history, she should now be considered the agent, handmaiden and stage of personal aggrandisement.'

The time had come for my holiday. Although I earned only nine pounds a week, opportunities for expenditure, other than at the hairdresser, were minimal. I had managed to save up a few pennies.

Carried on the wings of romance, I departed Venice by the

8.20 train one Friday morning bound for Lyon where David awaited me on his Vespa. He had somehow managed to drive, transport, convey or otherwise cajole it all the way from Paris.

'So what is life like in a Venetian palazzo?' he asked, as I leapt off the train into his arms.

His gaze burnt into my heart. 'Toad Hall with knobs on. What's life like in Paris?'

David turned to address his Vespa. 'Erm, the purest pleasure imaginable.'

'How are the frying pans?'

'Warming up. Hop on! Cling to whatever you can find.'

David had the entire holiday planned, the hotels, the restaurants, the sights and the scenic drives. So, heart swelling, spine tingling, I hopped on to the back of the Vespa and off we sped.

He never asked me where I wanted to go; I wouldn't have known. He loved underground rivers, so the itinerary took in the Grotte des Demoiselles, the Font de Vaucluse, the Gorges du Tarn, Yssingeaux, Pradelles, Mende, the Aven Armand, Abîme de Bramabiau, Mont Aigoual, Meyrueis, the Grotte de Dargilan and several other landmarks as yet unspoilt by hordes. We stopped often, but never at cafés: there weren't any in the primitive and isolated countryside that looked like a Cézanne landscape. Had we broken down or worse, Heaven knows how we'd have coped. I suppose David could have pushed.

This was my hourglass lifestyle: one day small-talking aboard *Christina O*, the next driving around the Cévennes on a Vespa looking for a cheap hotel. I can recommend the frisson you get from hanging on to the back of a scooter, especially being driven through the Gorges du Tarn. After winding up a particularly precipitous corniche for seemingly hours, I glanced at the sickening drop, and had to turn away. The only posh place we stayed at was Château de la Caze, a castle in the narrows of the gorge, which served a superb *crevettes* and duck sauce: goodness knows where they got hold of either the *crevettes* or the duck.

Although stubborn and manipulative, the Vespa grew on me. Even the slightest trip felt like an adventure. Whenever we arrived at a village, the locals, usually old ladies swathed in black, wearing out their days sitting in front of their houses, would stare as if we'd dropped out of the skies. I found that if you laughed (not at them, obviously) with a cheery *'Bonjour'*, tensions melted away.

None of the challenges that the Vespa threw up occurred to me until too late: rain, uncomfortable seating position, no crash helmet, and so on. Luggage was a perennial problem. What to do with it when you stop?

'I'll sort out the luggage,' said David, dismounting after we'd arrived at Le Puy. 'Meet me by the door of the cathedral.'

I must have waited by the door of the cathedral for three hours. No money. No passport. Just floods of tears and tumbleweed. Some nuns tried to comfort me. I explained to them that David must have been kidnapped or poisoned. The nuns listened gravely. Then one of them said, 'The cathedral is on two levels. Perhaps he is waiting for you at the other entrance.'

I had been waiting at the upper front door; David, equally anxiously, was waiting at the lower. There was a lot of rushing into each other's arms.

Too soon, it was time to wend our way back. Taking up the Contessa's kind invitation, David agreed to join me in Venice. Filled with magic, the divine spark pumped back into me, we travelled by train from Marseille, while the Vespa somehow made its way back to Paris. Chafing into Venice station, our train arrived in the early afternoon. No *motoscafo* awaited us so we took the *vaporetto* and alighted at Ca' Rezzonico, a couple of palazzi from Brandolini.

Over dinner, David charmed the Conte and Contessa with his understanding of music, art, literature, architecture, and his flair for languages; he in turn thought they were lovely. Standing on the balcony with him afterwards, drinking in the scene, I felt I was hovering between reality and a dream.

The Conte, Contessa and the entire household greeted David far more warmly than my own family ever did; even Nurse Rasch managed to extrude a smile. I drew strange comfort that my parents, unhappily married, disapproved of David, while the Conte and Contessa, whose marriage was evidently happy, approved. This helped resolve my attitude towards my future. The Conte and Contessa's warmth felt like an endorsement. The time was looming when I had to discuss my term at Brandolini. The Conte and Contessa would now know that I had good reason for wanting to move on.

My happiest memories of Venice spring from those three days with David. By the time he left, I felt I'd had a blood transfusion. Without him, I might have been more socially 'active', but I think the Conte and Contessa were glad that I wasn't. I was never a *problem.* I wasn't going to roll up at the palazzo hog-whimpering drunk after a night at La Grotta. I wasn't interested in looking for a boy. Mine was a slightly unusual situation for a young girl about Venice, but perhaps everyone's situation was more unusual than it seemed.

CHAPTER FOURTEEN

Villa di Maser

RUY e LEONELLO

BRANDOLINI d'ADDA

RICORDANO

LA LORO PRIMA COMUNIONE

SCUOLA DEI CARMINI

Venezia, 24 Settembre 1957

Previous page: *The programme for Ruy and Leonello Brandolini d'Adda's First Communion.*

RUY AND LEONELLO'S prima comunione (First Communion) on Tuesday, 24 September, was a chaotic affair. It took place at the Scuola dei Carmine, one of the chorus line of secondary attractions in Venice, famous mainly for its grisaille paintings by Niccolò Bambini and some rather loud Tiepoli. The service took place in the Chapel of Our Lady of Mount Carmel. While the Communion party waited in prayer and contemplation, one of the Scuola's scene-shifters clad in boots and dungarees leapt up on to the eighteenth-century marble altar dedicated to Our Lady of Mount Carmel, and, treading all over the holy linen altar cloth, unscrewed some dud electric candles and replaced them with wax ones. Shaking my head, I thought (somewhat priggishly, at the time), This would never happen in England; not even the working-party intern at the National Gallery would have behaved like this. From their expressions of faint amusement and stoic patience, the family appeared to treat the service as a formality to be endured rather than celebrated.

Afterwards, the Contessa announced that the following day we were going to a birthday lunch party.

'It's for Anna Maria Cicogna's niece, Diamanté Luling Boschetti,' said the Contessa. 'It will be held at their house. Do you know Villa di Maser?'

'It rings a bell,' I lied.

'And the day after tomorrow, Miss Payne is arriving for a

few days. She would love it if you and the boys could meet her at the station.'

What with services and inspections, receptions and send-offs, the boys' diary was not only becoming increasingly congested but also rather grown-up, serious and invariably urban. So it was a relief for them to take their leave of the ant heap and head into the countryside of *terra firma* for the day.

As I drove the Conte and a noisy Cadillac-load of excited children, including Nuno but not Nurse Rasch, the hour's drive north-west of Venice, the Conte filled me in on Maser's history. Also known as Villa Barbaro, Villa di Maser is the creation of Andrea Palladio and his patrons, the brothers Daniele and Marcantonio Barbaro. Daniele was the sixteenth-century mathematician, diplomat, philosopher, cleric, architect, Patriarch-elect of Aquilea and Venetian delegate to the final session of the Council of Trent – clearly another reckless, hell-raising defier of *dolce far niente*. He took a particularly keen interest in architecture. He translated the works of Vitruvius, the Roman architect from the first century BC, and commissioned Palladio to illustrate them. Vitruvius was the chap who promoted the idea that the proportions of classical architecture are based on the naturally harmonious proportions of the human body. Leonardo da Vinci famously illustrated this idea with his *Vitruvian Man*, who is depicted standing in a square overlaid with the same man standing in a circle. Is it a coincidence that Barbaro came up with the idea of Villa di Maser at the same time as he was translating Vitruvius's works in the mid-1550s? I can easily imagine him flinging down his pen, turning to Andrea Palladio, and saying, 'That's it, Andrea! I've had enough! Instead of sitting here translating this stuff, why don't we just go out and create the perfect neoclassical building?' And so they did.

Surrounded by fields and vineyards an hour's drive north of Venice, near the foothills of the Dolomites beyond Treviso, Villa di Maser is the architectural companion to *Vitruvian Man*, a paean to harmony, strength and elegance. That done, Barbaro went further. He commissioned Paolo Veronese to decorate the interior, and got Alessandro Vittoria to create some sculptures – making up a Renaissance grand slam. As the Conte continued his discourse, I thought of the Veroneses hanging in the National Gallery. They were among the largest paintings in the National Collection, usually depictions of beefy subject matter, kings and slaves.

In 1934, Count Giuseppe Volpi bought Villa Maser for his daughter Marina Volpi, sister of Nancy Mitford's friend Anna Maria Cicogna, and restored it to its full Renaissance splendour. Marina married Conte Enrico Luling Buschetti, a cavalry officer. Their two daughters were Diamanté and Esmeralda.

The Conte's exquisite exposition of Maser's history ground to a screeching halt when, on arrival, the first thing we noticed was not so much the villa, which stood on a steep, grassy hillside, but an iridescent child-sized merry-go-round among other garish rides, which had been set up at the foot of the hill, forming a children's funfair.

'Quite right too,' breathed the Conte, as he stared at the funfair. 'Last thing you want in Maser is young children.'

As the wheels of the Cadillac crunched up the gravel drive, I asked the Conte, 'How old is Diamanté Luling Buschetti?'

'Ten.'

As I entered Maser, I realised what the Conte meant. With its columns, pillars, arches, pediments, domed atrium, frescos and sculptures, and with its own Tempietto, which Palladio added some twenty-two years after the rest of the villa was completed and which was his penultimate work, this was not a house in which you want young children running amok. Every fresco and sculpture looked new, radiant and fresh; everywhere the eye came to rest, it fell upon some masterpiece of the Renaissance. With Veronese's frescos of members of the Barbaro family caught in everyday poses, and the trompe l'oeils that mimic Palladio's neo-classical architecture, I had a sense of the Barbaro family of four centuries earlier carrying on their lives and sometimes staring at me, as if I had interrupted them.

'It is as if Vitruvian Man had settled down and had a Vitruvian Family, and here they are depicted going about their everyday lives,' said the Conte, as we toured the villa.

Meanwhile, a difficult and exacting relationship was developing between me and Nurse Rasch. Her inherently isolated position in the household was aggravated by the fact that she was the only German-speaker. Certainly no conversationalist, she had the charisma and bedside manner of a broken sledgehammer. If she ever spoke, everyone stopped listening to her long before she stopped talking. The French chef regarded her with uncon-cealed suspicion, possibly a hangover from the war. No one wanted her advice on anything besides health, and only then with the greatest reluctance. She had no real authority except over Nuno, the angelic three-year-old. But a problem was brewing. Sensible chap that he was, Nuno seemed not to like Nurse Rasch. If I entered the room, he would wriggle out of her arms and run to me. Growing less and less amused with Nuno's desertions, Nurse Rasch intensified her repertoire of cold shoulders and muttered Teutonic oaths.

Matters took a fresh turn upon the arrival of a gruesome doctor from Milan, who appeared one morning unannounced and much to everyone's surprise. A small, balding man who wore rimless glasses, he seemed an unappealing prospect. He didn't look Italian. In fact, he scarcely looked like a man. No one could work out what he was for. Above and beyond his minimal clinical duties, which were vague and frankly supererogatory, he managed to insinuate himself into the household. I often found him moving about the palazzo with a noiseless and faintly predatory stealth. I thought he and Nurse Rasch might get along. But no. Nurse Rasch saw him as a threat that compounded Nuno's defections.

One evening, as I emerged from a chat in the ironing room with the laundry woman, I noticed the unmistakable silhouette of Nurse Rasch in the corridor before me. A sinister ray of light broke on her face. I got quite a shock. She looked unhappy and angry. Perhaps she'd caught herself in the mirror.

'So I think we need to talk, yes?'

'Oh, hello, Nurse Rasch. I didn't notice you there. How lovely to see you.' This was clearly an ambush. She had been lying in wait. She must have muffled her medals somehow.

Her stony, cold, injured eyes bored into me. Her thin lips were set in a taut line. I got a lungful of carbolic. 'We must talk.'

'What seems to be the matter?'

Nurse Rasch nodded faintly. 'You have no idea, do you? No idea at all. You float just in your bubble around.'

'Sorry, Fräulein Rasch, I have no idea what you mean.'

'Huh. Perhaps pretend you only.'

'Unless you tell me what you are talking about, I can't help you. Now if you'll—'

'It concerns the boy, Nuno.'

'What about Nuno?'

'*Du entfremdest seine Zuneigung von mir!* You are alienating his affections from me!'

'Am I?' I managed to make this contingency sound like the least possible thing imaginable, partly to try to calm down the inflamed Rasch.

'*Ja!*'

'Well, I'm not aware of it. I would never deliberately alienate anyone's affections, as you put it.'

'If you continue this way, become I mad.'

For a thrilling moment, Nurse Rasch seemed to hover on the brink of a major detonation.

'Mmm, mad,' I echoed. 'But why are you bothered by Nuno's affections? You're his nurse, not his mother. He is free to do as he pleases. Oh, don't tell me you are trying to bring down your own Ironic Curtain around him.'

Nurse Rasch's eyes narrowed at this slight. Through clenched teeth, she said, 'It is a question of who in charge is.'

'Ah, I see. Well, there is no question of who is in charge, because you are in charge, Nurse Rasch. Nuno is your responsibility. But if it is a power struggle you want, I can't help you. Why don't you go and have one with that charming new doctor?' Then I gave her a level stare. '*Er ist jemand, den Sie in einem Beliebtheitswettbewerb schlagen könnten, und – wer weiss? – vielleicht auch eine Kraftprobe. Aber in Wahrheit glaube ich, dass Sie gegen Dämonen kämpfen.* He's someone you might beat in a popularity contest and – who knows? – perhaps a trial of strength too. But in truth I think you are fighting demons.'

If Nurse Rasch looked horrified, I felt shocked. If she had had no idea I had that kind of German in me, neither had I. Not until it came out. I must have picked it up from my mother. Surprised at myself, I walked off.

Meanwhile, I was having my own problems with that doctor. From the moment he arrived, he was all over me. There weren't enough bargepoles in Venice not to touch him with. I tried to rebuff him. '*Ho standard incredibilmente alti. Nessun dottore potrebbe mai aiutare.* I have incurably high standards. No doctor could possibly help.' He wouldn't take the hint.

The Conte could hardly contain his laughter when I solemnly told him about the doctor. 'It's getting boring,' I added, 'and it could be affecting his health.'

The Conte greeted the idea of the doctor stalking me as being worthy of hilarity, but he assured me he'd 'have a word'.

The following morning, Thursday, 26 September, I took extra special care of the boys' appearance. I dressed them in their smartest outfits, trimmed and scrubbed their nails, brushed their hair and teeth, cleaned their ears, and checked that they wore each shoe on the designated foot. I didn't want Miss Payne to think I hadn't continued her exemplary work. That the Conte and Contessa should invite Miss Payne to stay, and that Miss Payne should accept, seemed to illustrate the mutual loyalty and affection that held family and the rest of the house-hold, past and present, together.

Under heavy clouds and intermittent rain, I travelled with the boys, Domenico and Angelo in the *motoscafo* to the station to meet her at twelve thirty.

On the platform, Ruy and Leonello ran to greet a woman not much older than me with wavy light brown hair, pale complexion, and a serious expression that belied a sparkle of humour in her eyes. She exuded energy, efficiency and a sense of no-nonsense purpose. Domenico held up an umbrella while Angelo collected her small suitcase. Having given the boys a long hug, she looked up at me.

'You must be the new me,' she said, swiftly running an eye up and down me, and extending her hand.

As we descended the shallow steps to the *motoscafo* and climbed on board, I sketched out the curious coincidence of events that had led to my position at Palazzo Brandolini. 'So Gertrude Maclean was my lucky break in childcare,' I concluded.

'Perhaps you were hers,' said Miss Payne. 'I bet Gertie got a real shock when you showed up at Universal Aunts. She probably thought you'd mislaid a tiara or fallen *orf* a horse.'

I laughed. 'I barged in on her lunch hour unannounced. I think she thought I was someone else.'

'I'm sure she soon had the measure of you,' she said. 'Did she ask for references?'

'She asked for nothing, no paperwork, documents, certificates or anything.'

'I expect she has spies.'

'I think she could tell that I wasn't "in trouble" or "on the run" or looking for an Italian romance.'

'How disappointing.' Miss Payne's 'serious' expression burst into a grin. 'I expect Gertie was wondering how on earth she was going to find anyone suitable for the job.'

'At least I didn't have to pretend to know where Venice is or fib about speaking Italian.'

I immediately felt relaxed in Miss Payne's company. I asked her why the Conte and Contessa had approached Oliver Messel. 'I mean he's one of . . . I mean what would *he* know about childcare?'

'The person matters more than the qualifications,' said Miss Payne. 'Oliver is someone whose judgement they trust, and in the world that the Brandolini inhabit, trust is an important but rare quality.' She looked me directly in the eyes, glanced at the boys, then back at me. 'Anyway, whatever method they use, it seems to work.'

To David Ross
Begun 24 September,
ended 25 September 1957

Palazzo Brandolini

David darling

I am starting this letter now, but I will no doubt find it becomes more or less a diary. I need not say I miss you, because you know that, but actually to-day has been such a hectic round, that I have had no time [to] sit and think. Altho' this evening I did allow myself to gloat over the pictures and the cards of La Caze and it all made me realise what a really <u>lovely</u> holiday we did have. I loved every moment of it, even when I felt I was falling down a precipice between St Enimie and Meyrueis. I do hope your journey did not seem too endless and that it was neither uncomfortable, nor smelly, nor noisy! I'm sure the Customs and ticket collectors did their stuff and awakened you each time the wheels had lulled you to sleep.

You will, I hope, be pleased to know that the Countess said to me very slyly, 'Of course I do not know David but I found him very charming – he has a great deal of charm.' Benissimo!

Now I must tell you about to-day's activities – the actual ceremony of the Prima Comunione was really rather a fiasco. We arrived at the Scuola dei Carmini at nine twenty-five, the thing being fixed for nine thirty. The florists were still busy sticking pink carnations into great pillars of flowers by the altar. After about ten minutes three tramps appeared carrying a harmonium! Finalmente, the proceedings got under way, and throughout the ceremony, the boys had a priest stationed beside them to stand them up and kneel them down and he even shoved their heads down when they were supposed to be looking particularly holy. They obviously understood nothing about the proceedings at all. It was very picturesque, but I didn't hear a word! Afterwards we had a splendid breakfast party with wonderful food, a cross between breakfast and tea – I was terribly hungry by this time, about eleven o'clock, as none of us had eaten before church. Then the children were given presents – and goodness what presents! Watches (Leonello three), pens, propelling pencils, gold cufflinks, tie pins (jewel-studded), silver objets, books, etc., etc. Two hours after all this food, we had an enormous luncheon party and I spent the rest of the day recovering from a surfeit of feasting. I am going to stop now but will continue anon – goodnight, darling.

Wednesday. David, to-day we went to a party at a place which makes these Venetian palaces seem like council houses. It is called *Villa di Maser*. It is situated in the country on a steep slope in the foothills of the Dolomites. The house was commissioned by two brothers Barbaro to be designed and decorated by Palladio, Veronese and Vittorio. It is supposed to be the most perfectly proportioned example of Palladian architecture – I wish I could describe it well or even draw it for you. It is really beautiful, of a warm yellow-coloured stone with most elegant statues by Vittorio and a wonderful ornamental formal garden on a steep slope with steps, fountains and statues. The house inside has ceilings and walls covered with Veronese frescos, but not in his heavy style, they are more like Tiepolo at his best. There is a guide written in English to the house and I looked at about twelve rooms, all Veronese, and all looking absolutely brand new. The present owners are very rich and it is all beautifully furnished – as it is on such a steep slope, there is a fountain garden set into the hillside on the first floor! The villa is surrounded by lovely green lawns, which must have been brought piece by piece from England! When I re-read this description, I realise that I have made the house sound too heavy and grand, but really the whole place gives a wonderful air of being light, airy, new and utterly charming. Maybe you have heard of it or seen photographs?

I took all three children in the car and it was [an] enormous party – over a hundred children and about as many grown-ups. Quite a lot of people I knew and several English, so it was great fun, all out of doors. There was a merry-go-round, donkey rides, hoop-la, gas-filled red balloons, tug o' war, treasure hunt, sack races, and endless ice creams – in fact everything to delight a child's heart. Nuno loved every moment of it and twice nearly drowned himself among the goldfish. Luckily I was able to place *him with a nurse I knew, while I did my tour of inspection and talked to people.*

Thursday. Today has been a depressing day – there was a thunderstorm all night and it has been grey and heavy all day, raining intermittently. We went to meet their ex-governess at the station and I find, contrary to expectations, she is charming. After lunch the Countess told me that that odious doctor has lost his job in Milan and she is going to have him to live with us and look after Ruy part of the time. The thought to me is indescribably repulsive. He is one of those completely unattractive men who thinks he is Rudolph Valentino and tries to rape every woman. Imagine having this permanently under one's feet – urgh! So there will be even less to do and no one knowing who's in charge – the Fräulein has already had a row with me about alienating Nuno's affections! So it looks as though we're in for a turbulent time. I do wish I really enjoyed having rows.

However, enough moaning – to look on the brighter side – Miss Payne is going to be here for ten days – so I shall have lots of time to go sightseeing and rubbernecking as she can have the boys.

. . .

I have just spent a fascinating evening being told by Miss Payne of all the immoral goings-on in Italian families – my hair is curling!

. . .

Think of me sometimes and love me a little, darling.

Gill

CHAPTER FIFTEEN

Confirmation

Mlle Giulietta Johnson
Palazzo Brandolini
S. Barnaba
Venice

ITALIE

Previous page: *David addressed his letters to 'Giulietta', showing the extent to which my Venetian identity stuck.*

DESPITE THE FACT – or because – the Venetians built so many churches (107 in the city proper), they have a reputation for being not particularly religious. As the old motto says, *Veneziani, poi Cristiani* (Venetian first, then Christian). It was therefore felt that a doubtful God might need some convincing on the matter of the boys' faith. Ruy and Leonello's Confirmation left nothing to chance. An elaborate spectacle of extended logistics, meticulous planning and lavish choreography was put on, culminating in a long, fully licensed lunch. In the eleven days that elapsed between their First Communion and their Confirmation on 5 October, a robed, bearded and wizened priest would arrive at the palazzo, and, amid great fuss, bless each member of the household individually, before conducting Confirmation classes. A private chapel at San Marco was prepared, and the Cardinal-Patriarch of Venice called upon to officiate. I took the boys to a tailor to have their all-white Confirmation suits fitted. Meanwhile, quite by accident, and echoing my earlier 'Firenze' embarrassment, I stumbled on the Church of Santi Giovanni e Paolo when a kind person pointed out that the signposts give its name in Venetian dialect: San Zanipolo. I'd already walked past it several dozen times.

To David Ross
[4 October]

Palazzo Brandolini

Darlingest David,

I have been having a very good time because I have been able to wander round Venice at my leisure gazing longingly at the shops, and planning what to buy when I have some money. I found some leather jackets but not the colour I want . . . However, I didn't think the cut was very good, I am sure the ones made in Paris are much better. These were trying to be English altho' made in Italy, which I thought rather phoney. The labels were written in incredible 'English'.

It is cold here . . . the Countess has already given me a lovely dark grey dress, which makes me look very voluptuous, Ruy says!, and a superb flame-coloured full skirt.

. . .

The Countess has now given me a gramophone for always and I do so wish I had my records here. I think my mother will have to send me some more winter clothes so perhaps she can add a few discs.

I have so much free time because the boys are having piano lessons, gymnastics, and lessons with the priest every day – and so I can do what I like.

. . .

This morning I had a charming letter from the American family I met at the Palace Hotel at St Moritz – they must be very rich to have stayed there and they live in New York. So I have written a very effusive letter back. I am sending one of the photos she sent me taken at S.M. of Ruy, Leonello and Les Girls Poo and Tweedy! I think it's charming – don't throw it away.

I visited San Zanipolo, but it took me so long to find it, that I only had time to be very impressed by the outside – so I must go again.

Here in Italy, Confirmation and First Communion are two separate things and R and L are being confirmed in San Marco on Saturday by the Cardinal of Venice, which is exciting as I expect it will be a very memorable ceremony in that remarkable God box.

I have been telephoned by a strange Italian I met on the Lido weeks ago and invited out – he is a friend of the Count and Countess – so I think I shall go, first to see what happens!

The Countess is staying at the Hôtel Ritz in the Place Vendôme from Monday, 6 Oct, until Thursday or Friday.

Love to your mother if she is still around, and to you.
Gill

P.S. Looking forward to seeing photos.

On the big day, the family and household dressed up and crossed the Grand Canal to walk to San Marco. Resplendent in white, the boys looked like escaped angels being escorted back to base. At the door of the great basilica, we checked and adjusted our sleeves and necklines before stepping inside. Twilit by candles and twinkling with altar lamps, with its mosaic-lined golden walls and arches, its richly inlaid irregularly undulating floor, its chapels and galleries and altars, the incense-smoked interior of San Marco looked and felt more like an ancient Oriental treasure chest than a temple to God.

We made our way past nuns, groups of children, knots of tourists and the inevitable pigeon strutting angrily about as if he owned the place.

'Well, he probably *does* think he has a right to be here,' said the Conte, when I pointed out the pigeon. 'Ever since Doge Enrico Dandolo sent news of the sack of Constantinople by carrier pigeon, the Venetians have had a soft spot for what other cities might consider flying rats.'

We walked up the main aisle towards the famous Pala d'Oro altarpiece ablaze with gems. There we waited. With a sibilant rustle of cassock and surplice, Cardinal Angelo Giuseppe Roncalli, the prodigiously paunched Patriarch, emerged in red from the vestry, followed by a cloud of incense. Candles danced in unison as he wafted past. There was much kissing of hands as lace-gowned stooges tripped over each other in their efforts to bow continually both to the high altar and to the Patriarch, who appeared to know little about what was going on.

Following a low-voiced consultation between the Patriarch and various permutations of clergy, we were ushered towards a steep, narrow, ancient stone staircase that seemed to tunnel its way upwards through the very structure of the basilica. With much puffing and wheezing from the Patriarch, we reached a chapel in an upper loft. After Roncalli had recovered his breath, the service began. Standing before the gleam of gold and polished pewter and silver, his fine eyes filled with candles, the Patriarch performed the Confirmation in a long, slow mouthful of strung-together Italian, like liturgical spaghetti, reading every word barely audibly from a book held beneath his nose (literally) by a lackey. He anointed the boys with oil, which was wiped off with (sacred) cotton wool carried on a (sacred) salver. Then each boy was slapped smartly on the cheek – the best part of the ceremony. After much swinging of incense, sprinkling of holy water, we lined up to kiss the Patriarchal hand, and were sent on our way. Back at the palazzo, incense-intoxicated we celebrated with an eight-course lunch at which I got slightly drunk. The following year, Roncalli was elected Pope John XXIII, so God must have been happy.

(Some twenty-five years later, feeling tired while visiting St Peter's in Rome, I sat down before a small altar, composed myself, looked up and saw Roncalli lying before me embalmed in a glass case. He had died in June 1963. I got quite a shock. In death, he looked exactly as he had in life twenty-five years earlier.)

At the palazzo, it was back to business as usual. The Contessa kept abreast of fashion but neither followed it nor set it except inadvertently. She was a woman whom I instinctively looked up to, even though she was two inches shorter than me. She was stylish, deeply sophisticated and ever so slightly jaded. She knew exactly where the line between elegance and ostentation lay. There was hardly an intriguing brand that she didn't consider overexposed. 'Fashion is for people without taste,' she told me. It is typical of her original and idiosyncratic style that she came up with her own ideas and created her own garments by choosing her fabrics and having her dressmaker run things up. Her wardrobe having been in temporary suspension due to pregnancy, she decided it was time to reinvigorate it, and that meant a dash to Paris. While the Conte and Contessa headed to the station, I took the boys to visit their aunt Clara at Villa Fürstenberg in Marocco.

A few kilometres north-east of Venice, Villa Fürstenberg was an elegant three-storey mansion set in a park reached by a tree-lined avenue. Its origins lie in the sixteenth century when Venice was diversifying into *terra firma* after cracks appeared in her maritime trading hegemony following the discovery of America and the rise of the Ottoman Empire. Over the years, the villa had undergone several transmogrifications. The present structure dates from the late eighteenth century when it belonged to the Carreggiani family. It later passed to the Papadopoli family and thence to Clara.

It merits a footnote in the history of the region. In an attempt to wrest northern Italy from the control of the Austrian Habsburg Empire, the Republic of San Marco was founded in 1848 following the fall of Prince Metternich; the republic was based on territories around the Venetian lagoon. It wasn't a success. During the First Italian War of Independence in 1849, the republic collapsed after a long siege. Julius Jacob von Haynau, the 'Habsburg Tiger', the fiercely reactionary Austrian general famous for his brutality, based his operations at what is now Villa Fürstenberg, and held negotiations for the surrender of Venice in the same building.

CHAPTER SIXTEEN

Vistorta

Previous page: *The villa of Vistorta di Sacile, seat of the Brandolini d'Adda family on* terra firma, *just outside Sacile in Friuli Venezia Giuli, north-east Italy. Brandino Brandolini d'Adda, who was born during my time in Venice, now makes organic wine there under the Vistorta label.*

THE PAGES OF my diary fluttered insensibly by as the year elapsed. The final curtain had come down on the season. The secret signal had been given: the jet set was on the move bound for Alpine resorts, the Caribbean, or perhaps, almost incredibly, the office. The Lido returned to a peaceful, golden strand picked over by beachcombers. One by one, the lights went out in the palazzi. A few astute householders moved back in, having leased their properties for lucrative summer residences. As the days shortened, twilight seemed to be perpetually gathering in. It was time for the Brandolini to decamp to Vistorta, their base on *terra firma* where I had met them on 5 June.

Set in a 500-acre estate, which included a working farm, vineyards, winery and several hectares of English-style parkland, Vistorta had been a seat of the Brandolini ever since 1780, when the family were *condottieri* or military leaders in the service of the Republic of Venice. In more recent years, it acted as an escape hatch from the Venetian autumn. The neoclassically inspired villa, which the Conte's great-uncle Guido had commissioned, was completed in 1872. A notable architectural feature was a large *barchessa*, a porticoed service building, adjoining the villa. Guido had also planted thirty acres of vineyards and begun to produce wine, notably an excellent Merlot, which became the economic mainstay of the estate. My previous visit had been barely a pit stop. This time, I was to stay.

Vistorta's rustic setting and park planted with limes, oaks, magnolias, beeches, elms, swamp cypresses, firs and cedars appealed to me, but there was little rustic about the interior. This luminous residence was filled with beautiful objects, pictures and pieces, offset with roses and rare orchids from the estate. The villa was more austerely elegant and comfortable than the baroquely extravagant Palazzo Brandolini. The palazzo was by comparison a summer house for parties and picnics; Vistorta was home. It was too large-scale for convincing domesticity, but somehow the Conte and Contessa pulled it off.

'We moved in after we got married,' said the Conte. 'It was a mess. It had hardly been occupied for three decades. I want it to evoke a country house from a story by Turgenev.'

The minds in charge of the refurbishment were Renzo Mongiardino, the Italian architect, interior designer and set designer, in collaboration with the Conte and Contessa. Mongiardino was almost unknown when the Contessa had met him at a party in Milan.

Almost unknown, but not for long. Thanks to the magic fairy dust that the Brandolini sprinkled on almost everyone who came into their orbit, he soon won a reputation as the aesthetically flawless decorator of the day, skilled in proportion and ornamentation. Circulated among the Rothschilds, the Onassises, the Agnelli, the Niarchoses, the Hearsts and the Thyssens, like a secret elixir, he glided through the dinner parties, drawing rooms and salons of the jet set, who caressed and applauded him, and looked to him as their in-house architect, designer and decorator.

With his elite vision and infallible taste, he suited an era when disparities of wealth were so exacerbated and polarised

as to be out of sight to either extreme end. He plundered the
architectural and decorative highlights of ancient Greece, classical Rome and the Renaissance, then wrapped them together
in perfect harmony and proportion, to capture a look of power,
glory and formal beauty that screamed Sumptuous Neoclassical
Imperial Gracious Living. In the 1950s, he was at his zenith,
and about to transition towards set design, which would later
yield him two nominations for Academy Awards. He was Italy's
answer to Oliver Messel, only grander and more serious. If
Oliver's designs looked like the vision of a child with impeccable taste, Renzo's looked more like an early draft of something
Vitruvius or Palladio might have conjured. At Vistorta, however,
he took his honorary role of in-house designer to the jet set to
an extreme and literal degree by living in an apartment on the
estate.

By the time I arrived, work was still in progress even after
two years. As the nursery floor was a building site, the boys
and I lodged in the ground floor of the guest wing. Early
one morning, I watched from my window as the quilt of fog
dispersed to reveal lawns, a lake, mature trees, espaliered
lemon trees, topiaried hedges, blown roses clinging to stone
walls, a network of small canals, weeping willows and a
sizeable swimming-pool all overlooked by mossy pigeon-
streaked busts of the fabled and the forgotten. Apart from
the swimming-pool, the estate seemed to be a real-life version
of the mythical gardens depicted in the frescos at Palazzo
Brandolini. The view gave a hint of further gardens in the
distance but with no suggestion of paths or gateways by
which to reach them. Soon, the surrounding wooded hills,
the shaded home of boar, roe deer and porcupine, shimmered

in misty *quattrocento* sunshine. In the far distance, ridge upon ridge receded to the violet Dolomites. No aspect of Vistorta was less than it seemed: the house, grounds and park were magnificent.

Through gaps in the estate walls, I glimpsed an altogether different way of life carrying on, one measured out not by the itineraries, schedules and agendas of the jet set, but by the slow wain of seed time and harvest. Bullocks hauled farm carts along the country lane that ran alongside. Horses drew crude tumbrils full of farmhands. Unbroken in centuries, the blunt, coarse, confined, low-centre-of-gravity, age-old skein of bucolic life, blue in dress and language, was insensibly and finally winding down, hastened by changes wrought by war.

'Historically, the Venetians didn't need peasants,' said the Conte. 'They stocked their larder by trade. But this is different. This is *terra firma*.'

I found it strange to consider the Conte as a living link to a feudal era. He seemed too well groomed for that, except perhaps in the most fantastic Hollywood interpretation of Veneto chivalry.

'Do you ride?' he asked.

There were horses and a stable block. Having ridden in Scotland during the war, I could just about tell one end of a horse from the other, but Miss Payne's joking aside about my prowess in the saddle proved prescient. The groom, a charming young fellow, did magnificently well not to laugh when I tried to mount the placid, glossy chestnut that was brought for me. When told to gallop in tight circles around the compound, I knew I was in for humiliation.

'*I cavalli ti insegnano ad essere forte, esigente e a prendere il controllo.* Horses teach you to be strong, demanding and take control,' said the groom, as he tightened the saddle and helped me remount.

I countered with, '*Può essere vero, ma i cavalli mi insegnano anche a mantenere la fiducia nelle machine.* That may be true but horses also teach me to keep faith in cars.'

I could drive but not ride. I felt that Giovanni Agnelli, who had pioneered the horseless carriage in Italy, would understand. Despite falling off, I persevered. It would have been a dereliction of *La Bella Figura* had I given up.

To David Ross
14 October 1957

Vistorta
Vistorta di Sacile
(Prov. di Udine)

Darling David,

I must first write to you about this house, which is even more palatial than Venice – from my fleeting glimpse of it before, I did not realise the extent of its grandeur. Considering the state of the alterations on the nursery floor – I think that there is no hope of one getting there before Christmas – there are just breeze blocks and gaping holes for windows – so I shall describe our apartment in the guest wing.

I shall start by explaining that the whole thing was re-done two years ago – but in early Victorian style! Least I think that's what it is, it might be a little earlier. The general effect is incredibly heavy and fussy and altho' it is superbly done and very comfortable, I don't really like it at all. Somehow the reason I don't like it is because it isn't genuine – all the furniture is reproduced – not real – but well done.

We have three large rooms and two bathrooms. The boys' bedrooms are on either side of my room, which is really a salon. Leonello's room has a four-poster bed hung with pink brocade and white net curtains drawn into a sort of coronet in the middle top. Both bedrooms are heavily hung with prints, mounted and framed in a very Victorian manner – and even the lamps are made to look like paraffin ones! It all reminds me very much of the guest rooms at Fiona Douglas-Home's home, the Hirsel, only there it was gracious and feudal and genuine and here is split-new and somehow rather grating and artificial.

My room is done in a far more elaborate style, being a salon. The walls are hung with real velvet and silk, bottle green stripes and oil paintings of unknown subjects which remain obscure, but I should imagine would be something like 'Esther before Ahasuerus', 'The Judgment of Solomon' and even perhaps 'The Rape of the Sabines'.

There is a lovely little writing desk, lacquered with painted panels by the same person as did all that painting on the panels in Venice – except this is much prettier and rather Renoirish. The windows are draped (curtains isn't the word) with gold brocade, as is my bed, which looks like a sofa during the day; and also a lovely big pouffe. There are some lovely china ornaments, a hideous clock with marble pillars and two enormous genuine Staffordshire dogs. And I have got to live in these completely unreal surroundings! You can imagine that the room is pretty big to hold all this; and then my bathroom – this is about twice the size of my bedroom in Venice. It is all done, walls and floor, in those tiny mosaic tiles – mauve – and it has a sofa about eight feet long and an armchair done in glazed chintz! It also has a lovely dressing table.

Both my bedroom and bathroom have French windows opening on to the best part of the lovely garden. A huge lawn with rose gardens down the side – v. English looking – and lovely trees in the distance and on two sides outbuildings and stables all beautifully painted and all with those lovely arched passages along the front – it really is quite heavenly. The colours in the garden and park are wonderful, reds, golds and greens and the sun was really hot to-day – cotton-dress weather and the smell from all the shrubs and roses is unbelievable.

I can't describe the rest of the house now, or I shan't have time to say anything else – but the whole thing is fantastic and most impractical: imagine the poor Schwester [Nurse Rasch] also coping with the baby and Nuno in similar surroundings!

I was very sad indeed to leave Venice. I had just had about four days of great gaiety, which was exactly what I needed since before that – I didn't tell you on the phone – I had been really ill for three days, sick all the time and unable to stop crying quite involuntarily.

I went to the Jacopo Bassano exhibition in the Palazzo Ducale – which I thoroughly enjoyed. It was most beautifully and artistically presented – I do wish you'd seen it. There were pictures from all over the world – lots from England. I know very little about Bassano, but he would appear to be a man of many parts, as he had three completely different and very distinctive styles of painting.

I went to about four films – all new English or American, but dubbed. I'm glad to say I now really understand most of what's said. I also visited a 'night club' – note the inverted commas please – called La Grotte. It was just a bit <u>too</u> Italian for me.

I have more or less made peace with my parents, which has eased my conscience . . .

Darling, this letter is terribly long and burbly simply because I have no one to talk to, so I should stop here and have a breather and read the rest later!

I went riding to-day – the groom came after breakfast and asked me at what time I'd like my horse! I just rode in the paddock – and he was very helpful, telling me about <u>all</u> the things I did wrong. I haven't had any instruction since I was about twelve, altho' I have ridden a lot since – so I have fallen into bad habits.

The grape harvest is over, and to-day I watched the last of the wine being made in hand presses with about three men turning a thing like a windlass. Then I went into the cellars with <u>vast</u> vats of wine all made from the estate – and I did a little tasting of about three vintages and rolled out into the sunshine!

David, if I were sixty with a squint and elephantiasis, this would be an absolutely heavenly life – but as it is I think this existence will pall very soon. We are miles from anywhere and the house is deserted in the evenings, because most of the servants live in this little village (called Vistorta on the estate) and they all go home. When I start talking to myself, I shall know it is time to leave. I know I have enough books and magazines for six months, wireless, gramophone and bowls of carnations and a bell by my side – but, but, but . . .

Nuno now follows me like a little shadow and I spend a lot of time with him and also with the baby, whom I adore – every morning he seems to be more grown-up and now laughs every time he sees me. I usually give him his bottle during the day, because I found that the hard-hearted Schwester just propped the bottle into his mouth in the cot. I remember being told that babies should always be held in the arms, even to be given a bottle, as it gives a sense of love and security – so I decided that this little thing needed a little mothering.

Everyone at Vistorta has Asiatic flu, including two servants in the house – so I don't see how we can avoid getting it. I'd like a wreath of love-lies-bleeding, please. The schools now aren't opening until 21 October – Ruy last went to school on 30 May!

The Count and Countess won't be back until Wednesday as they're staying in Milan for three days to buy furnishings and fittings for the new rooms.

I do hope I shall be able to borrow a car and go in to Venice occasionally – it is 64 kms and takes about an hour, as the roads are very fast.

I'm so glad you told your mother about getting married – but what are we going to do, darling? I have far too much time to brood over things and it would be far simpler if I knew what I was brooding over! Money is hell! I've decided that parents can be v. useful and it is pointless crossing their paths. Pa is really very doting – I have had a spate of letters recently from him. He keeps saying he wants me to be 'happy'. David, I do hope you'll write and tell me a little of what's in your mind for the future – otherwise this eternal solitude will get me down. I feel like a child dropped into a playpen full of lovely toys but quite

alone and just told to WAIT – but wait for what? Surprisingly
enough I still feel very sane, but it may not last.
. . .

God bless you love and XXX (long ones)
  Gill

In late October, my parents wrote expecting me home for
Christmas. *Expecting.* I preferred to spend Christmas in a luxury
building site in Friuli Venezia Giulia than in Victoria with them,
and I resented the presumption of their having a say in the
matter. The prospect of winter in Vistorta appealed to me. I was
perfectly happy to wear away the hours in my room composing
letters at my *scrittoio.* However, one quiet afternoon, while
strolling around the villa, I started at finding several slipped-
discs' worth of smart-looking suitcases, steamer trunks and
sundry equipage piled up in diminishing perspective by the
front door. I caught the sumptuous aroma of new *veau velours.*

Hello, I thought, what is this? A shooting party.

I knew that the Conte and Contessa had arrived back from
Milan that day, but these pieces weren't theirs. They travelled
jet-set light. The only sign of life was Daisy the corgi, lying on
a chaise longue, adding a heraldic touch.

I was craning my neck to read the name on one of the
luggage tags, when the Conte walked in briskly. 'Ah, Giulietta,
I must introduce you to a friend from Paris.'

Just behind the Conte, I could see a young, fresh-faced man,
spruce in pressed, creased flannels.

'This is Philip Van Rensselaer,' said the Conte. 'He will be
staying with us for ten days. He's a . . .' The Conte turned to

the young man for a cue. Then, with a slight deprecating gesture, said '. . . a – a writer. That's usually how he's described.' The Conte looked at the towers of trunks and suitcases. 'Luggage!' he cried, shaking his head. 'Hobgoblin of the insecure!' And with that, he executed a smooth about-turn and wandered off, cheerily calling over his shoulder, 'If you've never met Philip before, Giulietta, then you are in good company.'

Philip Van Rensselaer stepped forward and extended his right hand while keeping his left hand in his trouser pocket.

'How do you do?' he said. He spoke with an American accent and had a smile of infinite cordiality.

'I'm very well, thank you.'

'It's so lovely to be here in this magnificent place with such close friends,' he said, appraising me up and down as if to make me a suit.

A handsome, slightly too well-dressed man in his late twenties, Philip had such a smooth, clear complexion that he looked as if he did something special to his skin, like remove the topmost layer when shaving. I noted wristwatch, signet ring and diamond-studded gold cufflinks winking at me. He clearly wasn't afraid of accessories. He prolonged his handshake and overdid his smile.

I wondered what he was doing at Vistorta. There was no one else of his age. Except me.

It was unusual for the Conte to seek me out and introduce me to a guest. Perhaps he considered Philip an unmeritable figure and, not wishing to appear unwelcoming, had delegated him to me. Maybe the Conte thought Philip could do with being read *Swallows and Amazons*.

'Haven't I seen you before?' asked Philip, putting both hands in his trouser pockets while continuing to map and log my features and dress. 'I recognise you. Wasn't that you playing backgammon in St Moritz during the summer?'

'I don't believe it was. I don't play backgammon.'

'Or was that you aboard *Christina O* last month in Venice?'

'I'm sure I would have remembered you.'

'Okay, now I remember. It was you – wasn't it? – on Niarchos's yacht, right?'

'Mmm . . . I honestly don't think we've met. I'm sure that I would remember you.'

'No, wait. I saw you, I *definitely* saw you, by the Cicogna cabana on the Lido beach?'

What he really meant by this inquisition was 'I want you to know that I was on Onassis's yacht, that I was on Niarchos's yacht, and that I was in the Cicogna cabana.' Actually, I did recognise Philip. He was the young man on the Lido beach, looking lost in shorts and polo shirt. Perhaps I'd been living the life too long, and had picked up airs and graces, but something about him brought on an insufferably grand manner in me.

'You're getting warmer,' I replied. 'But, really, Venice is a small place. You see – and ignore – the same person two or three times a day.'

I wasn't won over by Philip's name-dropping, only mildly flattered that he thought me worth flattering.

'How do you fit in here?' Philip continued his inquisition as he intercepted a passing drinks tray with practised legerdemain.

'I don't. I glide under the radar. I look after the children and read them stories. Outreach to the infancy.'

'Do you read them fairy stories?'

'My morals keep getting in the way,' I said. 'Fairy tales are for fools. I prefer cautionary tales. What, may I ask, brings you here?'

'Oh, I'm just here for a rest,' he smiled, 'and to see the Tintorettos and Titians.'

I looked at Philip, and Philip looked at me, and from my look, he would have known that I didn't believe him.

Turning to the pile of suitcases and trunks, I noticed a name tag printed 'Philip Van Rensselaer'. On top of the pile of luggage was a binoculars case.

'Which other guests do we have?' I asked.

'None.' Philip beamed proudly. 'The luggage is all mine.'

'*All* yours?' I said, moving along the Himalaya of trunks. 'Are you moving house, or do you just suffer from a hyperactive wardrobe gland?'

'No such thing as too much luggage.'

'No such thing as too many closets.'

'This is capsule, for me,' said Philip. 'I normally travel with my full back-catalogue. My presence around Europe is usually heralded by trolley-loads of suitcases.'

'Do you have a chronic inability to say, "No," to tailors and menswear merchants?'

'I suppose I do. I have terrible self-discipline problems.'

I stared at the distinctive branding on one particular trunk.

'Louis Vuitton,' said Philip. 'Almost indestructible. Vintage is worth more than the new stuff.'

I looked up to see white-gloved Domenico and Angelo marshalling themselves before the trunks.

'*Solo i dieci bauli, Signor Van Rensselaer*? Just the ten trunks, Mr Van Rensselaer?' asked Domenico. Just then, he caught my eye and gave me half a wink.

'*Sì grazie, er . . .*'

'Domenico,' I whispered.

'*Sì, Domenico! Grazie, Domenico! Grazie mille!*' said Philip, overplaying his gratitude. He put a hand to his mouth, leant towards me and whispered, 'Should I tip?'

I minutely shook my head.

Angelo waited until he got a nod from Domenico, then began hauling the trunks away.

'*Ten* trunks,' I said, as I watched Angelo manage three in one go. 'One trunk per day.'

'Two on a good day,' said Philip. 'I hate to feel underdressed.'

'My entire family and all my friends could go on several world cruises with the luggage you have,' I said. 'I can see you're a one-man—'

'*Défilé de la haute couture?* Haute couture fashion show?' His French accent was perfect.

'Hand-me-down clothes shop in waiting,' I countered.

Philip smiled and took in his surroundings, the hall of Vistorta with its ancestral portraits, furniture, *objets* and real-life blazonry of the fierce Daisy, still *couchant*. 'Mmm, trophy-hunter stuff, eh?' he said, his eyes travelling about the beautiful room. 'It is lovely to see that my new friends have a real life away from the pleasure and the parties. This feels at one remove from the mortal coil.'

I could tell by his manner that Philip was already mentally deferring his departure from Vistorta. A current of sympathy passed between us. I felt glad to have someone of roughly my age to talk to, and who spoke English.

'Right, I must finish off a jigsaw with the boys,' I said, deliberately dropping an invisible safety curtain between us. As I went upstairs to the boys, whom I often found useful solvents for many kinds of social angst, I considered Philip's character on the basis of a few moments of his company. There was something unresolved about it. The more polished, refined and elaborate the shop front, the more anxiously he wanted to conceal whatever lurked behind. I feared that not even Domenico and Angelo could carry away Philip's heaviest baggage.

CHAPTER SEVENTEEN

Philip Van Rensselaer

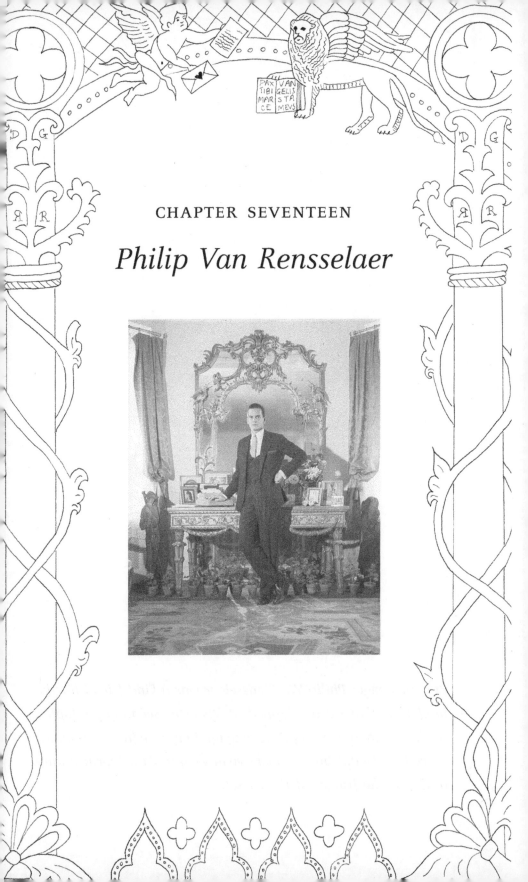

Previous page: *Philip Van Rensselaer was a kind friend for the brief time that we overlapped at Vistorta. Seemingly adopted by the Brandolini, he kept showing up. In life, he failed at almost everything he did, but his books vividly capture the febrile nature of life on the fringes of the jet set.*

THE LIFE OF the locals of the thirteenth-century *borgo* of Vistorta could not have been more different from that of the world I was inhabiting, even though both worlds were inextricably linked in a close, symbiotic relationship. 'Peasants' sounds disrespectful but it does the job. The locals belonged to the land, land that time and chance had delivered into the temporal custody of the Brandolini. The family looked after the locals. It wasn't a matter of tossing them a few potato peelings. The family fed, clothed, employed and educated them, in a latterday benign vassalage. In return, the locals held the Conte in a reflex of unthinking deep-rooted respect for the line and heritage he personified.

Vistorta felt like the middle of nowhere. By day, there were always members of staff quietly looking after the house and gardens; in the evenings, they went home to the *borgo*, leaving the villa vast, silent and brooding. The *borgo* of Vistorta was little more than a dormitory hamlet for the estate. Little seemed to happen there other than the slow gyre of the seasons and the eternal cycle of births, marriages and deaths.

Into this pastoral idyll, Philip might as well have arrived by spaceship. One of the first things he did was break the typewriter. This raised my suspicions: either he had no idea how a typewriter worked, or he broke it to expunge his guilt at not doing any writing. However, I was happy to have him around. With his debonair smile, careless chatter and *joie de vivre*, he was fun, and the more he tried to blend in, the more charmingly he didn't. If nothing else, his enthusiasm was 'infectious', as they say, except of course to Nurse Rasch who seemed to have had a lifelong inoculation. Supported by his splendid wardrobe, Philip always made an effort, always seemed 'on-stage'. One evening, he came on the full Noël Coward by making his entrance for cocktails wearing a silk dressing-gown with velvet lapels, a cigarette holder clamped between his teeth. He would often be seen indolently leaning on a table like the figure of Ralph Curtis in John Singer Sargent's *An Interior in Venice*. 'The dressing-gown?' he said, removing the cigarette holder. 'They also make them for men.' It was effortful, but everyone appreciated the effort.

I was entrusted with the keys to an olive green Fiat Millecento. Unlike the Cadillac, this miracle of Italian tinkering gave a real-world driving thrill. I treated it as my own, frequently ran errands and took the opportunity to tootle around the countryside, just for the sheer pleasure.

Francesca, the boys' piano teacher, lived in Asolo, a town of arcaded streets in the foothills of the Dolomites to the southwest. Just as I was preparing to depart Vistorta to collect her, I stumbled on Philip in one of the drawing rooms. He was scanning the newspapers.

'Hi,' he said. 'I'm just looking for bold-typeface mentions.'

I threw him a blank look.

'Headlines,' he said. 'Or, rather, HEADLINES!'

'Oh . . . I see. Why might the newspapers be interested? Are you being blackmailed by your luggage?'

'Oh, several reasons.'

'Must be a very quiet day in the newsroom for the papers

to be interested in you, or am I missing something? In between shopping trips, sightseeing and backgammon, did you manage to save the world from nuclear cataclysm?'

'Oh, something far more exciting.'

'Anyway, Philip, if you have nothing better to do, you are welcome to join me on a trip to Asolo.'

'As someone whose leitmotif has always been caving in, how can I refuse?' said Philip, folding a newspaper.

'The drive back might be a bit of a squash.'

'I'll go and change.'

'N-n-*no!*' I cried, following him out into the hall.

'Just a tie,' called Philip, over his shoulder, as he ran upstairs.

Fifteen minutes later, brandishing his cufflinks with a look of infinite importance, Philip stepped down the colonnaded double-staircase, angling his body at forty-five degrees so that he descended half sideways. He was wearing one of his signature costumes: navy crested blazer with a pocket handkerchief, polished black shoes, monogrammed shirt, and lustrously subtle grey flannels. At his neck flourished a gaily patterned silk foulard.

'Regimental tie?' I asked.

'Charvet, Place Vendôme. Same as the shirt. The shoes are by Peal. In case you were wondering.'

Philip's 'look' was a silky first cousin of the glib, studied, fetishistic stroking of the WASP establishment uniform straight out of Saks Fifth Avenue and Brooks Brothers. With his monograms and his effusive haberdashery, he dressed like an ignoramus's idea of an American gentleman.

'Philip, we're picking up a piano teacher, not going to a fancy-dress party.'

'Huh, sure,' he said, looking at himself in a mirror. 'But you never know who you might bump into.' He brushed imaginary motes off his coat and minutely inspected his fingernails. 'Freya Stark lives in Asolo.'

Squeezing ourselves into the Millecento, I fired up the engine, which sounded like a large hairdryer. We set off to the grinding of gears and the whirring of metal.

'I know about Freya Stark,' I said, as we kangaroo-hopped down the driveway. 'The war correspondent and writer. Thing is, Philip, the way you dress, no one could possibly *bump* into you. They'd see you coming from miles around. It would be more a case of an unavoidable collision caused by glare.' I caught Philip eyeing my dung-coloured autumnal jersey and trousers. 'Clothes look as good as they fit,' I said pre-emptively.

'It's important to make a strong first impression,' he countered. 'But trying to do so in gardening clothes seems like a handicap too far.'

'I'm not making a first impression!' I said. After driving in thoughtful silence for a few minutes, I said, 'Funnily enough, I agree with you. And every time I have judged ill of someone by their first impression, and have guiltily reviewed and softened my harsh opinion, I have often regretted it.'

'Have you ever heard of Anthony Trollope?' asked Philip, as he took in scenes of pastoral felicity on either side of us as we drove south-west towards Asolo.

'I've only read all of his novels, if that's what you're wondering,' I said. While Philip digested this intelligence, I pushed on. 'I rather enjoy Trollope's liturgical settings and language, the clergymen and the churchy milieu he describes so well. It's a bit like my own life.'

'Well, er, I haven't read all of his works,' said Philip, 'but apparently he wrote that the best-dressed gentleman is the one whose dress one never sees.'

'Oh, my God! We need an emergency copy of the *Chronicles of Barsetshire* now! Philip, don't go near your wardrobe until you have read at least *The Warden*. I don't suppose Nurse Rasch has a copy in her medicine cupboard. Maybe the Conte can help.'

'Hang on,' said Philip. 'I was going to say that Trollope is clearly a menace to the menswear industry, who didn't truly understand the language of clothes. Times have moved on. I don't do camouflage, except in gilded salons where I am happy to blend in. To me, clothes are not illicit pleasures, but statements and articles of taste. And I like to break rules: brown shoes with blue suit, straw hats before the Summer Exhibition, white dinner jackets before Royal Ascot, urban tweed, two buttons, cufflink stones before cocktail hour.'

'I'm sorry to disappoint you but I had no idea those were the rules.'

I noticed that Philip had adopted a slightly slumped posture in the passenger seat, and was ogling himself in the wing mirror.

'My point is that I believe in conspicuous spending. It encourages others to spend, and I take my responsibilities to the world economy seriously. So who is this piano teacher and why doesn't he have his own car?'

'*She* doesn't drive, and while there is a local bus, its timetable is indistinguishable from a calendar.'

I was being too chatty. Philip might think I was *interested*. But after a lull in the conversation while I concentrated on sorting out my hand–eye–foot coordination, and steered the Millecento around several tipsy grape-laden wagons, I couldn't resist coaxing more from Philip.

'Tell me about your writing.'

'Sure. I mean that's what I do.'

'You must be very successful. All that luggage and all those hoped-for bold-typeface mentions, as you put it. And yet I have never heard of you. Have you written anything I might . . .?'

'Not unless you take American magazines. I specialise in elite enclaves. I suppose I have what you might call a long, low, horizontal fan base.'

'I don't care much for magazines, or elite enclaves,' I said, avoiding a very relaxed-looking donkey standing in the road. 'Are you here solely to rest and take in Tintorettos and Titians, or will you be doing any work?'

'Oh, yes. I'm here to research and write a book.'

'But, in your caravan of luggage, there was no room for a typewriter of your own.'

'Well, I am a writer, but that's not the only reason I'm here.'

Swerving around a decoratively painted wooden cart that was being pulled by a horse, I glimpsed the rider wearing a wide-brimmed straw hat, smoking a cigarette and sitting next to a dog. 'Now you're confusing me.'

'I'm mainly here for the drawing-room sophistication, the dry epigrams, the tinkling laughter and the witty flirtations. But I've also come to find the answer to a question.'

'Isn't that why most people come to Italy?'

'I've come to work out whether to marry someone or not.' Thank goodness, I thought. He's not *interested*. Then I said, 'Is this part of your research, or are we talking about real life?'

'Real life. But it would make a great book. The woman in question is American.'

'Woman. Not girl.'

'She's slightly older. I can't say who.'

We sat listening to the whining of the car while watching the scenery rush past us as Philip's situation marinated in my mind. In every frame of vision, there was always something deliciously bucolic going on: a solitary farmer riding a horse, a boy tending a donkey, a frieze of women harvesting grapes, a dog barking at the sky, and so on. Sunlight gilded the very countryside that, 452 years earlier, Giovanni Bellini had depicted in *Madonna of the Meadow*, supposedly the earliest landscape painting (another Venetian first). Little had changed. Here was a wellhead; there was a raven; in the distance stood a hilltop fort. Bellini might as well have painted the picture yesterday.

'If you have come to Italy to ponder a marriage prospect,' I said, 'you have my sympathies.'

I sketched out my relations with my parents, my restless flight from London, and my extempore engagement to David.

'How odd to be engaged to someone you love,' said Philip. 'Got the financial settlement sorted?'

I shot Philip a glance. 'Settlement?'

'Who gets what when it doesn't work out,' he said.

'No need. Besides, neither of us owns anything valuable.'

'No second-guesses? No *arrière pensées*? What happens when it's too difficult to sustain the euphoria, when the romance is over, and when husband and wife are left staring at each other, face to face, every illusion vanished?'

'Doesn't enter my thinking.' I tightened my grip on the wheel.

'That's not how the world works. How faithfully does life ever reflect intentions?'

'You just have to keep your intentions real,' I said. 'One man's *arrière pensée* is another man's misjudgement or lack of focus.' An image of a woman sitting alone on a deckchair on a sandy beach filled the road ahead. 'It's odd,' I went on, 'you're the second expatriate writer I've met this year who is based in Paris.'

'Who was the first?'

'Nancy Mitford.'

'*Fish-knife anxiety!*' he chortled.

There was a pause while we took in a fine panorama of the Dolomites to our right.

I continued: 'How long have you lived in Paris?'

'A couple of months.'

'Whereabouts?'

'The Ritz.'

I shot Philip a slightly longer glance, to see if he was smiling or serious. He wasn't smiling. 'You *live* in the Ritz, or are just *staying* in the Ritz?'

'I'm happy to call the Ritz home.'

'"Home" for as long as it takes to work out how to avoid paying the bill.' I threw Philip a peep.

He was looking at me with mild disdain but I could have sworn he gave me half a wink. 'As I was saying, before you interrupted me, I may switch to the Meurice or the Plaza Athénée. I prefer hotels. I love the mysterious strangers, the sense of suspense, the frisson of impending drama and, of course, the Spode, napery and room service'

'David lives in a hotel in Paris.'

'Which one?'

'Er, let me see. It's not the Ritz, and I don't think it's the Meurice, and the last time I looked it didn't say Plaza Athénée on the outside.'

'That only leaves the George V, the Bristol and the Royal Monceau, unless you mean the Crillon?'

'Nope. None of those. In his hotel, the only sense of suspense is the laundry line in his room.'

'What does he like about this hotel?' Philip asked.

'Take your pick. Abusive service, rudimentary sanitation, nil décor, occasional mushroom harvests off the walls, and regular sightings of wildlife, but a tremendous sense of Bohemian squalor and low prices.'

'I've stayed in that one, too.'

While more flame-coloured countryside whizzed past, there was further mental marination.

'Forgive me for saying so,' I said. 'You don't sound Parisian.'

'How disappointing! Then again I'm not.'

'How come you live in Europe?'

'How much time do you have?'

'Asolo is about one and a half hours.'

'Let me plot out the grand arc of my career . . .'

Philip came from patrician east-coast Episcopalian old money. He was the remnant of a Hudson River dynasty and a kinsman of Herman Melville, author of *Moby-Dick*. The Van Rensselaers were New York's 'first family'. Their fortunes peaked in about 1835 when they owned a million fertile acres. In America, only John Jacob Astor was richer. What followed was a tale of Dickensian sadness and melodrama. Thanks to disastrous law suits, foolish marriages, bad luck and the Wall Street Crash, the family and its fortune were decimated.

'Clearly I've been reading the wrong cautionary tales to the boys,' I said.

'A friend tells me, "If you can overcome your backgammon . . . sorry, your back*ground*, you can overcome anything,"' said Philip. 'I think I've worked out how at least to hide my background for most of the time, from most of the people . . . Okay, from a few people for very little of the time.'

'Mmm.' I shook my head. 'Philip, have you ever thought of enrolling in acting classes?'

We laughed. There was more. The downward trajectory of Van Rensselaer was just beginning.

'My grandmother had two children: a boy, James, and a girl, Louise, who became my mother. In trying to trade her way out of one marriage and into another with a man who didn't want responsibility for her two children, my grandmother "sold" Louise to her childless sister, who died when her skirt caught fire after she'd fallen over drunk one evening. My mother, then four, inherited a fortune, whereupon my grandmother tried to claw her back. The courts intervened and entrusted my mother to her bachelor uncle, a millionaire playboy who proved a fantastically unsuitable guardian. After another court intervention, my mother, now eight, was entrusted to the care of two spinsters in New York City. However, her brother had kept in touch, and later introduced her to a friend, Charles van Rensselaer Junior. Charles and my mother married and had two sons, my older brother Charlie and me.'

'Honestly, Philip being with you is like being caught in quicksand. I can feel it sucking me in. It is horribly compulsive.'

We had arrived at the Pearl of Treviso. As Philip hadn't finished, I pulled over and switched off the engine.

'When I was a year old, my parents divorced. They'd only been married for five years. After the stock market crash wiped out most of her fortune, my mother turned to the great American answer to all problems: she packed up and set off with Charlie and me into the sunset, or sunrise, and Europe. We lived like gypsies in Spain and Italy, mainly Italy. I attended a series of schools for mentally disturbed teachers. We were forever packing, moving and unpacking, always on the road, from one flower-filled, balustraded, naughty-Cupid-carved villa to the next. I've managed to upgrade to hotel suites, but I've only ever known permanent transience. So . . .' Philip paused and sighed '. . . that's me. So many high hopes dashed, so much money squandered.'

'God, is that the time?' I said, my hand on the door handle.

Philip sailed on: 'But I can order the perfect Corpse Reviver Number Two in four languages. So long as I'm sober.'

I made as if to open the door and get out of the car.

'When we returned to New York,' pushed on Philip, 'a commodities trader bought my mother.'

'Bought?'

'He paid for her with flowers, diamonds, fur coats, limousines, chauffeurs, maids. He stole her away with trips to Europe aboard ocean liners.'

'Well, at least your luggage can't abandon you,' I said, trying to sum up.

'Whenever anyone asked me what I wanted to be when I grew up, my answer depended on the last movie I'd seen. I snatched at identities and pasted them on myself. I didn't have a clue who I was . . .'

'Right, Philip, it sounds like you've spun this tale many times

277

before, so if you'll forgive me, I really must find the piano teacher.'

I began to suspect that I had an escaped psychiatric patient on my hands, or someone on the edge of a major personality disorder. I wondered if Philip might be deep under cover for the CIA. His name, Van Rensselaer: was it an anagram or a code? Perhaps he was on the run. Vistorta was an excellent sanctuary.

I tugged the door handle and climbed out of the car.

Francesca the piano teacher was seated at a café, a neatly dressed senior figure, whom I had picked up several times before.

We *piacered*. 'I'm so sorry to have kept you,' I said. 'I have a friend of the Conte and Contessa with me, Philip Van Rensselaer. He felt he needed to dress up especially to meet you, so we were slightly delayed.'

Francesca looked Philip up and down, and turned to me. 'Whose national costume is that?'

'He's from America.'

'Philip,' I called to him, as he was taking in his surroundings in Asolo, 'you're going to have to squeeze into the back seat.'

On the drive back to Vistorta, I listened to Philip, who was lying almost horizontally and awkwardly on the back seat, limbs everywhere and at odd angles, try to explain to Francesca his reasons for being in Venice.

Francesca replied, 'That both of you have come to Venice to distance yourselves from aspects of your past shows that irony is not dead.'

'Please explain,' said Philip. 'I need more irony in my life.'

'La Serenissima is steeped in her past,' said Francesca. 'She is famous for her past. Her past is her future. But you are trying to get away from your past. For you, Venice is a kind of decompression chamber, no?'

'*Esattamente!*' cried Philip. 'It's a kind of therapy. I find decline irresistible. Being in decline is far more romantic and fun than being on the rise. I certainly wouldn't want to have been around during the *rise* of the Venetian empire.'

We had arrived at Vistorta but sat in the car still talking. 'You said "decline",' intoned Francesca, holding up a painted-nailed index finger, a finger that commanded silence as well as produced great music. 'I never mentioned decline. Yes, one day, who knows, Venice will go bye-bye, but Venice has pushed back that day so often that maybe, just maybe, she has worked out a way of avoiding it.'

For the first time, Philip seemed genuinely stunned into silence.

'So,' continued Francesca, moving to get out of the car, 'it takes a perverse mind – or perhaps just a journalist – to take seriously the idea that Venice is in decline.'

And with that Francesca peeled away to find the music room where Ruy and Leonello awaited her.

CHAPTER EIGHTEEN

The Contessa

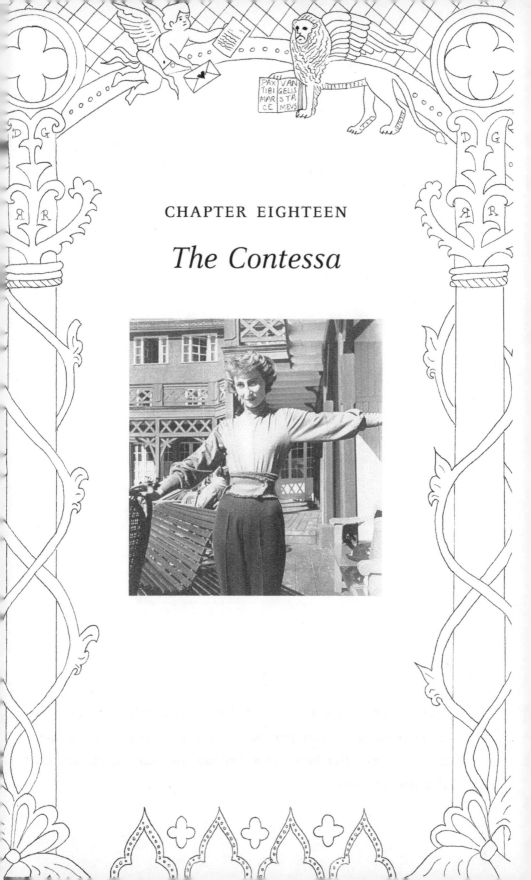

Previous page: *The Contessa Cristiana Brandolini d'Adda was a beautiful and lovely person, as well as a very good mother. She gave me a free hand when looking after her two eldest sons Ruy and Leonello.*

To David Ross
[18 October 1957]

Vistorta

David darling,

Sometimes I am bewildered by the unreality of the life which I am living, and pause to wonder how it is that I am living it.

It has become less desolate since the Count and Countess returned bringing with them a charming young American writer, whose European home is Paris, who has come here for ten days to make up his mind not to marry his girl.

Although this place is in the back of beyond, in a way I have much more freedom, which can either be fun or terribly boring, according to one's moods.

I ride every day with the groom, whenever I want – incidentally I have fallen off in the compound once already – I find it difficult to gallop in small circles! Then I have a Millecento Fiat that I can drive and yesterday, for instance, I drove 80 km to a place called Asolo (where Freya Stark lives) to fetch the piano mistress, 160 km in all, the last bit being in alpine country – you can see the mountains from Vistorta. You can imagine how much I love the driving, and the houses and small towns one passes through are so beautiful, and the countryside russet-coloured in the bright hot sunlight.

Apart from this, I sit in the garden and read, or take the dog

283

for a walk through the vineyards, with anyone who is willing to accompany me, and if I feel energetic, I put on my shorts and do gymnastics. In a corner of the garden there is a complete set of apparatus, bars, swings, ropes, the lot. What with the riding and the unaccustomed physical contortions, I have been very stiff – how painful, but how healthy! And then every evening candlelight dinners – six-course dinners – and afterwards listening to the gramophone(s). The Count has just bought two enormous new gramophones, each with separate cunningly placed loudspeakers. They are wonderful and can play fortissimo without any distortion whatsoever. He has an enormous collection of records at Vistorta – mostly opera.

Each morning from my window, looking out into the lazy morning sunshine and on to the lawn, made pearly-grey with heavy dew, there are two old peasant women in black, sweeping great circles of green on the lawn and removing every single leaf as if it were some abomination such as a bus ticket! And then in order that no leaves may presume to sully the lawns during the day, they hit all the branches they can reach with a long pole and sweep up the resulting downfall. And then they are gone and it is once more an English rose garden until, thro' a gap in the wall, I catch sight of a horse pulling a cart, driven by a blue-jacketed peasant wearing a straw sombrero.

I do think money is hell – why can't you fly to Milan and then come and stay here for a week or so instead of plodding the daily round in Paris? But don't take me seriously – I'm just <u>saying</u> it. But would you ever really think of working in Italy?

I have discovered that there is a US Airforce Station at a place called Pordenone, about 15 km from here – and the

Countess reckons I'll be able to get an introduction and go to the camp cinema, which has American films every night. I think perhaps I had better take my chauffeur (Domenico, his driving licence miraculously restored) with me to see how the land lies! But still it might be quite fun.

At the moment the Countess is doing everything she can to make life less lonely for me – so whatever I ask for, I get! I shall have the most enormous collection of scarves, because she keeps giving them to me.

I must still be enormously fat, because the other day, three-year-old Nuno announced to the world at large (several people being present) that, 'Miss July ha due paupau, uno gli e uno gli' indicating my posterior and my bosom! Roars of laughter all round. You see, these Italians start very young in their appreciation of the female form!

. . .

To describe this place a little more, Vistorta itself is a tiny village, about 200 inhabitants, all belonging to the Count! They all work on the estate. There is a tiny church and a school for toddlers and one shop, just like an English village shop. The Palace, as this house is called, is in an enormous walled garden.

I can't remember how depressed my last letter was – anyway, I've cheered up now. It does help to have the odd human being to talk to – especially if male! Anyway, I'm having a great sort of pro-American culture session – there are so many American magazines here too, that I am subconsciously becoming Americanised!

The reason why I have so much time for these extra-mural activities is because the children have lessons all the morning.

I hope you are well and happy and enjoying singing and everything else – I should so love to have dinner with you at the Saint Père.

Please write, darling.

Love

Gill

Ruy began school on 21 October, not having darkened an academic institution for nearly five months. No one seemed bothered. The school was half an hour's drive from Vistorta. It was all very informal and low-key. He didn't wear a uniform. I drove him there every morning and picked him up in the afternoon. He seemed perfectly happy. This meant that during the day I had even less to do than before. Some days were vegetable days when literally nothing pierced the suspended bucolic sequestration.

Talking to myself aloud, I strolled across the spreading lawns, skirted the lake where dragonflies on the wing darted and hovered, picked my way through enchanted glades and threaded along narrow paths that wove among the great trees that stood in gracious silence, casting an ancestral spell.

Often I would take Leonello and Daisy with me. After playing ball-fetch with Daisy, we would stop and listen to the squawk and whirr of game birds, and the soft music of the wind sighing through the trees, broken only by the sudden emphatic agitations of birds playing their version of Monopoly among the upper branches.

On the lake and the canals that fretted the estate, we watched swaggering ducks, perky moorhens, squabbling coots, hunched stilt-walking herons and crested grebes with sea-urchin haircuts.

My favourite time was early evening, the so-called *attimo fuggente* (fleeting moment): the sun turned a deep red-gold and threw a lateral light that struck richly across the park, extending gleaming fingers through the branches of the trees. A group of swans would land on the lake in formation, like returning bombers. The countryside soon darkened, and an air of mystery descended.

Despite the isolated setting, life at Vistorta continued on a grand scale, as in a great English country house. Dinner was always candlelit, always six courses, and always finished with a Christmas-type pudding of nuts and dates washed down with port. The soft light, the sparkle of glass, the gleam of silver, the shimmer of jewels and the attitudes of the heads of the men and women as they leant and listened, and the muffled footfall of servants all added luxurious touches. Afterwards, in the drawing room, we would play games, listen to opera and discuss the latest perturbations of salon society. Philip, legs crossed, ankle on knee, gave full scintillating value. He had perfected a line of small-talk that rippled effortlessly from his tongue, covering films, books, theatre, furniture, fine art, and other people's appearances, inheritances, breeding prospects, jewellery and clothing. In a performance of considerable breadth and nuance, he had a way of making things seem much more amusing and entertaining than they were. With an innate sense of a certain style that was beyond me, he seemed expert on all the accoutrements of fine living.

Many of the famous names tossed about were international stars known to me only from newspapers. Philip seemed closely acquainted with them all. He wore his contacts like a diadem. The expanding concentric circles of the Brandolini's and Philip's networks seemed to go on for ever. One evening, however, I managed to slip in a mention of my cousin, Anthony Dawson. If Aunt Ida had several sides to her, her son Anthony was multi-faceted in a literal sense.

Several pairs of eyes locked on to me when I mentioned his name.

A Hollywood actor, Anthony played Charles Swann, the contract murderer in Alfred Hitchcock's *Dial M for Murder* (1954). In the late 1950s, he was set to enjoy a purple period, playing Professor Dent, the villainous geologist in *Doctor No* (1962), then Ernst Stavro Blofeld in *From Russia with Love* (1963) and *Thunderball* (1965). To star in three Bond films in as many years proved Anthony's acting prowess, charisma and entertainment value. On-screen, he had a slightly villainous look; off-screen, he was the jolliest member of my family, and my favourite cousin. A gifted pianist, he could harmonise and improvise any tune, in any key, in any style. In later life he roguishly stayed single until well into his forties. He even claimed to have had an affair with Grace Kelly, his co-star in *Dial M for Murder.* Anthony inherited much of his presence and forcefulness from Aunt Ida.

'*Bravissima!*' applauded the Conte. 'I'm sure you share some of your cousin's innate qualities that translate so well outside England.'

Every day, Philip placed long-distance telephone calls. I'm not one to eavesdrop, but I couldn't help overhearing that the voice at the other end of the line was always the same: a mournful, weary-sounding female. The calls lasted about thirty minutes. Neither business-like nor chatty, some of the dialogues inspired Philip to stand and raise his voice; other calls, conducted from a seated position usually on the largest sofa, sounded as if he was listening to a lengthy shopping list. Sometimes, in mid-call, he'd do a cross-word, wanly muttering, 'Whaddaya know? . . . Huh! . . . Isn't that something? . . . Whyncha call a doctor?' On one occasion I could have sworn he'd nodded off. He would emerge from these calls either gazing starrily or looking deflated and confused.

I observed Philip with increasing puzzlement. He was amusing and entertaining, as were most of the Conte and Contessa's friends. What *else* they saw in him was hard to fathom. Perhaps the Conte and Contessa, whose family fortunes had travelled in the opposite direction to those of Van Rensselaer, felt a twinge of sympathy, mindful of the transience of wealth. Besides, given the Contessa's American roots, it would be poor form were word to seep back to the States that she was anything other than a generous and welcoming hostess.

Meanwhile, a vicious fever struck. The intangible visitation caused a number of deaths in Sacile. When I fell ill, the Contessa, herself seemingly impervious to illness, told me to stay in bed. This, however, opened the door not only to Fräulein Rasch but also to the sinister doctor from Milan. Alive to the friction between me and Nurse Rasch, the Contessa took charge. This would have irked Rasch more than ever. The rest of the staff stood wide-eyed at my treatment. Friendly and chatty, the Contessa shared with me her views on marriage, other people and the world in general. She told me about her wedding in Rome 1947.

'It was not a grand occasion. Italy was going through dark times, so we kept it *piano*. After the ceremony at the Basilica of St. Bartholomew, a tenth-century basilica on Tiber Island in Rome, Gianni hosted a reception just for the family at his house in Trastevere.' I noted that the Contessa did *not* get married in Turin, the Agnelli stronghold.

I sometimes sensed that she felt a twinge of loneliness. Perhaps she imagined that more interesting things were going on over the horizon and that she was, in some curious way, missing out. This may have partly explained her ceaseless travelling. The Conte also travelled, but that might simply have been a reflex, in the time-honoured tradition of Venetian noblemen travelling widely in search of new opportunities or crusades.

The Contessa once asked if I thought people were having more fun in places like Biarritz and Monaco.

'I'd be genuinely impressed if anyone knew *less* about Biarritz and Monaco than I do,' I shrugged, 'but I doubt it, unless you believe what you read in magazines.' Then I remembered something Aristotle Onassis had said to me on the *passarella* of *Christina O*. I paraphrased it, adding my own spin. 'I suppose some people are just trying to kill time while they find their way to the next shiny object or hunt down the next most fashionable myth or chase down something they think looks like something they might want. Time always gets its revenge.'

The Contessa nodded slowly. 'And how do you find Philip?' she said, switching tack. 'Do you have difficulty taking him seriously?' The Contessa's cool blue gaze settled on me.

I had noticed that her stately ambiguous reserve towards Philip contrasted with the Conte's jollier disposition (I sometimes felt there was a bit of a love-you-to-death vibe) so I felt able to unbutton.

'I have no problem taking him seriously,' I said. 'He's delightful. He seems perfectly harmless, except perhaps to himself. We are completely different kinds of people. We want different things. There's an air of boom-or-bust about him. I think he's more susceptible to smoke, mirrors, bells and whistles than I am. We are not, as it were, in competition. The gap between where he thinks he is and where he wants to be is far, far greater for him than it is for me. He's all about the journey. I'm about the destination.'

The Contessa nodded slowly. 'Most of us are not impressed by . . .' a silence momentarily fell on her lips '. . . optical illusions of wealth and taste, but we do like a new face, now and then.'

'Yes,' I said. 'I think he genuinely enjoys dressing up and going to smarter, grander parties. It seems to be who he is. But if you are asking *why* he is . . .' I raised both arms in a gesture of despair. 'Goodness knows!"

Smiling thinly and pityingly, the Contessa once again nodded slowly, then added wistfully, 'Exactly. He's not alone in having had a difficult upbringing. Both my parents died in their forties. Everything changed when my father died. I was eight . . .'

After the Contessa's father died in a seaplane accident in 1935, not only did Giovanni Agnelli, her grandfather, try to wrest control of her and her six siblings, but he also tried to freeze out their mother, Virginia. Scooping up her brood, Virginia fled south to Rome. The tug of war between Virginia and her father-in-law was tragically resolved by the death of Virginia in a road accident in 1945, and the death of Giovanni Agnelli fifteen days later, which left Gianni Agnelli as head of the family and of Fiat at twenty-four. Two years later, Cristiana married the Conte, a man who disliked driving, came from a wheel-less city and was charming and cultured.

The Contessa gave me a significant look. 'And then,' she said, 'Brando's parents died in their fifties. Our early losses are why we can live like this.' She gestured vaguely and slightly dismissively at the room around her. 'But the price has been high.' The Contessa turned her head away and looked down at the floor.

I thought of a comment she made at Villa Kechler nearly five months earlier about the importance of a 'mamma' figure, a figure her grandfather had tried to deny her. Perhaps the sympathy that the Conte and Contessa evidently felt for Philip had something to do with Philip's own traumatic and scattered upbringing.

The Contessa looked up, smiled a beautiful, radiant and completely uninhibited smile. As it subsided, she elegantly turned and looked out of the window so that I saw her in profile. With a hint of ice in her voice, she continued, 'We all have choices. The difficulty is often in making the right one.' She turned to me. 'I'm an intuitive person, but among my many faults, being wrong is not one of them.'

To David Ross
Wednesday, 23/Thursday,
24 October 1957

Vistorta

David darling,

I have been in bed with a slight 'something'. I don't think it can be Asiatica, because there is a very virulent form of it here, and

three people have died in Vistorta. It didn't feel very virulent,
but I just enjoy being spoiled. The Countess herself took my
temperature. I am in bed surrounded by books, wirelesses, maga-
zines, fruit and pills, which a doctor has given me for my malady.
I have a constant stream of visitors and the dog Daisy suffocates
me by sitting on any stationary part of my person.

I am writing another rambling letter, because I find that
writing to you is a pleasant pastime – I like the sound of the
scratching of my own pen, and trust that you won't be taken
aback by the resulting nonsense and might possibly be amused.

I have just been reading one of last week's Daily Expresses,
all the papers arrive about five days late here, and I see that a
girl I knew quite well once upon a time called Jennifer Harris,
alias Sally Weston, has been jailed for twelve months for fraud
amounting to £524! She was a friend of Shelagh [Cooper], knew
Pete [Collins] and Mike [Hawthorn] and among many other,
doubtless similar, activities, she was Stirling's [Moss] mistress
for three years. Poor Sally – I bet this Katie Molson whom Stirling
has just married is a madly proper little thing. Maybe GOOD
does triumph in the end – does it?

I'm so glad you found Lance [Macklin] at the Salon de l'Auto
– what did you think of him? I hope Shelagh writes to me,
because I can't write to either, as I haven't got their Paris address.

. . .

I expect you know how it is: in some extraordinary way if you
learn a new word or learn of a new person or place, you imme-
diately hear it or them mentioned again several times by different
people within a very short time. In the same way I have just
found two articles about the Gorges du Tarn – one in Elle *and*

one in the Tatler. *After reading these articles, I came to the conclusions that we definitely saw all that was most memorable. La Caze was mentioned with bated breath as being only for the very rich! Ha! Ha!*

That awful young doctor is arriving to take up residence on Sunday . . . however I have taken the bull by the horns and told the Co. and Co-ess that he made advances (!!!) and the Count, amid gales of laughter on all sides, has promised to speak to him, and he is not going to sleep in the house – so at least I shall be safe in bed!

I really have been getting on so well with the Countess recently – and we have been having real woman-to-woman gossips. All the down-to-earth advice she has meted out to me on marriage is fantastic. I fear I have made a life-long enemy of the German Fräulein, because she is never asked to sit in the drawing room – let alone have dinner with them. But it is fascinating listening to their conversations with names like Elsa Maxwell, Greta Garbo and Onassis being talked and bandied about like the Smiths or the Joneses. Luckily I know just enough about this sort of thing to put in the odd remark and take an intelligent interest.

Do you know that for every evening for about eight days we have had different wine glasses? Some of them are quite beautiful. We have individual toast-racks and butter dishes. Never again will I know such luxury and sometimes I even think that in about thirty years' time it will be quite unusual even to be able to recall such feudal grandeur.

Darling, I don't know about you coming for Christmas – it hasn't been mentioned again – and the new rooms may not be finished, in which case there won't be much room. But do you really want to? I am sure it will be quite an experience – if you really _want_ to, but I don't _want_ to find you have some other ideas.

Next day

I woke up this morning so surprised to see snow on the mountains, which I can see from my window. I had no idea that they were so high. In the sunlight they look absolutely lovely – it is so extraordinary, as there are still figs and late grapes ripening in the sunshine.

I don't know what I shall do if I have that awful doctor trailing me round all day, as I'm sure he will – but if he for instance wants to bath the children with me, I just won't stay. For one thing, I am going to have even less to do, and as I have virtually nothing now – it will be just so boring.

Thank you for your postcard – I'm afraid this letter has got somewhat belated. I have thrown off my sickness and am rushing round again.

I have been driving a lot – oddly enough in this large household there are few people who hold a driving licence so I have even been getting some night driving. Last night we went to the cinema in Pordenone – the nearest town of any consequence. We saw a wonderful film – it won at the Cannes Film Festival and is directed by the same man as La Strada. You must see it if you have a chance – called Le Notte di Cabiria with Giulietta Masina as a prostitute in Rome. Hers was a magnificent performance. She is a fascinating and lovable character, but the story is very pathetic.

. . .

Lots of love,
Gill

CHAPTER NINETEEN

Bubbles and Mirages

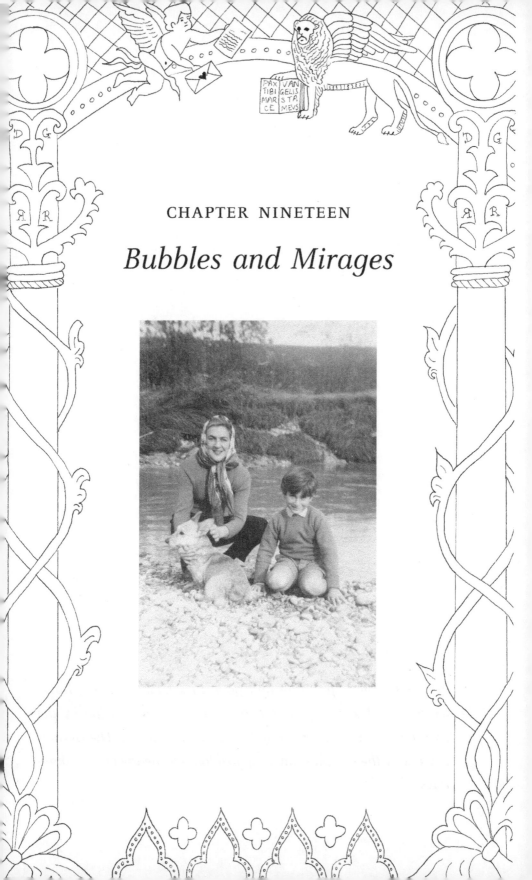

Previous page: *After Ruy had gone to school, Leonello, Daisy (corgi) and I were left on our own. Here we are posing by the river Livenza which ran along the estate at Vistorta. The Hermès scarf was the* ne plus ultra *of fashionable headwear in those days.*

THE CONTE HAD two brothers, Guido and Tiberto. I never wittingly met Guido, but Tiberto would drop by. He seemed in awe of his eldest brother, and rose whenever the Conte entered the room. Always friendly, he would often prefer to take supper with me and the children than dine with his brother and sister-in-law. Anglophile, industrious and sociable, Tiberto owned a palazzo and ran his own estate in Pieve di Soligo, some thirty-five kilometres east of Sacile in the province of Treviso. Here he grew grapes and produced wine. When I took the boys to visit, he told me a harrowing war story, which I recounted in a letter.

To David Ross
[Sunday, 27 October 1957]

Vistorta

Ruy, Leonello and I set off in the Fiat for Pieve di Soligo, a village in the foothills of the alps, to visit Conte Tiberto – who, you may remember, is the brother who likes to think he is a British cavalry officer and talks huntin', shootin' and fishin' non-stop. He welcomed us with open arms (literally). He really is a kind man, because he had bought some English cigarettes for me in Austria and presented them to me – most welcome, as I have just exhausted all supplies. They cost 400L a packet here (Senior Service), approx. 5/-. However, I smoke so few now that I suppose I could buy the odd packet. However, I digress.

Maybe you know that only the main roads in Italy are tarmac – and to arrive at Soligo we had to go over ten miles of virtual cart-track – altho' passing thro' several sizeable and v. attractive towns perched on cypress-dotted hillsides, with pink-washed churches in profusion. The countryside is still very green, only some of the trees have changed colour, and the sun was hot, hot, hot . . . and grapes, grapes everywhere – the grapes in the hills being the latest grapes to be harvested.

Count Tiberto is enormously proud of his palace, which dominates a little town of 450 inhabitants, and I will preface my descriptions of it by telling you its history. Before the war it was the main country seat of the Brandolini – they all lived there when not in Venice. The war came, and the widowed mother and her daughter [Maria della Grazie or Graziella] went to the country, taking with them all the best treasure from the palace in Venice – several Guardis, Canalettos and some Brunelleschi stuff, etc. After Italy capitulated in 1943, all three sons fought in the British Army – but the hill country in northern Italy was a German stronghold and also the hideout of the Partisans, who lived in the depths of the hills, only coming down for surprise attacks on German convoys. The leader of the Partisans happened to be a friend of Count Tiberto, and thro' him the mother was always kept informed of the well-being of her sons, and in return she would do what she could to help the Partisans. This band of Partisans ambushed and completely destroyed a German convoy nearby – and the Germans, wishing to revenge themselves, decided to punish the surrounding countryside, only old men, women and children, because the men either hid in the hills or were soldiers. So the German general called on Contessa Brandolini and demanded whether she knew where the Partisans hid – she would not answer, but in the salon, the general saw proudly displayed photographs of her three sons in British uniforms; whereupon the general said he gave her ten minutes to get out of the palace before he set fire to it – during which time he hanged the only four able-bodied men in the village. She escaped with her daughter, and her palace and the whole village were burnt down – out of 116 houses, 104 were burnt to the ground. Everything in the palace was lost – it being the third time it was burnt – in 1917 and once before.

Now Soligo is a rebuilt and charming little village, with only a few remaining ruins to remind one of the tragedy. The palace itself, completely rebuilt, is charming, with a lovely sun terrace looking over the hills and a fountain playing in a big lawn shaded by cedar trees. The rooms were all very light and airy yet perfect foil for some of the lovely furniture, but genuine and not overdone like here.

There was a lovely garden and then vineyards as far as one could see, covering all the hills. With great pride the Count showed me how they made the wine in an enormous cellar, twice as big as the one here. He is the biggest private wine producer in northern Italy. I saw the enormous vats – which are just like rooms (they were empty) – where the new wine is left to ferment for a week and then put in the smaller wooden vats. He showed me the machine for de-skinning the grapes for the white wine and another for straining it. It was fascinating. In the afternoon we all went shooting [Remainder of the letter is missing.]

'Morning, Philip,' I said, the following day, as I breezed into the main drawing room at Vistorta. Philip was standing by a set of French windows, lost in thought. 'I'm off to take Ruy to school.'

Philip remained silent. I noticed he was staring at the view but not taking it in. Some reverie engrossed him. Snapping out of whatever it was, he mumbled, 'Oh, hello. Good morning, Giulietta.'

'Are we all right this morning? Do we need any help polishing our tie pin?' I often found myself talking to Philip as if he were one of my younger charges.

'No, thank you.' Philip smiled with his mouth only.

Something was bugging him. I pressed on. 'After I've dropped off Ruy, I thought I'd visit Farra di Soligo. Apparently there are some frescos in the church of Santa Maria Nova.'

'I've never heard of Farra di Soligo or Santa Maria Nova, but I have heard of frescos,' said Philip, in a monotone, slowly turning towards me. 'What's the interest?'

'Nothing really. They're just old frescos.'

'What is it about frescos that you like?' The light from outside broke on Philip in a strange way. He looked several years older. There was a haunted mien to him.

'Oh Philip, do you really want to know or are you just filling the air with words?'

'No, I'd really like to know. What is the intrinsic interest in frescos?'

'For a start,' I said, folding my arms, 'appreciating a fresco requires a more subtle instinct than I suspect your average tourist can muster, an instinct that is well within your capabilities. Second, frescos have an authenticity that paintings can never match: with a painting, you never know who has done what to it or where it has been stored or hung. None of that applies to a fresco. A fresco is there, on the wall or ceiling, in plain sight and immovable.' I noticed that Philip was taking everything in with a 'serious' look.

'Hmm, I guess so,' he said, drooping slightly. He turned to look out of the French windows, and slowly added, 'Are you suggesting that I might pick up a few tips on authenticity?'

'I'm not saying that, Philip,' I continued, cheerily but firmly. 'I'm merely saying that when staring at a fresco you stand on the very spot that the artist stood, you see what he saw, and perhaps feel something of what he might have felt when he painted the fresco. Who knows? It might even give the writer in you an insight into the creative process.'

'Hm, yes,' conceded Philip. 'Or perhaps an insight into the *quattrocento* fresco industry. Must have been booming.'

'The further attraction is that these frescos only came to light when they were uncovered during the Great War.'

Philip's face congealed suddenly. 'Giulietta, I'd love to join you but I've gotta take a call.'

'Fine. Remember, this evening we're going to the cinema in Pordenone.'

'Of course.'

After dropping off Ruy, I set off for Farra di Soligo in the heart of Treviso's Prosecco belt. Travelling fairly long distances to peep inside obscure little churches and look at art is, I find, one of life's pleasures.

Returning four hours later, I found Philip lounging on a sofa in the main *salone*, engaged in an intense telephone conversation, oblivious to his surroundings. He ended the call soon after I entered, and looked up at me with mild surprise. 'That was quick,' he said, slowly getting up from the sofa.

'How has your day gone so far?' I asked.

He gave a long, deep sigh. 'I'm having problems trying to find the answer to *The Question*.'

'Is this the question that you came to Italy to help answer, about whether to marry this girl or not?'

'Yes.'

'What's the problem, if you don't mind me asking? Can I help?'

'I doubt it. The girl in question is being difficult.'

'Would I have heard of her?'

'Probably. If you have envy, prepare to go green now. She's Barbara Hutton.'

Once I'd picked myself up off the floor, I cried, '*Barbara Hutton!* Not *the* Barbara Hutton, Baroness von Cramm? Not multi-millionaire Barbara Hutton?'

'There's only one Barbara Hutton, thank God,' said Philip. 'I should point out that this is not breaking news.'

'She must be old enough to be your mother. Anyway, she's already married.'

'Oh, she's been married several times. It looks like sponge number six is about to be hung out to dry.'

'Is it game, set and match?'

'Baron Von Cramm is struggling with his serve.'

'How do you hope to fit in? Ball boy?'

'It's kind of complicated and a bit cloak-and-dagger, as opposed to dagger-and-cloak, which is a completely different thing, by the way.' He managed to crack a wan smile.

'That's incredible,' I said, still reeling, 'but at the same time very credible. Is she the woman you keep speaking to over the telephone?'

'Yes. She's in Paris.'

'I thought that that was your doctor or psychiatrist on the line.'

'I think I'm *her* doctor or psychiatrist. I can't deny that our relationship has its ups and downs,' he added, with a rapt far-away look, 'but I believe she may be interested in auditioning for husband number seven.'

'And you think that's going to be you. Is that right?'

'I'm working on it. At this stage it is more of a subjunctive conditional possibility. I suppose you might call me her newest prince consort in attendance.'

'Sponge-in-waiting, more like.'

'I intend to marry her, and then obtain a fairy-tale divorce settlement of a million dollars, as all her previous husbands have done, and several other men too.'

I shook my head in disbelief. 'So this is the great *dénouement*, the stroke of fortune that puts your life right.'

'Yes, this is my ultimate vocational objective,' he said, 'my "Grail" if you like.'

'I'm sorry. It's all just too eyebrow-stretching for me. That's a revolting way to live. How long have you known her?' I asked.

'Oh, slightly less than two months.'

'Two months!'

'We met at a party at Palazzo Brandolini. We stood on the marble balcony on the Grand Canal, held hands and talked intimately, while the fragrance of tuberoses filled the air and candles flickered in the stately rooms.'

'If it doesn't work out you could always try your hand at writing cheap romances.'

'She told me,' continued Philip, 'that we were like two drowning people desperately grabbing any rope that someone might throw us. We both hope to be each other's saviour.'

While I stared in disbelief, Philip looked at me and, seeing my disbelief, added, 'Sometimes you just have to think the unthinkable.'

'I unthinkably think that you stand a better chance of being killed by a squadron of falling pigs. Just suppose, Philip, just suppose that, having married Barbara, you find you're suited to each other and that you discover it isn't just about the money, and that, incredible though it may seem, you fall in love with her. What then?'

A look of horror filled Philip's face. 'There's unthinkable and there's unthinkable. Falling in love with Barbara would definitely fall into the second category. This is not *Romeo and Juliet*. That would be beyond a disaster!'

'Maybe, just maybe, you're wrong.'

'It couldn't possibly happen. She's not capable of it. Nor am I. The two of us are displaced and a little mad. Neither of us is capable of what you'd call a "normal" relationship. Ironically, this is what has drawn us together. We are quite similar. At least, that's what I think.' Philip looked away and exhaled deeply. Turning back to me, he said, 'When feeling charitable, I think she's misunderstood. When feeling realistic, I think she's manipulative, and has the will and ability to fall out with anyone *meteorically*. She's fundamentally unstable. Her mother committed suicide. Oh, and just don't hold a lighted match near her dress or hair. Or breath, for that matter. I mean, she only has to pass someone with a lit cigarette and . . . *Kerboom!*'

I stared in utter bafflement into the depths of his eyes. 'You're just a sad extension of Barbara's handbag, Philip,' I said. 'You seem myopically obsessed with baubles and superficialities. You are simply chasing bubbles and mirages. What about love, trust, empathy, honesty? Does love mean anything to you? Is it just a form of merchandise? Can you buy it by weight? You probably don't even think it exists.'

'I'm on a perpetual quest for shinier things, sparklier people, smarter invitations, and something greater than a return to the place from which I came. I want higher goals, higher vibrations.'

'So you're looking for the full sonic boom?'

'I despise anyone who settles for less than an immense expansion of ordinary life.'

'Oh dear,' I said. 'That's me.'

'If the sort of love that you are referring to does exist, then it is even less substantial than bubbles and mirages. It's just a word. I have an idea that love means selling something precious, like good looks, charm and energy and, of course, getting well paid for them. As for the desire for expensive clothes, jewellery, furniture, art and first-class travel, these are as much a natural instinct for me as . . . as food and drink are to you. Riches and happiness are one and the same. Well, they are for me.'

'You certainly win the prize for mad inventiveness. What about values? Principles? Ever heard of them?'

'Huh.' Philip gave a derisive snort. 'They're for fools. I don't believe in such abstracts. I don't aspire to them in the conventional sense. I aspire to role models, like Becky Sharp, Scarlett O'Hara and Wallis Simpson, although I admit I may come on more like Blanche DuBois.'

'Never mind Blanche DuBois, I'd say more a tailspinning Walter Mitty. Where is your soul Philip?'

'This is the *real* world,' replied Philip.

'No, Philip, it's your world. It's your choice. And it's a choice I don't believe you can afford. Being you clearly doesn't come cheap and is most likely unhealthy.'

Philip gave me a startled look, as if, for the first time, something I'd said had pierced his psychological armour. I pressed home my advantage. 'And I see substantial risk, bordering on absolute certainty, that well before Doomsday you will be due a good test of nerves.'

'I can't wait!'

For the first time since we'd met two weeks earlier, I saw in Philip's face a look that I hadn't seen before, a look of someone on whom a new and terrifying dawn had broken. I think he realised that the machine he had set in motion when he met Barbara Hutton had now turned on himself and was hunting him down.

To David Ross
Giovedi [31 October 1957]

Vistorta

David darling,

. . .

It's useless going on living the life I'm living – now that the doctor is here, I have even less to do, <u>nothing</u> at all in the mornings, just driving to meet Ruy from school, about fifteen miles, and studying a little Italian, reading Bonjour Tristesse *in French, which is <u>very</u> good for me – wandering round the estate. I have found quite a sizeable river about ¼ mile from the house and I go and sit on the stones by the river in the still <u>hot</u> sunshine and read or play ducks and drakes. My other almost full-time occupation is studiously avoiding being with the odious doctor. Imagine, he kept a book of matches which I gave him in Venice*

– just to remind himself of me! Urgh! But it's so awful having to live with this romantic Romeo and you know I always hate men who think I'm wonderful. I didn't know I could be so foul to anyone – I snub him thoroughly at least three times a day and he comes back for more. I'm supposed to teach him English, but I keep saying I'm busy! Luckily Philip, the American, is still here, and I stick to him as much as possible. David, do you know that the 'girl' he doesn't know whether to marry is Barbara Hutton? (Baroness von Cramm at the moment.) She rings him up about twice a day from Paris, usually drunk, and talks for about half an hour. She is forty-five or so and he is twenty-nine. I tell him not to do it, but he says she will give him a million dollars and want a divorce within a year, so why not? I tell him that he'll never be happy if he sells his soul – because he's a nice type, not a gigolo at all, and we have great jokes together about this materialistic life that goes on here.

To cheer you up, I will send you a book [The Towers of Trebizond], *which I have just been reading by Rose Macaulay – I laugh all the time and adore the style it's written in – you must tell me what you think of it. It's the Count's, but I'm sure he won't mind – he's been very matey lately.*

I have heard all about Barbara Hutton's 'love life' – it's fascinating – I must tell you about it.

This won't be one of my marathon letters, as I'd rather post it at once – in case you're still feeling miz[erable].

. . .

Leonello's latest thing which he thinks is <u>so</u> funny and keeps telling everyone is that in a film he saw recently with his father, Marilyn Monroe complains that her pants get so hot that she *keeps them in the fridge between whiles. He tells all and sundry this and goes into peals of laughter, which the Count thinks terribly funny and so do I, but none of us can make out whether he has the slightest idea what the joke is!!*

Yesterday was Brandino's christening – so we had another full-scale family party with the works. The christening robe was lovely – with yards of train of Valenciennes lace. The children threw confetti for all the peasant children in Vistorta. Do you know what real confetti is? Sugared almonds!

To-day is the last day of October, but one could easily wear a sundress and my face has definitely got brown again.

. . .

STOP PRESS I have just this moment while writing had an 'EXPRESS' letter from my ma, saying that she and pa are motoring to Geneva on 15 Nov and so think they will come on here to see me, as it's only 400 miles. So I think they really want to know what's up. I must say something, darling – please tell me what. Actually my mother is always far more human out of the house, because she's happy only when travelling. I'm going to tell them that I'd love to see them and the Countess will have them to stay a night or so.

I rushed off to tell the Countess that they were coming and she said anxiously – 'Will they take you home with them?' However I reassured her on this point and then she asked me again about staying. Evidently this amorous doctor has been offered a job in a London hospital for two months from January and if I will stay to the end of March, she will let him go, and would like him to go to learn English. However, I did not want to commit myself until then. But I must say something definite

310

soon. So please really answer somehow quickly. I think it's better to say I will leave at the end of December – I don't really want to go to Cortina. I could always go to London and stay with Jean or someone. At the moment two months stretches out like an autostrada – but I know I'm having a wonderful time really and I will have £70 and have bought things at the end. November is the end of my contract.

. . .

Philip says the States are the only place - and people with professions and good degrees still have an enormous advantage there.

X

Gill

The next day, Friday, 1 November, was All Saints' Day. I found Philip darting about the villa, rushing up- and downstairs, a streak of haberdashery, heels click-clacking importantly on the floor. 'Still here, Philip? I thought you were only staying ten days. You've been here more than two weeks. You look like you're on a mission.'

He wore a broad-shouldered, double-breasted suit, dark blue and white striped shirt, and silk floral tie.

'I suppose I am, in a manner of speaking. I couldn't resist staying on for the Fürstenberg party, so I've been getting ready.'

Clara von Fürstenberg was holding a *festa* at her villa in Marocco. I was to take the boys. And Philip, it seemed.

'Oh, so you're coming with us?'

'Of course. Parties like these are the soup kitchens of the professional gigolo,' he said, straightening his tie and face before

311

a mirror. 'I leave for Paris tomorrow morning. I've spent the morning helping the maids do my packing. From Paris, Barbara and I sail for America. I need to resume my courtship. I love it here, but domestic bliss isn't for me. The Conte has lent me some of his clothes. Now that I have lost a bit of weight, we are almost exactly the same size.'

'That's nice of him. It must be very expensive, for someone with as many clothes as you, when your weight and wardrobe get out of line. The replacement cost must be immense.'

'Do you know what my greatest fear is?' said Philip.

'Moths.'

'No. Missing out on something. Fear of hearing voices off. Fear of the invitation getting lost in the post. Fear of extinction.'

'You *are* a moth looking for a richer, younger, more beautiful moth.'

We squeezed into the Millecento and set off on the hour's drive south to Marocco. In truth, for all his flaws and faults, and against my better judgement, I didn't want Philip to leave. He was the antidote to gilt-cage loneliness, and provided cover against the doctor from Milan. I enjoyed his company. He could be funny. His honesty was disarming. He was such an egregious character that I couldn't resist playing him out a bit more rope, just to see what would happen. While trying to concentrate on the road, I casually asked Philip, 'What are you doing for Christmas?'

'Hopefully living until then.'

CHAPTER TWENTY

Fever

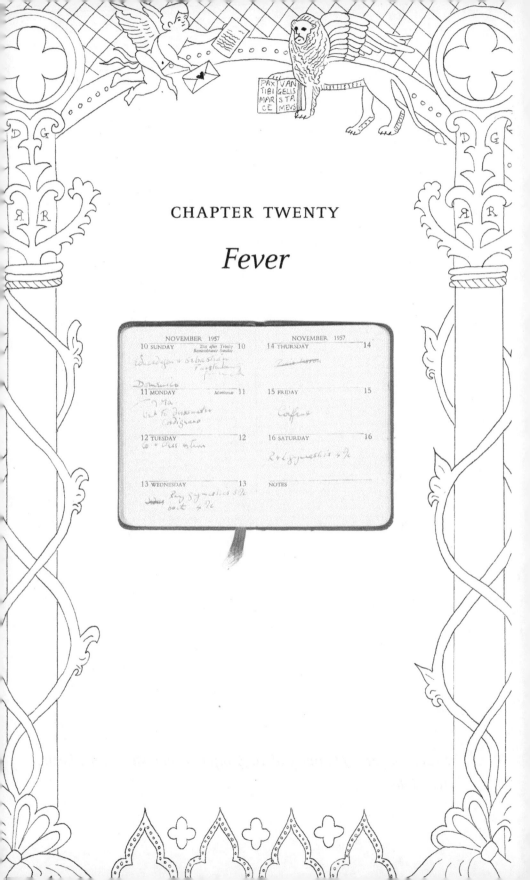

Previous page: *My diary of 1957 offers a snapshot of my hectic schedule!*

To Mr and Mrs Guy Johnson
Friday, 1 November 1957

Vistorta di Sacile

My darling Mummie and Daddy,

Thank you for your letter, I am thrilled that you might be coming to see me – I have told the Countess and I think that you can stay here, if not there is quite a sizeable town called Pordenone where you could be fixed up, only about twenty minutes from here . . . This is a very pretty place, with the foothills of the Alps about five miles away and last week they were covered in snow. Although at the same time, for the last week or so the sun has been hot enough for me to wear a sun dress, but the nights get cold, because of the snow in the mountains, I suppose. By the way, your EXPRESS letter took three days – I can't send this express because it is All Saints' Day and everything is closed – but we are going to the Princess von Fürstenberg's this afternoon, that is to say I am driving the boys in the car, so I will post this in Mestre at the station, and evidently it goes from there even on festas – so I hope you get it soon.

About my clothes – thank you v. much, it sounds splendid. No, I don't think I want any jerseys, I think that they would all be too small for me. Yes, the skirt is the one from the old suit – the pleated one.

. . .

This really is a lovely life and it is such a beautiful place and the Countess is being so sweet to me. I have dinner with them every night, and at the moment there is a young American writer staying, which makes life more amusing – but on the whole the trouble is that I do not have enough to do because school has started. However, I am getting a lot of driving, which as you know I like almost better than anything else.

The other day we went to a wonderful marionette show. They were world famous and were fantastically good – so big, almost lifesize. There is a very good cinema at Pordenone, too. I saw the prize-winning Italian film the other day, and enjoyed it very much indeed and was so pleased because I understood so much of it.

Last Sunday, I drove the children to their cousins who live in the lower Alps – it really was a beautiful spot, with all the hills covered with vineyards and the grape harvest had only just begun and I saw the whole process of how wine is made.

Wednesday was the baby's christening here in the village, and we had a big party for it. The children gave sweets to all the village children.

I am giving both boys piano lessons, which actually I find quite absorbing – I think that really I would be quite good at teaching children.

The main blot on the landscape is that the young Italian doctor who is going to look after the children when I leave has already arrived, and I can't stand the man. He is obsequious and ingratiating and tries to follow me around, which I find most boring. But it means that I can leave the two boys with

him any time I want – so I can always push off in the car.
Sometimes, when I think I'm being paid to live here, I just laugh
to myself and think how ridiculous – but it does have its draw-
backs, and when the post is so slow, I feel miles away from home
and everybody. My last letter from David took a whole week
just from Paris.

But, do try and see this place if you can . . . We could go
shopping in Venice for the day, because it is only an hour
from here – or we could go and have a look at the mountains.

I hope to hear from you again very soon to know if you really
are coming.

Lots of love xxx
Gill

'Let's be honest,' said the Conte, as he stood at the front door
of Vistorta and waved at the luggage-crammed taxi in which
Philip was departing for Sacile station and ultimately New
York. 'This is going to be unbelievably fun to follow.' He was
referring to Philip's strange dalliance with Barbara Hutton.

'I've never known anyone to say goodbye so many times
without actually leaving,' said the Contessa, turning indoors.

'Let's hope he finds Barbara before she snaps out of her Titania-
trance,' said the Conte, changing the record on his gramophone.

As Philip's taxi disappeared, I wondered what more I didn't
know about him. Perhaps he was someone's illegitimate child.
Maybe an influential but distant American connection had
leant in and whispered, 'Be kind to Philip.'

To David Ross
8 November 1957

Vistorta di Sacile

. . .

To go back to R and L's flu – a very good course in child nursing for me, penicillin, inhalations with syringes and electric atomisers, medicine and pills galore and suppositories, and I did it all myself, including taking the instructions from a monolingual Italian doctor! Really it was quite a relief to have something to do. However, under my expert care, they are now both fully recovered.

. . .

My dear American friend Philip has left and I really miss him – we had a lovely friendship! He gave me his address in New York with instructions to be sure to visit him if in the States.

. . .

The weather has deteriorated disappointingly – torrential rain has made my private river quite exciting – but one afternoon I drove into Mestre, about ¾ hour from here, and on the way home in the dark I got stuck in a thick London-type fog and it took me three hours to get back.

. . .

Also I have just had a letter from Fiona [Douglas-Home], in which she says that she met Oliver Messel at a party the other evening, and as Fiona put it, 'he rhapsodised and eulogised' about me for a quarter of an hour.

I dread the Countess going away, when I shall be left with the difficult company of the jealous Fräulein and the wet doctor. She is going to-morrow for four days or so – the amusing thing is that the Prince [Tassilo zu] Fürstenberg (Ira's father) is coming to lunch with me and the boys on Sunday! He is the one who has been cuckolded for the past seven years. However, he is v. pleasant and talks excellent English and rather bad Italian. I am also told he talks rather strange German, which is his native tongue.

. . .

Good night and love
Juliet

Conflicting messages flew in from my mother, whom the Contessa had kindly invited to stay. She was agonising over whether to travel by car, train or air, as if I could summon the effort to care. I hoped that her indecision might reflect a lack of motivation. However, I panicked when a telegram arrived, saying she was arriving by air on Monday the eighteenth. Ten days' time! After I'd told the Contessa 'about' my mother, she and the Conte diplomatically decided to coincide my mother's arrival with an urgent trip to Paris. Half of me looked forward to seeing my mother, the other half dreaded a barrage of questions about David.

David's photographs of our summer holiday aboard his Vespa had arrived by post. My parents knew that I'd been in France, but not *with David*. I suspected they suspected. If my mother asked to see the photographs, I'd need a fully backstopped legend. David and I even discussed the idea of concocting a cover story. Philip never bothered with cover stories. Quite the opposite, he seemed happy to be paraded as a credible suitor to the much-married Hutton.

Before their trip to Paris, the Conte and Contessa managed to squeeze in a four-day visit to Turin. I was once again 'in charge'. Princess Clara's sons, Prince Egon and Prince Sebastian zu Fürstenberg, came to lunch with their father, Prince Tassilo, whom I found delightful. Egon and Sebastien's ages more or less matched those of Ruy and Leonello. They were charming and naughty.

To David Ross
Lunedi matina
18 November 1957

Vistorta di Sacile

Udine

Darling David,

. . . And now to answer your serious letter – I feel quite confused but I will endeavour to express my point of view. To start off with: Christmas. I have now more or less promised the Co'ess to be here for Christmas, as she says the children won't enjoy it if I have left! Humph! Then almost immediately after Christmas, they leave for Cortina and skiing. I think that this really would be the moment to leave – altho' the idea of Cortina for skiing is attractive, I can just imagine the social set-up. I don't imagine there will be a spare bed for you here at Xmas – and it wouldn't be worth coming if there wasn't. Ruy has suggested to me and his mother that you share mine – I thought it an excellent idea, but

the Countess just laughed! I should love to go to Cortina if you could come too – but I suppose you really can't afford to take another holiday – and I hope we can have a honeymoon too. Otherwise it would be too exhausting!

. . .

Philip's name is splashed in all the papers including photos of him arm in arm with B. Hutton. However he's left her already and is flying back to Paris and I think coming here for Christmas.

The Count and Countess leave for Paris today – isn't life unfair that I can't just pop into the train as well? I shall give this letter to Laura, the maid, to post on arrival in Paris. One must think of some way of outwitting the post. They will be staying at the Ritz for about ten days and then are going to Claridge's in London for a week, and then I imagine another couple of days in Paris on the way back. So if you should feel like exchanging any pleasantries with her, you know where to find her, the Countess I mean – she is still feeling very well-disposed towards me!

And so I will have my mother to myself for a week. I plan to make a few excursions in the car – for instance, Cortina is only two hours' drive and there is already lots of snow, so I should love to go and see it. This evening I am driving into Venice in the car to meet her.

I cannot imagine what my mother is going to say to me, whether she will immediately start flapping about weddings – when? Where? Etc. I believe all mothers go slightly potty on these occasions. I will keep you informed.

I'm sending two photos of me and Leonello; taken a few days ago in <u>hot</u> midday sun. I look as though I'm expecting twins!

I have had a slight slimming campaign and I'm happy to say that I can lose it again v. quickly – but why bother at the moment when there's lots of lovely food and nothing better to do than eat?

. . .

Yesterday evening the Co, Co'ess, two guests and I laughed ourselves silly playing puerile private drawing-room games. I listen to lots of records, and when my mother brings some music for me, I hope to be able to learn to play the piano again. I must stop and give this to Laura and dash to meet Ma.

God bless you, darling,

Tanti baci e amore,

Giulietta

It was a more rounded and nuanced mother who greeted me at Venice airport than the one to which I was accustomed in London. She found ordinary life tiresome, but loved to travel, mainly because it involved staying in hotels or grand houses and being looked after. (She and Philip would probably have got along.) Travel was one of the few activities she deemed worthy of her self-image and her cosmopolitan outlook, and she was perfectly capable of travelling on her own to Italy. She was actually a more pleasant person when abroad. She considered herself European; having a German father, she could hardly pass herself off as English, not with the dust of war still settling. In this respect, she was completely unlike David's mother who, despite being entirely Russian, considered herself absolutely British.

I was anxious to avoid any Teutonic clashes with Fräulein Rasch, so as soon as my mother arrived at Vistorta, I drove her on to Cortina for a spot of sightseeing. I expect Fräulein Rasch breathed a sigh of relief to see the Millecento disappear down the drive.

In contrast to the alpine scenery that we drove through to get there, studded as it was with ancient villages, Cortina proved a large town dominated by a series of giant 'Minibrix' hotels. Over lunch at a suitably inexpensive restaurant, I asked the waiter if it was possible to reach the snow line by car. He told me that people were already skiing on the Falzarego Pass. After lunch we took the road, a defile between red sandstone crags and through larch forests, and climbed 1,100 metres in sixteen kilometres, emerging on the roof of Europe, bathed in brilliant sunshine. Pulling over, we walked in the pure keen air of Nature's monumental exercise ground. Better than the views and the air was that my mother never once asked about David but warbled on about London, my brothers, Nanny, and the minutiae of home life, none of which interested me.

Arriving back at Vistorta, I had a slight head cold and was almost completely deaf in both ears either from the altitude or from my mother or both. It was nothing that a few glasses of Glühwein, grappa, and several pills, couldn't cure.

Asiatic flu struck hard, again. As it efficiently went about its business, first Ruy succumbed, then Nuno and Leonello. We had to isolate them from baby Brandino. Rising to the occasion, Fräulein Rasch made an enormous fuss, and mobilised her arsenal of prescriptions, applications, poultices, inhalations, surgical spirit, aniseed cough sweets and kaolin. The doctor – oh dear – visited every day. The Conte and Contessa sensibly kept away.

Domenico drove my mother and me to Venice airport. I wasn't exactly relieved to wave her goodbye: I was feeling lonely.

We parted on better terms than when she had arrived, but still not enough to enthuse me about going back to live in my parents' flat. I reckoned I could tolerate one week, no more.

I marked my mother's departure by shopping in wintry Venice: a yellow and grey jersey, coloured stockings, shoes, slippers and gloves. The arcades of Venice were no glistering troves of elegance and sophistication. Far from it. Once the rich had departed for their winter resorts, Venice lapsed into feeling quite a poor city.

Back at Vistorta, I fell to Asiatic flu. Confined to bed with high fever and aching body, I subsisted on pallid, inert Italian invalid food: boiled potatoes and olive oil. Every morning, Fräulein Rasch bathed my temples – the only softening of her otherwise obdurate loathing – and then, grinning dentally and horrifically, would shove various aspirin-like things up my bottom (few medicines in Italy were taken by mouth). Thrice daily she took my temperature. For two weeks, I saw no one but Fräulein Rasch (shows how redundant my position was). She was in her element and seemingly immune to the flu herself. It was hard to tell which was worse: the disease, the remedy, or the Schwester's bedside manner. Would Nurse Rasch snatch at every opportunity to add to my misfortunes? It did occur to me that she had a material interest in diffusing fever throughout the household, since it reinforced her position.

For peace, and proximity to bathroom, I moved to Leonello's room where a great four-poster brass double bed awaited me, like a gilded barge that might lead a pageant down the Grand Canal. If you must be ill, be so on a double bed: you can have your wireless, books, magazines and papers all scattered beside you, leaving plenty of room for encumbrances like arms and legs, of which one seems to have so many when ill in bed.

I would graze through the radio stations, pausing here and there to listen. One set of stations that came on loudly and clearly were those blaring out anti-American propaganda, delivered in the Queen's English. The clipped Oxford accents would have embarrassed Nancy Mitford. It was a reminder of how close the Communist frontier was to the Brandolini bubble and of how tenuous loyalties were. The rise of Communism and socialism lent a *Twilight of the Gods* feel. People lived right, but talked left. Even if in their lives most people fell short of left-wing ideals, the zeitgeist aspired to socialism. But this topic was not to be mentioned, never mind discussed. Politics were unsympathetic to *La Bella Figura*.

At night, lying in bed in the halfway house between sleep and wakefulness, with the radio switched off, I tried to interpret the sounds that filtered in from the outside world. The stillness of the Friuli Venezia Giulia countryside was punctuated by the hoots of owls, the occasional crack of branches, the bellowing of distant livestock, farm-to-farm canine colloquy, the settling of old timbers and the gurgle of central heating. Occasionally, out of the darkness, the distant clip-clop-clip-clop of a horse and cart could be heard on the road. The sound would slowly swell, then just as slowly fade until silence closed in and was fully restored. Sometimes I heard men's voices singing tunelessly and boisterously, occasionally breaking from their song to lapse into loud incomprehensible exchanges. They might suddenly fall silent as if a terminus had been reached, and then, from nothing, burst into song again before receding into the distance.

It was hard to tell if these reports from the real world were actual, or figments, inventions, drug-drowsed dreams, harbingers, or tricks conjured by the strange combustions and alchemy of the night-time brain. I would get out of bed to peer from the window for anything to substantiate these sounds. All I saw was inky night and the moon flickering through the trees.

To David Ross
3 December 1957

Vistorta

My darling David,

I don't seem to have had a letter from you for ages – and as I have been in bed for six days, isolated, it seems like a hundred years. This Asiatic flu hit the household like a tornado and nine people got it – I nursed Ruy and Leonello for three days, until they were better and then got it myself. My temperature has hovered around 101 degrees for five days and then yesterday it shot up to 103, so they gave me injections and I feel better to-day but very small and miserable not having been out of bed or eaten anything for six days. Yesterday I couldn't think how to talk anything but English, so Ruy had to come and interpret. As so many people are ill – I don't often see a human face but I now know all the strange stations on the wireless and listen to all sorts of anti-American propaganda from Moscow by people with terribly Oxford accents, my dear!

I have moved from my own room to be quieter and I am in a wondrous brass four-poster bed. It has rose brocade and white hangings.

I have had a telegram from my father when my mother got home to say he was so glad we were going to get married and I have since had a sweet letter too.

As you will gather from this letter, I am wallowing in self-pity, so I had better stop before I soak the paper with crocodile tears.

Lots of love

Gill

After sixteen days, my temperature returned to normal.

Preparations for the Festa di San Niccolò on 6 December were under way. The *antipasti* to Christmas, this feast marked the occasion when St Nicholas rewards children for their behaviour, good or ill, during the previous year: sweets and toys for the good children, lumps of coal for the naughty ones. In the morning, I joined Fräulein Rasch in immersing ourselves in the job of wrapping presents for the impeccable children of the *borgo*.

Domenico invited me to visit his house. He lived with his wife and child in a simple property in the *borgo*. The interior was dominated by a large living room with a kitchen in one corner. There was almost zero décor and little by way of furniture. There was no upholstery, no soft furnishings, not even cushions, just hard chairs and an empty grate. My eyes kept wandering about looking for a three-piece suite. England was comfortably ahead of Italy in the furniture league.

Domenico turned to me and, with a shy expression that I hadn't seen before, produced from his pocket an object.

'*Un piccolo regalo*, a small gift,' he said, and gave me a box, little larger than a matchbox.

I took it, opened it, to find a small parcel of tissue paper. I unwrapped it to find a gold charm.

'*Per il tuo braccialetto,* for your bracelet,' said Domenico. '*Qualcosa che ti aiut'a a ricordare il tuo tempo a Venezia.* Something to help you remember your time in Venice.' He then confessed his love for me.

I felt shocked. Shame and deep embarrassment battled against gratitude and heartfelt thanks. I'm hopeless at hiding my feelings. Domenico must have noticed. I wanted to refuse, but felt I had to accept it. Domenico stood still for a few seconds, then turned away. I knew the staff at Vistorta weren't paid much, so this gift would have cost a great deal. Perhaps the other staff had contributed. There was no way of knowing. Should I give Domenico something in return? Surely not. That wasn't the done thing. Or was it? Sixty-six years later, I still feel acute embarrassment at the memory.

CHAPTER TWENTY-ONE

Palazzo Papadopoli

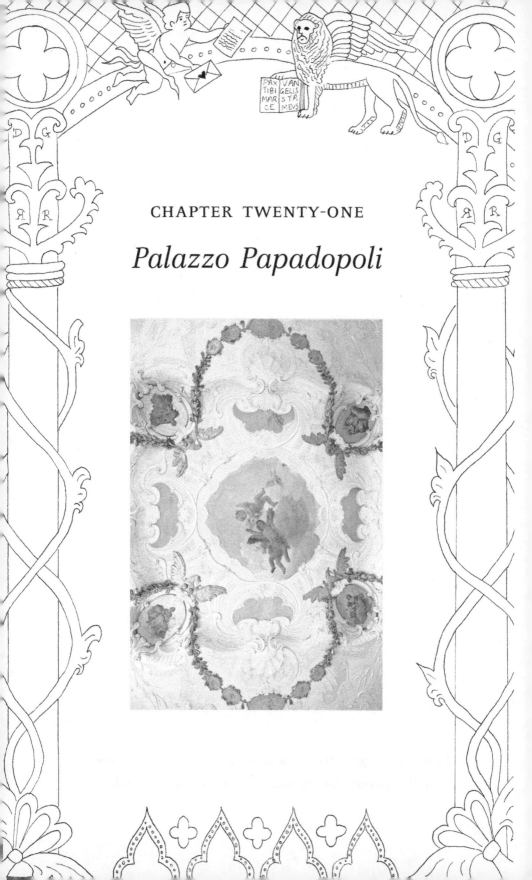

Previous page: *I felt honoured to stay a night in the palazzo that the Tiepolo family had lived in and decorated.*

GRAZIELLA GONZAGA, THE Conte's suavely elegant sister, rang one morning for no apparent reason other than a friendly sociable chat.

'When will you return to London?' she asked.

'Just after Christmas,' I said.

'Ah, yes,' replied Graziella. 'It is so much easier to leave *after* the party is over. Perhaps you would like to come to Venice for one last time next week. As Palazzo Brandolini is closed for winter, why don't you stay as my guest at Palazzo Papadopoli?'

'I should love to. Thank you.'

'Come on Tuesday the seventeenth for one night. I will make arrangements with Cristiana.'

I had little idea of what to expect of Palazzo Papadopoli. I was wavering between excitement at the prospect of moving on to the next phase of my life, and dread at saying goodbye to Venice.

Just as the Conte and Contessa prepared to go away to Milan for a few days, the weather began to deteriorate. Somehow, they always managed to dodge the vicissitudes of weather and fever.

Rain-laden mauve-blotched cauliflower clouds rumbled heavily down from the Dolomites, spitting lightning and weeping bitterly and loudly over the darkening Friuli Venezia Giulia countryside. I watched from the ground-floor windows.

The prolonged roar of rain beating down on the roofs of the villa and on the great trees of the estate sounded like applause. The water gushed, spouted and writhed its unaccustomed way around the topography of the villa and the estate, cascading down the contours of the garden, forming unprecedented pools and errant streams. The gargoyles of the church vomited water. Occasionally, a member of the gardening staff, foliated in wet-weather clothing, dashed for cover from one outbuilding to another. Meanwhile, indoors, the household staff, holding baskets of laundry, piles of ironing and cleaning implements, stared in alarm at the false twilight and elemental drama unfolding outside. While Vulcan's smithy hammered out lightning bolts, Daisy the corgi hid under a chair. The only calm presence was Domenico who toured the ground floor switching on lights, firing candles and stoking hearths.

After three days, the storm blew itself out. I ventured outside to see the havoc. *Terra* supposedly *firma* looked like a blasted battleground of felled trees, broken branches, denuded bushes and leaves everywhere. Squawking birds wheeled about in shock, looking like the contents of all the wastepaper baskets of Vistorta thrown to the winds. The entire estate was filigreed with rivulets and streams. The river Livenza, which touched the estate, had swelled into a furious brown torrent, bearing away trees, detritus and the carcasses of drowned animals. In the gardens, several pumps were at work draining waterlogged lawns and beds.

The Conte and Contessa calmly returned from Milan. In their wake came a caravan of luggage, parcels, boxes and bags. They had done their entire Christmas shopping not only for the family but also for the village.

'Coming home is one of the best reasons for travelling,' said the Conte, as Daisy greeted him with rapture.

To David Ross
Saturday, 14 and Sunday,
15 December 1957

Vistorta di Sacile

. . .

For the last three days a most splendid storm has raged and to-day I ventured forth to look at my river. It is in full flood, fields under water – dead dogs, sheep, the lot – most impressive – and tons of water rushing noisily. I just stood and watched it for ages while Daisy barked like a maniac and water trickled off Leonello's mac into his Wellington boots – then we squelched home. This evening I hear that the road to the village is closed because the water has flooded the bridge. We haven't seen the mountains for days – but I expect there is lots of snow.

. . .

Christmas will be strange here. The peasants have already had theirs – S. Niccolò on 6 Dec – I have been helping Fräulein Rasch pack up Christmas parcels for the peasants – 150, all in different colours with sweets, toys and clothes. It was great fun.

<u>Sunday</u>

You cannot imagine the mountains of luggage and parcels, packages, etc., which they have brought with them – heavenly chaos. Two cars full! Luckily I have sent off all my Christmas cards because I can see that between now and Christmas I am

333

going to be fully employed – doing the Contessa's Christmas cards, writing her letters, shopping for her, doing up hundreds of parcels and helping to decorate the whole of this enormous house. I think it will be great fun. It will be one long round of parties from 23 Dec onwards. But she announces that she is leaving for Cortina on 27 or 28 Dec, so I shall book a sleeper for the twenty-eighth, I think – in which case I shall be in Paris two weeks to-day!!!!!!

. . .

We will spend the twenty-fifth at Villa Maser, the lovely Palladian palace I told you about almost in the mountains.

. . .

Philip may be coming for Christmas.

I am most embarrassed because Domenico has just declared his undying devotion and passion to me (he looked after me when I was ill) and he has presented me with a gold charm to put on my bracelet and remember him for ever – it's all most awkward as he kisses my hands at every opportunity! I'm sure I didn't provoke it – but it's a great strain having <u>no one</u> to flirt with! And then I have my perpetual cold war with the doctor – so boring and he's so thick-skinned. Imagine the cheek yesterday – he followed me into a shoe shop where I was trying on something I'd seen in the window and said he'd come to help me choose and just stood there watching. As soon as we got outside I told him he was very ill-bred and he just shrugged his shoulders and went on talking.

Hope you are well and in good form
Love Gill XXXXX

'I have some Christmas cards to send,' said the Contessa, the day after I wrote to David. 'They are mostly in English. I wonder if you'd help.'

The Contessa had a marvellous line in velvet persuasion. She managed never to sound like she was giving orders, but there was never any doubt as to what she expected. As far as I could tell, she didn't do handwriting other than to sign letters and documents. She often asked me to write notes and letters on her behalf. Today's task was to work through a pile of Christmas cards. I wrote out the name of the recipient; she applied the power squiggle. I also wrote the Conte's Christmas cards. The names of the recipients passed me in a blur of Devonshires, Onassises, Niarchoses, Lambtons, Callas, Olivier and all the most celebrated 'ofs and froms' in the *Almanach de Gotha*. If the recipient was someone the Contessa knew only faintly, I would sign the card on her behalf. My diary entry for the day reads, 'Busy all day'. It was the first time I'd been busy in months.

Given that Christmas was only nine days away, I kept thinking that if all the cards were bound for England or abroad, the Contessa was expecting a great deal of the local postal service, unless she sent the cards 'express' or via a special network of couriers.

What a difference two months makes. A subfusc wintry gloom had descended when Domenico drove me to Venice and dropped me off at Graziella's *motoscafo*. In the thin December light, the Grand Canal seemed drained of colour, turning the city into an aquatint. The *calli* and canals were almost deserted, each as black or dark grey as another. Most of the palazzi were shuttered. The occasional boat glided silently through the wraithlike *caigo da mar*, the sunless Venetian mist that hung dankly in the air. The golden aura of the gay and trifling summer city had dissolved into a grim, spectral *grisaille* of fog. Nothing has more tones of grey than a Venetian December. It makes you realise how exciting grey can be, and what a rich spectrum exists from silver via wet sheep and wolf to elephant.

Canaletto definitely painted his famous scenes of Venice during summer. In fact, the Venetian winter put Venetian artistry of brush and palette into a new perspective, as if the colour and exuberance of so much great Venetian painting was intended partly as an antidote and equipoise to the dour winter.

Palazzo Papadopoli was located about four hundred metres from Palazzo Brandolini, on the same side of the canal and some three hundred metres from the Rialto. Graziella was waiting for me as the *motoscafo* drew alongside.

'Welcome,' she said, as I stepped on to the stone quay outside the palazzo. She greeted me with a kiss.

The palazzo was an unusual L-shape, and had a garden that looked directly on to the Grand Canal. The interior was gloomy and, in those parts not gloomy, dimly lit.

Graziella took me carefully around the florid but faded *piano nobile* with its virtuoso flourishes, scallopings, mouldings, scrolled ceilings and gildings, and its usual vistas and enfilade of doorways. It was smaller in scale than Palazzo Brandolini, and some hundred years younger.

'Let me show you my bedroom,' she said, switching on the light as we entered a modest room overlooking the Grand Canal. The bed was to the right, the dressing table straight ahead. It took me a while before I was able to focus on my surroundings. The walls were painted with a light, airy scene of clouds and figures wearing red and blue, who appeared to be skiing in the clouds – precisely the sort of scene to cheer one up in a Venetian winter.

'I expect you know that the Tiepolo family used to own this palazzo in the middle of the eighteenth century,' said Graziella.

This came as a jolt. I now realised what I was looking at. All four walls had been painted by Tiepolo, with clouds, cherubs, flowers and what looked like saints. He'd even painted the dressing table, the bedhead, the chairs and a hand-mirror. I felt privileged to see before me in plain sight something that few people in Venice had ever seen. I also appreciated the irony that while most people who wanted to see a Tiepolo had to travel to a gallery, Graziella simply had to wake up.

'These frescos are the most beautiful thing I've ever seen!' I blurted out. Graziella looked at me with wild surmise, as if I'd let the side down. 'Of course,' I added, trying to recover the decorum of patronage, 'you can see where he has been trying to experiment with perspective.'

'Ah, so you are an expert too,' said Graziella, with an indulgent smile. 'I'm sure you noticed that the *piano nobile* is done by Giambattista's son, Giovanni Domenico.'

'Really my time in Venice has simply been an extension of my time at the National Gallery in London,' I said. 'The director of the Gallery was right when he said I would "hardly notice the difference".'

'You have spent the last seven months watching paint dry,' smiled Graziella.

'Yes, and fortunately in a series of colours that I love.'

Graziella then gave me some suggestions for shops to visit if I wanted to do some Christmas shopping for my family. 'I'd come with you,' she said, 'only shopping in Venice can take hours.'

'Oh, I'm normally very quick. I don't actually like shopping unless I really have to do it.'

'That's not what I mean,' said Graziella. 'Walking around Venice, you meet so many people you know, and you have to pay them your respects or they get upset. Venetians are always very friendly to each other, because we know we will see that person again and again and again, usually on the same day.'

I found it romantic to be misted over and shadowed. I wanted to explore Venice on a winter's night, and see the city as only Venetians would – that is, without tourists.

'Walking around the city at night is easy,' dismissed Graziella. 'It doesn't matter which way you go, you'll soon hit a canal. *Sempre diretto!*' Graziella shared none of her sister-in-law's qualms about me going out alone after dark.

Nothing is quite as mysterious as a winter's night in mist-swirled Venice. Wherever I went, I heard the drip-drip-drip of water. Although Venice was the first European city to experiment with street lighting (in 1128), she still hadn't perfected the illuminations even by 1957. There was no room in the *calli* for stand-alone light fixtures, so the lamps were bolted to the sides of buildings. The intermittent light they threw was sepulchral and untrustworthy. It made the darkness darker, and cast grotesque, distorted shadows across walls and streets. There was always the peril of tripping over something and falling headlong into a canal. I was haunted by a sense of someone or something following me, even if it was the echo of my own footsteps.

Besides the occasional necessary cat staring at me malevolently and a few muffled figures flitting about among the *calli*, the only signs of life were in the small narrow shopping streets between the Piazza San Marco and the Rialto, which were lit and decorated for Christmas. For the first time in months I found myself looking forward to the bright lights of London.

A voice inside my head kept telling me to move on, or someone might turn into a pumpkin. The surpassing food and general inactivity of life at Vistorta had begun to tell. I was piling on the pounds. If Nuno had picked up on my spherical aspects, what would David think? They say travel broadens the mind. In my case it broadens the stomach.

The days leading up to Christmas were dominated by the substantial logistics of people, food, drink, presents and decorations, while outside in the Friuli Venezia Giuli countryside, thick snow descended like a lace shawl. The last thing I needed was another dose of Asiatic flu, which made its return like a malevolent Santa. Thanks to, or despite, the ministrations of Fräulein Rasch, I managed to shake off the symptoms after a couple of days in bed. I emerged to find that most of the population of the *borgo* had turned out to join in with decorating Vistorta with baubles, tinsel, glitter, candles and still-lifes of fruit bowls artfully wreathed in holly. A fir tree from the estate was marked, felled and dragged into the entrance hall of Vistorta.

CHAPTER TWENTY-TWO

'All That Glisters'

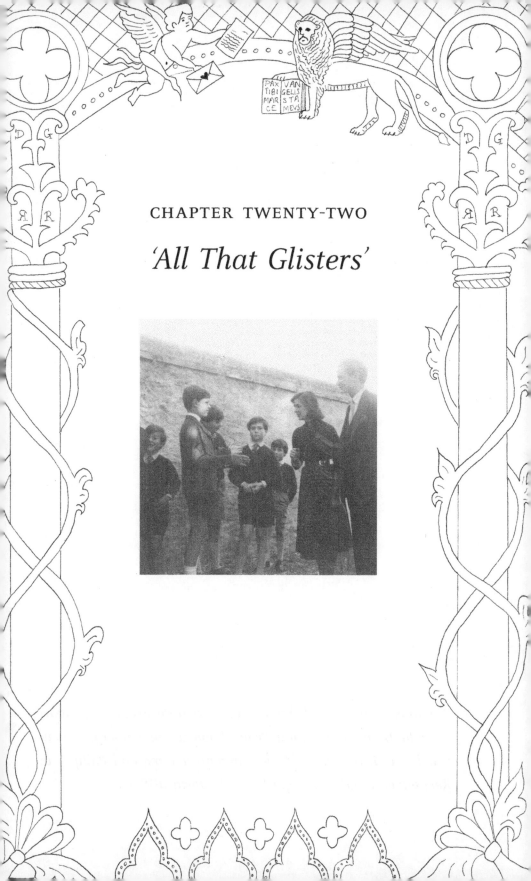

Previous page: *A family reunion on Christmas Eve: (left to right) Leonello Brandolini d'Adda, Prince Egon zu Fürstenberg, unidentified, Ruy Brandolini d'Adda, unidentified, me and Philip Van Rensselaer stand in the garden at Vistorta di Sacile.*

'*FIAT LUX!*' CRIED a familiar voice from behind me.

I could scarcely believe it. He was back.

'Hello, my name is Philip "Your Cheque Is in the Post" Van Rensselaer!'

'Ah, the man in motion,' I said, slowly turning around while peering over a small tower of parcels that I was carrying away for wrapping. 'The myth! The legend! Good afternoon. Which elite enclaves have you been probing?'

'None as elite as this.' He grinned as he turned to see Domenico and Angelo sizing up the mountain of trunks in the hall. 'I have allowed my luggage and me to be lured back to Vistorta. More packing, more moving, more unpacking – the story of my life! Still, when I'm on the move, my life doesn't seem so pointless.'

Philip had turned up at Vistorta with an even greater baggage mule train than before.

'Huh!' I carefully put down my tottering load. 'No fixed abode, no fixed ability, just a lot of fixed baggage, Philip.'

'Deliberately so. Specialisation is for insects. My luggage is my most constant travelling companion. Everything else in my life has to audition.'

'And you have no destination.'

'The journey *is* the destination, although you don't always end up where you want.'

'Indeed. But you generally end up where you *ought*. Don't

343

you ever want to get away from it all, shed the baggage, settle down, get a job?'

'Oh, but I have a job.'

Philip then articulated the *modus operandi* of his, for want of a better word, career. His idea was to prove himself so superior in pedigree, intellect, attire, looks, grooming, name-dropping and improvised sophistication that the social points thereby accrued could be 'cashed in' for an invitation, to be parlayed into a better invitation, and so on, until his vaunting was substantiated, whereupon greatness would finally gather him into its circle.

'Ten out of ten for optimism,' I said.

'I've painted the blue-sky scenario.'

'Not even Tiepolo could come up with your shade of blue.'

'When life doesn't make sense that is when it is beautiful. Nothing makes me feel younger and more vital than flying with the jet set. It makes my brain change shape. It's like belonging to the best kind of club. I could never be a commuting drone, but I'm happy to watch commuting drones. I'll jump at any serious income unencumbered by the need to understand anything or do any hard work, until, that is, a better offer comes along. I believe luck trumps hard work or merit.'

'Surprised you believe in luck. It hasn't done your family much good.'

'The bad luck is out of the way. Let the good luck roll in.'

I looked at Philip's luggage. For a swift but terrible moment, I thought that Philip was being hired to pick up with Ruy and Leonello where I was about to leave off, but then I came to my senses. 'I hope you have a Father Christmas outfit in that lot.'

'I look terrible in red. Having a red bank account is quite enough.'

'I hear the Grail of Barbara Hutton's hand eluded you. Cock-up? Over-reach? Part of the plan? Or just a nosebleed?'

'Star-crossed love.' He sighed. 'Actually, I'm quite relieved. The drink and the pills were too much. Barbara has apparently found a cheaper, less discriminating, less handsome crash-test dummy, with a stronger liver. I assume he is hoping to be paid handsomely in return for having to listen to her interminable life story over and over again, until both of them hit the brick wall of reality.'

'She got bored. You got the boot.'

'Whatever it was, I managed to avoid check-mate. I've taken myself off the project.'

'No more experiments with the high life?'

'I've hardly started! I'm still livid that I'm not a millionaire and that I have to strive for a living. I'm determined not to go back to sobbing uncontrollably while staring at the walls of dismal *pensione* rooms. Oh, to be higher up the food chain!'

I wondered if David was sobbing uncontrollably in his room at the Hôtel Danube.

'Well, while you've been away, I've been working my fingers to the bone and the hours are insane, but I've somehow managed to survive.'

'Well, it's jolly lucky you don't have any friends, isn't it?'

'Philip! Look, I have no time to cross-examine you on what you've been up to. It's all-hands-on-deck here. Now, I don't suppose you can help.'

'I don't suppose I can.'

'So you'll just do your usual thing of hanging around and waiting for the next meal, will you?'

'Rude not to.' He chuckled.

'You're like Asiatic flu – hard to shake off, and with a tendency to make repeat visits.'

Later, when I told Philip about my night at Palazzo Papadopoli, he shrieked, 'I would sell a kidney on the black market and pay, *pay* to sleep in a Tiepolo-painted bedroom. Who do I send a blank cheque to?'

Christmas Eve night was cold and clear. Beneath quivering stars like brilliant jewels and the moon bathing the countryside in a silver light, the Brandolini, various Fürstenbergs, and the Arrivabene (Graziella's family) gathered to walk the short distance to the church at Vistorta. The crisp crunch of leather soles on frosty ground beat time to the chatter and laughter.

After midnight mass, we returned to the villa. It was two o'clock in the morning when we took our seats to feast on roast suckling pig.

Villa di Maser was a sight to behold when we arrived there slightly bleary-eyed on Christmas morning. Gone were the children's funfair, donkey rides and tug o' war of my previous visit. So tall that it could have been a present from Norway, a Christmas tree stood in the domed atrium.

It was the scene of a great party, the glitter of diamonds answered by the sparkle of champagne. Happy at the prospect of returning home, I name-dropped, joked and small-talked my way around the rooms.

'And suddenly,' Philip was saying to a woman alight with jewels, 'with total clarity, I knew it was time to leave.'

Philip was on campaign. Oozing unearned entitlement, tripping on his own brilliance, terrifically *ministering*, proficient in every protocol and form of address, his features composed into a rictus of politesse, he worked the villa like a neurotic eel, and was lightning across ten yards. To see him in action was like watching a piece of performance art. *What* he did, he did exceptionally well, improvisation of the highest order by a gifted actor. He could assimilate himself into any group, and could skilfully bait and fish the many casual and fragmentary conversations for information about other guests, usually speaking in italics and CAPITALS: '*So I told my driver to KEEP THE ENGINE RUNNING . . . I fly from Paris to NEW YORK in two weeks . . . How long are you here for? . . . Do you know the Birchington-Strangewayes? Now there's a man whose SUCCESS hasn't gone to his wardrobe, MWHA-HA-HA. . .*'

I couldn't resist intercepting him in mid-flow: 'That's one difference between you and Nancy Mitford. She's not trying to prove she can make a hundred friends at a cocktail party in one evening.'

'Ssh.' He put a finger to his lips. 'This is what due diligence looks like in the jet set. Nancy writes about it. I put it into practice. Ah, there's La Principessa.' He glanced over my shoulder. 'Don't let me monopolise you.' And off he flew in the direction of a bejewelled woman I vaguely recognised.

Afterwards we all stayed overnight at Maser, exhausted.

Philip would later remember and regret his luxurious prodigality in his amusing, stylish and frank memoir, *Rich Was Better*: he portrays the Conte and Contessa thinly disguised as Count and Countess Maestriossi. Ruy and Leonello appear as Gia and Lazzilo. The Conte's sister Graziella is Theresina

Coraggioso ('She has the most beautiful eyes and the most beautiful voice imaginable'). Vistorta is Rosalia. Gianni Agnelli is Cecco Pallido, his wife Marella Badia. Ever since he first met the Conte and Contessa, he wrote, 'over the next decade they were to be my haven in the storm'. Although I never once saw either the Conte or Contessa actually handle cash, I sometimes suspected that Philip survived off the odd cash hand-out.

Back at Vistorta on Boxing Day, I felt tired and overexcited. I was suffering from various injections that Fräulein Rasch, eyes burning like dark-red coals, had administered to alleviate the symptoms of flu. I did wonder what they contained – maybe they were her way of getting her own back on me.

The time had come to say farewell. I hugged Ruy and Leonello, and told them I looked forward to seeing them make their mark. Did they learn anything from me? Hmm, I told them about London, the English and the war. I hope I amused them. Perhaps I was the Doodlebug in their lives: much noise and screaming overhead but falling to earth equivocally. I said goodbye to the Conte and Contessa, to Domenico and Angelo, and finally to the other members of the household whom I had grown to love.

'I and my trunk (singular) are leaving Vistorta and Italy,' I said to Philip.

His parting words were, 'Play the game. Join the club.'

'I'll have those words stitched into a cushion.'

Philip saved his 'best' until last. His long hoped-for redemp-tive arc failed to land safely. For one who set so much store by his own fitness for survival in a world of social Darwinism, he failed to evolve, which is always a problem for those who consider themselves close to the top of food chains. His salutary 'test of nerves' and long-awaited karmic reckoning took place several years later. He had always enjoyed a drink, and was not averse to popping the occasional pill. His already unstable condition dissolved into a pathology of snobbery, entitlement and greed, fuelled by specific substances, resulting in a constitutional crisis. In 1973, while staying as a guest of the Conte and Contessa at Vistorta, he succumbed to an irresistible compulsion and disgraced himself by stealing twelve suitcases full of exquisite *objets d'art* of inestimable value, eggs, boxes, statues, figurines and precious bibelots, in an over-medicated, vodka-fuelled frenzy. Somehow, he and his haul made it to the airport and on to a flight to the United States. With his irresistible charm and innate sense of don't-you-know-who-I-am-ery, he managed to blag his way through US Customs, but got little further. 'To the knowledgeable, the objects were as well known as the *Mona Lisa*,' he wrote in *Rich Was Better*, 'and any attempt to sell them was an act of indescribable naïveté or arrogance born out of the strange flowers that grew wild in my head.'

The loot was returned, legal action stayed and, as the Conte and Contessa eschewed the vulgar notoriety of newspapers, the matter was hushed up. Philip had filed for moral bankruptcy. It was a rude Darwinian dawn. His name was for ever blackened. He had a streak of escapism, blind and wilful behaviour, grandiose attitudes, poses and narcissism. He promised only to betray, flattered only to deceive and put his interests squarely before his conscience. Never mind social Darwinism, he simply added another chapter of social Dickensianism to his family history. That said, I'm sure he gave some people some pleasure. He was the picture in the gallery that no one had noticed was hanging the wrong way round.

As the Brandolini prepared to head to Cortina, I was bound for Paris and then home. The Conte took me to the station. As I looked out of the window and waved a tearful goodbye, I prepared to return to a very different kind of reality, that of creating a family with David.

La dolce vita was fun, up to a point, but I was keenly aware of its risks and costs. Behind the sparkle, the parties and the balls, personal calamities seemed to loom, many of them beginning with D – divorce, dependencies, depression, 'distressed circumstances' and worse. The deeper I immersed myself in this world, the more I recognised it as one to which I didn't belong. For a woman not born to it, the only way of authentically accessing it was by marrying into it, which wasn't for me. It was too rich, too superficial, too facile. I'm the antidote to wealth fantasy. Money didn't pump my glands. *La Vita Dolce . . . Figura far Niente . . . La Bella Niente . . .* in the end, none of it meant much. It scarcely occurred to me to aspire to anything beyond what I already had. Although fascinated by the people, the ideas, the values and the relationships that I had encountered, I left Italy with exactly the same ideas and values, in much the same order, as when I arrived. So much for my 'adventure'. You can be fascinated by something without wanting it. I could not have learnt more thoroughly that happiness does not come by the kilo or the square metre; it cannot be leased, hired or chartered. It seems to elude many of those who have every worldly advantage: they seem always to want more – but of what?

As one phase of my life came to an end, a new phase was about to begin. While the train clattered across the Veneto, I felt Giulietta fading away as Gill Johnson took over – but for how long? It was time to get on with the serious business of living, which meant marrying a man with no money who lived in a hotel room in Paris.

David and me at our wedding, 11 April 1958, St Bartholomew the Great, Spitalfields, London.

ACKNOWLEDGEMENTS

Very like La Serenissima herself, *Love from Venice* began as a blank expanse and a few fugitive ideas. It has slowly and painstakingly been built up, added to, decorated and adorned from a multiplicity of sources.

My great thanks go to my son Rory Ross. The idea of *Love from Venice* came to him on a family holiday in Italy in 2015. Five years later, he had the opportunity to immerse himself in the project during Covid. After many days spent pummelling me with questions, and many weeks spent researching Venice, he finally chose the right words, wrote them down, tore them up, started again, and again, and so on. Without his hard work, diligence and determination, this book would never have been written.

I thank many others for their support, suggestions, advice, memories and ideas, even if it was simply a word uttered here or a phrase spoken there, that stuck in my mind. My special thanks go to my brother Hugh for being an unfailing source of wisdom, encouragement and understanding; to my sister-in-law Disie Johnson for pouncing on unsuitable modern coinages and correcting me on the finer points of Italian art, culture and lifestyle; to my daughter-in-law Sarah for her kindness, loyalty and brilliant insights; to my grandchildren Isabella Ross for creating the frontispiece to the chapters, Emily Ross for offering her thoughts on the cover; and Alexander Ross for his close scrutiny of the text. Margaret and Fred Lyle deserve special praise for the great lengths they went to in helping research this book, for the amusing ideas they came up with, and for generally buoying my spirits. I cannot thank the brilliant Fred Waterman enough for the many days that he spent poring over the text while sitting in my garden, dispensing invaluable advice and ideas on the essential ingredients and dynamics of narrative. Thanks also go to Bradley Adams for shrewdly spotting mistakes and offering suggestions; to Prue Mosselmans for reading an early draft and giving encouragement; to Hugh Joseph for offering his suggestions; to Nigel Tisdall who, in the dark days of Covid when the book was in early gestation, reached out to Rory and with him toasted better times with beers on a bench in Green Park; to Professor Munro Price for correcting several points of European history; to Fiona Douglas-Home for rekindling our time at the National Gallery; to Shelagh Montague Browne for sharing her memories of Formula One in the 1950s; to Mary Killen for her support and ideas; and to Rachel Kelly for her astonishingly quick and thorough critique of the book. Finally my thanks go to Tom Perrin of Hodder & Stoughton for his enthusiasm, professionalism and brilliant editing. With infinite skill and tact, he suggested reducing the original typescript by about one fifth to make a more manageable work. It has been an absolute pleasure to work with Tom. If I've left out anyone, I apologise; as I approach my 92nd birthday, my short-term memory isn't what it once was.

GILL JOHNSON
London, October 2023

PICTURE CREDITS

Chapter 1: Author's collection
Chapter 2: Author's collection
Chapter 3: Sueddeutsche Zeitung Photo/Alamy Stock Photo
Chapter 4: Author's collection
Chapter 5: Author's collection
Chapter 6: Author's collection
Chapter 7: David Ross
Chapter 8: Author's collection
Chapter 9: Roloff Beny/Library and Archives Canada/PA-193744
Chapter 10: Author's collection
Chapter 11: Gill Johnson/Badrutts Palace Hotel
Chapter 12: David Ross
Chapter 13: Author's collection
Chapter 14: Author's collection
Chapter 15: Author's collection
Chapter 16: Author's collection
Chapter 17: Slim Aarons/Getty Images
Chapter 18: Henry Clarke/Condé Nast/Shutterstock
Chapter 19: Author's collection
Chapter 20: Author's collection
Chapter 21: Courtesy of Aman
Chapter 22: Author's collection
Page 352: Author's collection

ABOUT THE AUTHOR

Born in 1932, Gill Johnson grew up in Hampstead and Selsey. Evacuated to Scotland after the fall of Dunkirk, she returned home in 1943 and narrowly escaped being hit by a Doodlebug rocket in Buckinghamshire. Leaving St Mary's Calne school, she joined the Bach Choir in 1949, and is now the choir's longest serving member. After marrying, she worked in the British Embassy in Paris, then returned to London to assist Kenneth Clark, the art historian. To fund the education of her four sons, she imported sorbet from the Rhône Valley. Having lived in the northern Auvergne, Italy and Hong Kong, she has settled in west London. *Love from Venice* is her first book.